Sustaining the
Family Business

Sustaining the Family Business

An Insider's Guide to Managing Across Generations

Marshall B. Paisner

BASIC
BOOKS

A Member of the Perseus Books Group
New York

Library of Congress Catalog Card Number: 00-102394

ISBN 0-7382-0320-3

Copyright © 1999 by Marshall B. Paisner

Previously Published by Perseus Publishing.
Published by Basic Books, A member of the Perseus Books Group.

Text design by Rachel Hegarty
Set in 11.5-point Garamond by the Perseus Books Group

10 9 8 7 6 5 4 3 2

Basic Books titles are available at special discounts for bulk purchases in the U.S. by corporations, institutions, and other organizations. For more information, please contact the Special Markets Department at the Perseus Books Group, 11 Cambridge Center, Cambridge, MA 02142, or call (617) 252-5298 or (800) 255-1514 or email special.markets@perseusbooks.com

Find us on the World Wide Web at http://www.basicbooks.com

To
Mathew, Jason, Alex,
Terri, Ian, and Connor

Contents

Acknowledgments

I began this project as a small essay for my grandchildren about the personal and professional ethics needed to make it in the twenty-first century. I wanted to share my excitement for our family business and help them decide whether they wanted to join the business eventually. Even if they chose another course, I hoped my essay might help prepare them to excel in their work and find satisfaction in it. As I wrote, I realized that my entire adult life had been dedicated to building a successful business that could be passed on to my children. So the essay turned into a book about that process.

Along the way, a few people, some knowingly, others unknowingly, helped shape the book's content. When I served on the first board of the Northeastern University Center for Family Business, its director, Paul Karofsky, read the first outline and said, "This should be your family business succession story." Paul Cole, national director of the Customer Connection Team within the management consulting group of Ernst and Young, also read the first outline and sent me off in yet another direction. Barry J. Nalebuff, of the Yale School of Management, bluntly told me that unless I was willing to tell our family story, no one would take seriously the conclusions I had reached. So I must thank my wife, Elaine (who also put up with me for the two years it took me to give birth to this book), our daughter, Carol, and our sons, Bob and Dan, for letting me share pieces of their life with you.

The first draft was reviewed by Joseph F. Blum of MassMutual Life Insurance Company; Richard Narva of Genus Resources; Robin Weaver of New York Life Insurance Company; Patricia Annino of Peckhan, Lobel, Casey, Prince, and Tye; Jeremy Weir of BankBoston; and Wendy Handler of Babson University. Their comments were invaluable in broadening the scope of the book and enhancing its value to the reader.

I am especially grateful to two professional firms that helped shape our family succession plans over the years: the accounting firm Forman, Itzkowitz, Berenson and LaGreca, and the law firm Lourie and Cutler. In addition to their guidance and good ideas over the many years of our association, Carl LaGreca of the former firm and David R. Andelman of the latter reviewed the final manuscript for accuracy.

I want to thank Richard Luecke, my agent, who believed in me and the project from the very beginning. He guided me through the proposal and contract stages without a hitch.

No amount of praise could do justice to the contributions of my editor Sara Laschever. I'm going to miss her weekly e-mail messages asking me to do more research on a particular subject or prove my conclusions from other sources. Her talent for helping me to organize my thoughts and make the manuscript more readable was invaluable.

Just when I thought I was finished, along came Nick Philipson, the executive editor for business of Perseus Books, who gave additional editing suggestions.

Introduction

Not long ago, on the lush greens of a Florida golf course, I met a man most Americans would envy. Jack had started a freight-forwarding business in the Midwest during the 1960s. He'd entered the business at an opportune time for trucking: Railroads were in decline and the federal government was pouring millions of dollars into improving the interstate highway system. By working long hours, taking risks, and making some savvy business decisions, Jack earned a lot of money. At the same time, he and his wife raised three children and sent them to college. They happily paid their hefty tax bills every year and contributed both time and money to several civic organizations in their community. Jack's business provided employment and benefits for dozens of people, and two of his three children joined their father's company when they reached adulthood.

Shortly before I met Jack, a competitor approached him with an offer to buy his business for $15 million. His lawyer, accountant, and friends thought this was an offer to seriously consider, since trucking is a regulated industry and Jack was concerned about how his business would fare in the future. He discussed the situation with his banker, who suggested that before he accept the offer he talk to the bank's investment-banking division. Officials there brought in a public company looking for successful small businesses; the company offered $30 million for Jack's business. The offer was partly in cash and partly in stock but nevertheless way over the market value of the business. Since Jack calculated the book value of the business at around $9 million and the terms of the sale included five-year consulting contracts for both his sons, he thought the offer was too good to refuse. His wife and children agreed. He and his wife could enjoy their retirement without business or financial worries, and their children's jobs would be secure.

Jack's story interested me because my own situation was similar. He and I were close in age. I too had started my own business in the mid-1960s—the ScrubaDub car wash chain—and we had enjoyed similar success. My two sons had joined the business shortly after reaching maturity, and I also had received sizable buyout offers. But there the similarities ended. While Jack sold his company, I resisted this option and passed my business on to my sons.

Jack's decision was more typical. Despite the promising future many family businesses enjoy, very few survive beyond the careers of their founders. In the past three decades, less then 30 percent of family businesses in the United States have made it to the second generation before changing hands, and less than 10 percent have reached the third.[1] Some of these businesses lacked the resources to compete or to adopt new technology as their markets changed; others had no capable successors to carry the enterprise forward. Still others, like Jack's, received offers they believed were "too good to refuse." In 1996 the acquisition of private firms reached an all-time high, totaling nearly $80 billion. This represented an 84 percent increase over 1995, and made up 12 percent of all U.S. mergers and acquisitions for the year.[2] Investment bankers evidently believe that these family firms have very sunny futures, since family businesses nationwide continue to be bombarded by public companies that see them as prime mergers and acquisitions (M and A) candidates.

Since family businesses make up 90 percent of the 15 million businesses in the United States, a lot of businesses will soon be on the block. Some analysts predict that family assets worth as much as $10 trillion (half in the form of family businesses) will change hands in the next decade.[3] Although many of the owners who sell out may believe, like Jack, that they would be nuts to turn down the generous offers they receive, I'm convinced that more than half of those businesses would be worth more in dollars and cents to their owners and families if they continued to operate them. After all, the corporation that acquired Jack's business invested $30 million in Jack's company rather than using that money to expand its own operations; clearly, its top managers expected Jack's business to grow at a faster rate. A study of the twenty-year performance of family businesses by the Family Business Stock Index supports this assumption, indicating that the percentage annual return produced by family businesses exceeds those of the Standard and Poor's 500 stocks.[4]

But more is lost than mere money when family businesses are sold. The business usually loses, the community and the local economy lose, and

American society as a whole loses. Once again, research supports this view,[5] suggesting that acquisition by large public companies frequently destroys many of the positive qualities that characterize family owned and managed businesses, such as concern for quality, commitment to long-term investment in the company, and strong community relations.[6] Large bureaucratic companies often care more for the short-term interests of management—such as boosting annual earnings to satisfy Wall Street and stockholders—rather than the longer-term best interests of the business and the community. They emphasize efficiency over quality, institute standardized procedures that limit the variety of products or services the company can provide, and often shut down or move businesses to avoid competition and to centralize operations. Communities lose a vital economic resource, local bankers lose an important customer, and employees lose their jobs. Even when the acquiring company doesn't close down or move a family business, hired managers rarely share the founding owners' commitment to the community, and since they are often transferred from location to location, local charities and civic organizations suffer as well.[7]

Beyond the loss to the community when a family business is sold, I believe that there is also a loss to the family itself. In my experience, family businesses not only teach good business skills, they create strong families. Family members in business together must feel concern for one another's welfare and share similar goals. If they do not begin by sharing values, they must work together to reach consensus about what is important—for the business and the family. Because they spend more time together than the members of other families, they build stronger family ties and traditions. As a result, they are typically better able to cope with crises when they occur.[8]

But when the family business is sold, children lose the opportunity to carry on what their parents worked so hard to build. They miss the chance to witness the direct impact their values and their decisions can have— on other family members as well as on employees, the community, and the market. Rather than seeing their parents' business as a legacy of opportunity, tradition, and strong values passed from generation to generation, they see it reduced to its simple cash value. And even on these terms, the family frequently loses.

Although it would be foolish to insist that all family businesses should survive from generation to generation, I do know that when family businesses are sold, the only sure winner is the IRS. Despite the good intentions of the Taxpayer Relief Act of 1997 in increasing the estate tax exemption for family businesses, few family businesses will gain much relief from this excessively complicated legislation. And with the reduction of the capital gains tax, more and more financial advisers are likely to recommend that family businesses accept those offers that seem too good to refuse.

Because they are not well-enough informed, many family business owners are likely to take that advice. A 1997 survey conducted by Arthur Andersen and Massachusetts Mutual Life Insurance Company demonstrated that many family-owned businesses had not taken the steps that would enable them to make educated decisions about business succession. One in four had not completed estate plans. Two in three had not written a strategic plan. Nine out of ten did not have a written investment policy for managing the family's personal assets. One in five owners over the age of sixty-one had not selected a successor. These were all well-established companies averaging forty-six years in business, each employing over fifty people and having annual revenues of over $9 million.[9]

This survey, comprising three thousand family businesses, also reported that 42.7 percent expected their leadership to change hands within five years. More than half expected the CEO to retire within ten years. Almost one-third of those planning to retire within five years had not named a successor, and of those that had chosen a successor, 86.7 percent had selected a family member. But over 90 percent—whether they had taken steps to make this happen or not—expected to be succeeded by a family member. If recent history is any guide, however, two-thirds of those founders will be disappointed, since current trends suggest that less than 30 percent of their firms will make it to the next generation unless planning and changes take place.

My intention in this book is to help family business owners start that planning and make those changes. To do this, I will use my own story as a starting point. In the process of figuring out what to do with my business when I retired, I encountered most of the problems that family businesses struggle with in planning succession. Several times, I was tempted, like Jack, to sell out and focus on my golf game. But because I had begun researching succession issues early—as soon as I realized that one of my sons might want to enter the business—I hesitated. Which is not to say that I found much useful information or real guidance when I started thinking about business succession. Although I attended numerous seminars and read all the existing literature on the subject, I discovered many clichés about the difficulties of running a family business (no one had to tell me about these) but few specific ideas for successfully passing the torch of ownership from one generation to the next. Nothing I heard or read, to my mind, adequately stressed the importance of continual renewal of business competitiveness, without which succession isn't worth attempting. Frustrated, I made it my business to learn more, drawing on the knowledge of consultants, academics, lawyers, tax specialists, and other business owners whom I respected. What I learned persuaded me that many more family businesses could be successfully passed on to succeeding generations if their current owners had a better grasp of the factors that make bridging generations of ownership possible. These include:

- understanding the elements that create a family culture and learning how to build family traditions of value creation, ethics, and quality;
- bringing children into the business in a positive way;
- handling conflict between family members;
- keeping ownership in the hands of the people directly involved in the business;
- recognizing the difference between market value and "inherited" value;
- creating opportunities for nonfamily employees;
- using outside directors;
- constantly renewing the business in order to build a solid customer franchise and create a business that can survive;
- understanding the tax laws that discourage passing on family businesses;
- planning tax and estate strategies using a family business plan;
- preparing heirs to take the reins;
- having a retirement plan in place;
- knowing when selling makes sense.

This book treats each of these topics in detail, using my own experience as a starting point and drawing examples from other family businesses in a variety of industries, including Johnson Wax, the Legal Sea Foods restaurant chain, Steinberg Supermarkets, Kiplinger Washington Editors, Rosenbluth International, the Saunders hotel chain, and others.

It is my hope that this book will help many family business owners recognize that there are alternatives to those offers that seem "too good to refuse."

Sustaining the Family Business

1

Creating a Family Culture That Promotes Business Succession

The chance to live well without having to go to work every day persuades many family business owners and their heirs to sell their businesses. For many Americans this represents total success: They believe that the goal of starting any business is to sell it, eventually, for a lot of money. Many people also think that a life of luxury and ease is the most desirable human state, and that the person who has the most money at the end of their life somehow "wins." Certainly many business educators and professional advisers subscribe to this idea.

The argument against this point of view gets into moral, as well as psychological, issues. In simple terms, are we doing future generations any good by leaving them large sums of money? I'm not suggesting that inheriting money prevents people from becoming successful. Like most parents, I want my children to have the best of everything, and I wouldn't deny them the luxuries my hard work can buy them. But I think that giving them such luxuries without the chance to earn them themselves is denying them something far more valuable than material goods: the opportunity to live the life that I have lived and continue to enjoy. And that is a life that business ownership has made possible for me—a life built on pride in my accomplishments, a strong work ethic, a family tradition of fairness, concern for employees, and involvement in the community.

Unfortunately, the "start, grow, and sell" ethic is deeply ingrained in American culture. For more family businesses to make it to another generation, a change in culture is necessary. How does one change culture? As with anything, private beliefs must change before public behavior can follow. For the culture of American business to change, the private culture of family business owners—their values and attitudes—must change first.

Let's Talk Business at the Dinner Table

A common joke told about family businesses has it that the first generation builds the business, the second generation lives off the business, and the third generation kills the business. The truth in this derives from the expectations and training that family business owners give to their children. In too many families, parents send signals to their children that running a family business is a stressful and unfulfilling endeavor. For example, wishing to spare their children unnecessary worry about problems they can't understand, parents unwittingly turn their children against the business by banishing business talk from the dinner table, closing off opportunities to share both disappointments and triumphs. Or, in their efforts to bequeath the American Dream (whereby their children will be better off than they are), parents cave in to the temptation of selling the business to ensure their children's financial well-being, while ignoring the intangible benefits that are gained by instilling in them the values of hard work and social responsibility.

A 1992 study by Douglas Holtz-Eakin of Syracuse University and David Joulfaian of the U.S. Treasury, which was based on IRS records, found that only 4.5 percent of those who received an inheritance of less than $25,000 dropped out of the workforce, but one in five dropped out when they received more than $150,000. Another study conducted by economist David Weil of Brown University in 1994 showed that the mere expectation of an inheritance can cause people to spend more and save less.[1]

Contrast this with the values presented when a family business is not sold. Discussions around the dinner table center on satisfied customers or pride in a new product. Children are shown a full, rounded picture of the life their parents enjoy; they see for themselves the daily, nonmonetary rewards of hard work; and they come to understand that by joining the family business they can anticipate a similar life for themselves and their future families. How young people feel about their parents' business starts at a very early age. When the time comes for them to make a career choice, their early impressions can have profound results. Leon Danco, the dean of family business consultants, feels that children should not be pushed into the family business. I agree. But there are a few things you can do to give the family business a better than even chance as a career choice.

By making a conscious effort to discuss the positive and interesting things that happen during the day, you can leave wonderful impressions on the minds of your children—impressions of the pride you take in your work, of the integrity with which you try to make decisions, and of the enjoyment you feel every day because you're building a company of your own. As a business owner, you regularly see illuminating and instructive dramas acted out in the workplace. In recounting these at the dinner table, you can give your children a better understanding of what the workplace is truly like. This kind of discussion is not only healthy for young children, it's healthy for the whole family. Both your spouse and your children will be more likely to sympathize with you on difficult days if your conversation doesn't give them the impression that every day is a trial. (Needless to say, maintaining a positive mental attitude about your work is healthy for you too.) Sharing your pride in the family business, and communicating that it is their business too, can help shore up your children's sense of their place in the world. Discussions about the business can also help them to see the difficult choices they must make in a larger context. I'm not suggesting that dinnertime conversation be about business every night, but that when possible you use the business to demonstrate a point concerning the values you want to teach your children. I suspect that the common practice of families not allowing business conversation at dinner has caused many young people to turn away from their family businesses. The mere exclusion of the subject sends a negative message; at the same time, a great opportunity to pass on cultural values is missed.

The dinner table is also an appropriate place to discuss money. Giving children an allowance and responsibility at an early age, giving them weekend or summer jobs in the business while they are growing up, and communicating the importance of a strong work ethic help safeguard them and prepare them to be productive adults. By the time they must decide whether or not to enter the business, they will have some understanding of what will be expected of them and enough information to make an informed choice.

Leading writers and thinkers in the family business consulting industry agree. David Bork, in *Family Business, Risky Business,* writes, "Grooming children for entry into the family business can begin at an early age. The attitudes of children toward the business will be formed by their parents' discussion of the business at home. When parents are positive about the challenges and demands of their work, the children will adopt a similar viewpoint."[2] John Ward, in *Keeping the Family Business Healthy,* feels that "parental grumbling about business problems like poor help, fickle customers, unpredictable suppliers, can . . . discourage children."[3] He also believes parents should make clear that they want their children to enter their business. "If parents fail to actually communicate their desire to have their children in the business," he writes, "it is easy for those children to assume they are unwanted. They back away from the business into another career."

Benjamin Benson, in his book *Your Family Business,* reports: "[One] owner, overly concerned about unduly influencing his children to enter the business, didn't allow any discussion about the business at home. As a result the family viewed it as 'dad's business,' and didn't identify with it. When the kids grew up and sought careers in other fields, he couldn't understand why."[4]

In other words, by giving children the opportunity to go into the family business and properly preparing them for it, parents can instill in them the values that have made their own labors so rewarding. This is not to say that children should be cut off from other opportunities or discouraged from following the path down which their talents may lead them. And you should be careful not to convey the message that your heart will be broken if your children don't enter your business. The idea is to present the family business as a potentially rewarding career, rather than as a miserable time-drain that keeps Mom and Dad too busy and etches furrows in their brows.

The ScrubaDub Story

Most entrepreneurs start their business when they discover an opportunity to fulfill a need. I was an account executive working for a national sales promotion firm. While on a business trip to California, I drove by a new car wash that was having a grand opening. Banners, colorful streamers, and balloons drew my attention to the property. The contrast between this new car wash and what I knew of such businesses in Boston made me stop my car. Here was an ultramodern cement building that could win an architectural prize. In Boston, car washes were typically housed in old garages and relied on manual labor (mostly the unemployable). They had a reputation for sloppy work and rudeness. The general impression was that a car came back from a car wash looking worse than when it went in. But the car washes I saw in California were beautiful! I started paying attention to how these businesses out West operated. They were housed in modern, custom-designed buildings, the property was landscaped, the facilities were partially automated, and they were run by uniformed employees. The idea of no inventory, no receivables, and no traveling appealed to me, and I returned home wanting to build this kind of car wash in Boston.

Reluctant to give up my job until the new business was up and running, I kept working while I convinced three investors to go in with me on the company. We set about applying for permits. It took two years to clear the rights to what we thought was an appropriate lot, and we were finally ready to build the first "modern" car wash in Massachusetts. Over the next few years, we made every mistake possible. The location we'd chosen turned out to be second-rate. Our equipment supplier did not deliver what he had promised, and what he did deliver could not clean the New England dirt off our customers' cars. The labor we hired was undependable and the customers we served were impatient and demanding. My investors quickly lost patience, and with the car wash on the verge of bankruptcy, I had a decision to make: give up and stick with my "day" job, or buy out my partners and commit myself to solving the new business's problems. With the encouragement of my wife, Elaine, I chose the latter.

This experience taught me one of the most important lessons a business owner can learn, and that is the value of persistence. While still employed by the sales promotion firm, I sold the car wash and used the proceeds to purchase an older one in need of repair. Using our family savings and all my spare time, I remodeled the car wash and started to experiment with solutions to the problems encountered at the first location. Working with a new manufacturer and drawing on my own mechanical ability, I helped to develop a conveyor that would allow customers to stay in their cars during the washing process. This new concept, the roller-on-demand conveyor, opened up all sorts of possibilities for speedy exterior washing and increased automation. It substantially reduced the amount of labor needed to run a car wash and eventually revolutionized the industry. Two years later, I remortgaged our house, quit my regular job, and set out to build a new car wash that separated labor and equipment to achieve efficiency and speed.

With the introduction of fully automated exterior washing, we'd been able to clean cars in high volume. This was great after a good New England snowstorm, when almost everyone wanted the exterior of their cars cleaned. But sometimes customers wanted their car interiors cleaned too. This led to another principle that I've relied on throughout my business career: "Give the customers what they want." I surveyed our customers and learned that they indeed wanted more service options, such as interior detailing and custom polishing. In planning the new car wash, I envisioned a facility where customers could stay in their cars during an exterior wash cycle, and have the job done completely by machine—using no labor and at high speed. If they wanted the added service of interior cleaning (called "full service" in the industry), they could go to another part of the building and leave their cars. Labor would be concentrated on the interior cleaning service, allowing for higher-quality work and multiple added services.

Elaine entered the business at this point. My wife and I worked together for endless hours designing a comfortable, high-quality facility to serve our customers. The car wash we built according to this plan was a success from the beginning. Today, after several remodelings, it remains the flagship of our chain and ranks among the top ten highest-volume car washes in the world. Keeping labor out of our production line prompted me to find new ways of cleaning cars at high speeds and opened the door for many innovations. These included computer controls, the use of cloth brushes, and new chemistry and water reclamation measures to lessen the environmental impact of the business. At the same time, we were able to change the image of the industry from one that paid little attention to customers to one obsessed with customer satisfaction.

The rewards have been steady and plentiful. By consistently reinvesting our profits, we have grown to ten locations in the Boston market, washing over one million cars a year. The business was written up in the business section of the *Boston Globe* in 1988 because of its total commitment to customers. In 1994 ScrubaDub was named the first winner of the *Inc.* magazine/MCI Positive Performer Award recognizing superior customer focus. The American Management Association magazine *Manage-*

ment Review published a customer service case study focused on the firm; two management texts, *Grow to Be Great* by Dwight L. Gertz and Joao P. A. Baptista and *Customer Connections* by Robert Wayland and Paul Cole,[5] used the company as an example of superior customer focus. ScrubaDub has also been featured on CNN (1995) and MSNBC (1996) and most recently was given the Blue Chip Initiative Award for the State of Massachusetts. I have served as president of the International Car Wash Association and received numerous awards and honors from both inside and outside the industry. Although I have passed the business on to my two sons, Bob and Dan, ScrubaDub continues to be considered a leader in innovation in our industry.

All of my ideas about how to keep a family business viable stem directly from my own experience. These experiences, especially the early setbacks and difficulties I encountered, helped me withstand the pressures that force so many family business owners to sell. In addition, one of the ways in which I built a family culture that could withstand those pressures was by telling these stories to my children while they were growing up. I used their natural curiosity about their father's past to communicate the values that had brought us success and enabled us as a family to lead the life we were leading. Those values include respect for hard work, a determination to excel, persistence in the face of setbacks, and a dedication to family life.

I began preparing my children when they were very young by trying to convey that the hours I spent away from them were devoted to an effort that I was very proud of. Wanting to share my excitement about work, I tried to bring the family into discussions about what I was doing and the problems I faced in trying to build the business. My enthusiasm must have been infectious, because everyone got involved. Whenever I heard about something new being tried in the car wash industry, I would jump on an airplane to see it for myself. Back home, the whole family would consider what I had learned and discuss whether we should change the ways we ran our business. (From the beginning, I referred to the business as "ours" rather than "mine.") On one trip, for example, I noticed the manager of a car wash wearing a shirt and tie. In a business dealing with dirt and grease and heavy mechanical equipment, putting an employee in a shirt and tie did not seem very practical. My wife and I, with the kids chiming in, went back and forth about this issue. My wife felt that putting a manager in a clean uniform would have the same impact that clean, well-landscaped grounds had: Customers would feel more inclined to have their cars cleaned by a service person who looked clean himself. Through the course of several family discussions, we decided to go one step further and put all our employees who dealt with customers into a ScrubaDub shirt and tie.

This important family decision, which was made at our dinner table when my children were ten, twelve, and fifteen years old, helped create a new value for our family and our business. It was a commitment to keep a business that specializes in dirt looking at all times spotlessly clean. This decision also helped us solve another problem that had plagued our industry since its inception: how to keep good employees. Traditionally, to control costs, car washes kept employees on the payroll only when the weather was good and traffic through the facility was heavy. At the same time that we decided to put our staff in uniforms, we resolved to keep our main staff employed for a forty-hour week and use low-traffic times— whenever the weather was bad or business was slow—for keeping our facilities clean. We even went so far as to wash and wax our washing equipment on rainy days.

We discussed other issues regarding our treatment of employees at the dinner table too. Should ScrubaDub offer health insurance and retirement benefits? In most homes, the input of children on an issue of this sort would never be solicited. In ours, my wife and I saw it as a way to teach ethical issues to our children.

I was able to report, soon after we had implemented our employee benefits plan, that our turnover rates had improved and that employee morale appeared to be at an all-time high. Less turnover meant a better-trained staff that could be more attentive to customers' needs. The business continued to grow and repeat customers kept increasing. As we expanded, we began receiving job applications from more qualified people, and our customers started asking me where I found such nice workers. By pointing at the direct impact on our bottom line of policies my children had endorsed, I was able to teach them a wonderful lesson about how doing the right thing for your employees tends to be good for business.

Our family discussions found their way to other ethical issues as well. What do you do when a customer complains about something missing from their car? How should we handle employees caught stealing? Some parents might feel that these are inappropriate topics for children, but they turned out to be very important in creating a value system that built strength into the business. Take the issue of items missing from a customer's car. We could have taken the position that any items left in a car were the customer's responsibility. Posting a simple sign announcing this policy would have been enough to settle the issue. Our children objected to this tactic, however, saying that they would never go back to a place where they'd had something stolen. Through our dinner-table discussions, we realized that this was an opportunity to make a value statement to our customers about the honesty and integrity with which we ran our business. We resolved to make it our policy to take total responsibility for any automobile turned over to our care. If a customer complained about something missing, we would stop the car wash and involve all our employees in finding the item. In addition, we would inform all our employees on their first day of work that stealing would result in immediate dismissal. Furthermore, if we could not find a missing item for a customer, we would pay to replace it.

Family discussions led to a similar policy regarding customer complaints about damage to their cars. In the view of a child, there is no alternative but to fix something that may have been damaged in your care. Most car washes post a disclaimer listing all the types of car damage for which they will not take responsibility. But our children's vision of this policy as unfair was so clear that their mother and I could not persuade them to debate the issue. They felt that it was wrong to break someone else's property and not fix or replace it, and that there were no circumstances under which they would change their minds. As a result, at every ScrubaDub car wash our disclaimer sign says "We are responsible for everything except nonfactory-installed equipment."

Another discussion that affected both our family culture and our business practices concerned charity. As our children grew, we frequently sponsored the athletic teams with which they were involved. One day, my son Bob asked me why we didn't help other teams. I launched into an explanation of limited resources and the economics of being practical. But Bob and his siblings weren't satisfied, and after much discussion we figured out a way to donate something to every community charity that had a fund-raising campaign: We would offer free car wash passes for door prizes and raffles. This helped a lot of local organizations without breaking our bank. Further discussion about helping people in our community led us to develop a "haunted car wash" event on Halloween that has raised thousands of dollars to clothe homeless children in Massachusetts shelters.

I am convinced that these family discussions helped build a family culture that centered around being the best we could be. As our children grew older and began to work in the car washes on weekends, they were always on the lookout for quality suggestions and brought many useful ideas to the business. In retrospect, it's clear to me that rather than burdening the children with my business "troubles," the stories I brought home from work led to conversations that influenced not only our business policies but our children's values; our dicussions also made business—from policy making and brainstorming to day-to-day management—seem creative and rewarding rather than draining and dispiriting.

I now see signs of the value of exposing youngsters to business decisions among my grandchildren. Last year, my son Dan took his son Mat out for a lobster dinner after Mat returned from summer camp. Dan and his family went with another family to a new seafood restaurant on the banks of a beautiful New Hampshire lake. The restaurant had been open for only a few weeks, since the middle of the summer season. At the conclusion of an excellent meal, they were approached by the owner and asked if they had enjoyed themselves. One woman in the party asked the owner if he would like some constructive criticism. He replied, "of course." She suggested that he consider serving a fresh salad with freshly baked bread, instead of corn bread. His reply shocked the table. He said, "We want to get them in and get them out. If you'll notice, we don't have seat cushions on the seats, because we don't want you to get too comfortable. Don't you see how busy we are? People are lined up waiting to get in here. So if you want a salad and bread, go somewhere else." With that he walked away. Mat turned to his dad and said, "That man doesn't understand anything about customer service." The point of this story is that my eleven-year-old grandson knew the difference between good and bad customer service. Where did he pick up this idea? How did he learn to distinguish good customer service from bad? The answer is that his parents had discussed customer service issues in front of him, and he had begun to realize what good service was all about.

Family and Business Life Cycles

Psychologists and family business consultants have written extensively on family life cycles and business life cycles and where the two intersect. In my view, these cycles go side by side and generally include three stages.

The first stage, which can be called the entrepreneurial stage, covers the founder's struggle to get the business started at the same time they are struggling to bring up a young family. During this period, there are plenty of ways for the demands of the business and those of the family to collide or conflict. During this first cycle, entrepreneurs usually spend much more time in the building of their business than they would have spent at a job; this prevents them from playing their full role in what is typically the most demanding cycle of their family life. Being away from home a great deal may limit their participation in the bringing up of their children and put a lot of pressure on their marriage.

Those entrepreneurs who successfully balance their family responsibilities with the demands of their businesses go on to the second life-cycle challenge. This second cycle involves the running of a successful business while instilling good values in the growing children. During this stage, the family is beginning to enjoy the results of all that early sacrifice and effort. This is a critical juncture, for it is here that entrepreneurs—making up for their early neglect, or heady with the power of their new position—can spoil their children or overindulge them instead of helping them understand and adopt a set of strong values that will serve them well through their entire lives.

In the third cycle, both the business and the family must face the linked issues of retirement and business succession. Although ideally the entrepreneur has planted the seeds that will ensure the future of both the family and the business in the first cycle and reaped them in the second, it is here in the third cycle that most of the business mistakes are made. Often, the goals of the first generation collide with the goals of the second. Where the founder wants to pass on the business to his or her heirs, the heirs want to sell it and live the high life. Or the founder feels it is his or her prerogative to name a successor, but some members of the next generation prefer a more democratic or meritocratic process. Or they simply disagree with the choice of successor. These are difficult conflicts to resolve, especially since, in the early years, the entrepreneur made all the decisions and grew used to making decisions. Even when family members joined the business, the founder may have continued holding on to authority, leaving their roles, their responsibilities, and their accountability poorly defined. Since family roles are conditioned by a lifetime of family interactions, and the way a family member is perceived within the family may differ markedly from the way he or she is regarded—by colleagues, clients, and employees—on the job, this can be especially difficult.

Perhaps the most significant and potentially destructive third-cycle conflict arises between those family members who want to keep the business and those who would like to see it sold.

Market Value Versus Family Value

Second-generation family members who want to sell the business often convince the rest of the family to sell because no advanced estate planning was done. They make a good case that the business cannot survive the death of the founder and payment of the estate taxes. The business has reached that wonderful point where its market value far exceeds its book value, and the proponents of selling out argue for taking advantage of the moment by converting this asset (the business) into a diversified portfolio of treasury notes, bonds, and mutual funds. The family will be rich; no one will have to work any more; and everyone will live happily ever after.

But let's examine this decision to sell the family asset when its market value seems to have hit a high point. I am not suggesting that a family business should never be sold. Certainly there are cases when it is prudent to sell. My assumption here, however, is that we have a viable, successful enterprise and have no immediate economic reason to sell. We are only considering it because the business's market value is much greater than its book value (let's assume $5 million book value) and a national public company consolidating the industry wants to move into the area. Investment bankers retained to represent the family come up with a selling price equal to two times assets, or $10 million. At current operating levels, the company earns a 10 percent return on assets after taxes, for an annual yield of $500,000. We are the leader in our industry and have no reason to believe we will not continue to stay there. Market research confirms these assumptions. So what would the business's value be if we did not take the $10 million offer and the business prospered for one more generation? With a reinvestment rate of 50 percent of our annual earnings (or $250,000 a year) our family business could be worth as much as $10 million (book value) in twenty years, or in just one generation. During those twenty years, it could provide several family members with employment, as well as give them respected standing in the community and the satisfaction of owning a piece of the job they do every day. For everyone who has toiled long and hard in someone else's employ, the rewards of ownership cannot be underestimated.

But, you may ask, why wait twenty years for the business to be worth on paper what it's worth in the marketplace right now? First of all, I want to point out that if the business were sold, the family would net only around $7 million after taxes and conveying costs. Most family businesses that have grown under the leadership of the first generation have a very low basis for their stock value. They achieved growth by reinvesting profits, and a lot of the business's value resides in intangible assets such as goodwill. In a sale, the IRS taxes these intangibles and any recapture of depreciation on appreciated assets. When you add in all the other costs of a sale, you can lose as much as 50 percent. Although it may be easy to live off the $7 million net proceeds, after estate taxes this sum could shrink by another 50 percent. By then, reduced to its cash value, a $10 million business could be worth less than one-third of the original business value to the next generation.

Even more important is the loss to the family. To understand this we need to come to a new understanding of a business's value. If our primary goal is not to get rich but to pass on to our children the life that the family business has made possible for us, then we need to communicate to the next generation the idea that market value is only the score of the game and not the goal. If we distinguish between the market value of the business and what I call its inherited or family value, then we will have achieved the spirit of family business culture. Far more important, to my mind, than the dollar value of the company is its family value—with all the attendant opportunities and benefits.

I am convinced that a conservative return on a going business is so far greater than the return on after-tax dollars from the sale of a business, and that the return is even greater for the next generation after the net sale value passes through estate taxes, that I believe entrepreneurs with large-enough businesses should consider passing their businesses on to another generation through professional management if no family member is capable or ready to take the reins today.

An Offer Too Good to Refuse

Let's return now to the story of Jack, the man I mentioned in this book's introduction. At the time I met him, in the afterglow of the sale of his business, it was too soon to know how things would turn out for him and his family. The two sons who had worked with him to build the family business would each have a five-year ride. But it is unlikely that they would have any influence or standing in the company they had helped their father build. The new corporate managers would probably tolerate them for five years and then ask them to stay at home and clip bond coupons, which would be unfortunate, since the two young men, according to Jack, were capable of running the business. Now they wouldn't have that opportunity.

After achieving his ultimate goal of a six handicap in his golf game, Jack could anticipate leaving an estate valued at approximately $18 million. (Of course, it could be less if the value of the stock he received went down.) The net proceeds to his family after the settlement of his estate would be no more than half that—somewhere between $8 and $10 million. His sons would find themselves with a pretty chunk of change but nothing to do—no purpose in life other than pampering themselves and spending their father's money.

But let's backtrack and devise an alternative scenario that would have guaranteed Jack his comfortable retirement and that six handicap while offering his sons their rightful inheritance: a chance to run the business. All of the principles used in this example are detailed in Chapters 5 and 6 on tax and estate strategies.

Assuming that the managers of the public company that bought Jack out were no dummies, we'll agree that Jack's business possessed genuine growth potential and therefore represented a real opportunity for his sons. Anticipating this, what if, back when Jack's sons first came into the business, Jack's accountant had suggested that he begin giving them stock in the company on the expectation that they would eventually inherit the business? Through a recapitalization, Jack could have changed his common stock to two attributes, 90 percent nonvoting and 10 percent voting common stock. If the real estate was not already a separate entity, Jack could have separated it from the business at this time. This might involve some legal and tax costs up front, but would be well worth the effort. Jack could then begin gifting $20,000 per year of the nonvoting stock to a trust for each of his sons. Because this stock represented a nonvoting minority interest, Jack could have discounted it by as much as 50 percent. (Note that valuation is fact-based and must be backed up by appraisals that consider the specific factors on which the discount is based.) In other words, each gift might represent close to $40,000 of the business's net worth but be valued at only $20,000—and therefore within Jack and his wife's annual gift exclusion—by the IRS. When it became obvious to the accountant and to Jack that the boys had the potential to run the business, as Jack proudly told me they did, he could have increased the value of the gifts by using some of the $600,000 (or with his spouse $1.2 million) exclusion available to him at that time.

The long-range plan would have been for Jack and his wife to retire on the income from the real estate and the sale of the voting stock. When they felt the urge to move to a warmer climate for the winter months, they could have done so knowing that they were giving the boys more room to learn how to run the business. Having already given away 60 percent of the nonvoting stock, and with the net worth of the company around $9 million, Jack could have sold his remaining 40 percent to his sons at market value for $6 million. The boys could have borrowed the money using their own stock as collateral, and taken out a last-to-die insurance policy on their parents to cover the loan.

After taxes and expenses, Jack would have netted $3 million plus the title of chairman of the board, with all the perks that might bring. He and his wife could live very well on the interest from $3 million (at least $150,000 a year) plus the rental income from the business real estate ($300,000 a year). Jack's wife would have been happy knowing that provisions had been made for her and her husband to retire comfortably; she probably wouldn't have cared about selling the business as long as her future remained secure. Far more important to her would have been the peace and harmony of her family. She would have wanted reassurance that no conflict would arise from these transactions.

At the day of reckoning, under this scenario, Jack's sons might inherit a pittance rather than the $8 to $10 million they could expect if the business were sold. But look what they would end up with instead: a business worth at least $15 million, the pride and satisfaction of working for themselves, and the rewards of a fulfilling, productive life that cannot be measured in dollars. Wow! What a difference.

On the other hand, since Jack did sell out, after a few years his sons may start to feel that they never received legal recognition for helping their father build the business. Jack had obviously taken the early steps that made passing on the business possible because his sons wanted to join the business in the first place. They presumably entered the business thinking that it would be theirs someday, and I'm sure Jack said as much from time to time. After all, he had never intended to sell—it was that "too good to refuse" offer that raised the issue in the first place. Had Jack made a commitment to his sons by passing along some nonvoting equity stock, they would at least have had some say in the sale and received some of the proceeds. But instead they ran the business never expecting to be out of their jobs while their father enjoyed his senior years. When the $30 million offer came in, they may have been mesmerized by the size of their potential family wealth without thinking about the cost of the sale and the after-tax results. They probably assumed some of the wealth would rub off on them—and, again, if they had owned some stock this would have been possible. But once the net results were in from the sale, it became very difficult for Jack to pass on any large amounts to family members without incurring additional taxes. Jack could loan them money to go into another business, but this would mean taking on lots of new responsibilities and risks just when he felt like playing golf. The benefit of a business to shelter income would be gone and he would have to pay heavily to pass on any of the proceeds. Stuck in the uncomfortable position of waiting for their beloved father to die so that they could claim their inheritance, Jack's sons may well come to the conclusion that after all was said and done they should have kept the business.

If Jack had chosen not to sell the business but to pass it on through an orderly succession plan, does this guarantee a happy ending? Of course not. Lots of things could go wrong. His sons might not have his work ethic, might play too much and blow the business. Competition from a larger public company with cut-rate pricing could force them out of business. Technology might change and the railroads once again could become the dominant way of delivering goods. Even with these possibilities, let's look at what would have happened to the family. The entrepreneur and his spouse would have gotten what they wanted, a secure retirement with a contented family. Jack's money would be in the bank. The real estate value would only go up regardless of its use. Jack wouldn't have $18 million in the bank, but so what? Uncle Sam would take most of that anyway. His sons would have gotten a great opportunity to build a business and a lifestyle. At the very worst, they could sell the business and get the money if that's what they really wanted. At the very least, they would get more than its $9 million net worth. No one would be beholden to the other, relations between parents and children could be open and unstrained, and each family member would be free to chart his or her future course. Whatever happened to the business would be in the hands of the next generation. That, after all, is their inheritance: not a transfer of wealth but of a means to a lifestyle. I think that this is a much better ending, one that this book seeks to help you realize.

Key Messages from This Chapter

❖ Start early to develop a family business culture.

Unfortunately, the predominant American culture supported by higher education has been to start, grow, and sell a business to become rich. Only recently because of the recognized opportunity in family businesses have some institutions started to encourage young people to take a closer look at the family business. It is difficult to change the ways you think and operate to accommodate the possibility of a child wanting to take over the family business. Unfortunately, the statistics bear out how difficult it is, so a change in culture is necessary.

❖ Use dinnertime to teach ethical values
through positive business experiences.

Generally, discussions at home about business are an unwelcome subject. What we must realize is that what we say and do affects the lives of our children starting at a very early age. Not using dinner-table conversation to teach is a missed opportunity. A lot can be accomplished at the dinner table.

❖ Consider market value versus family value.

Accepting the notion that family value is far more important than market value is a key step in wanting to prepare a business for another generation. The goal should be to live the desired lifestyle and then give the next generation the opportunity to do the same thing.

❖ Question offers that seem too good to refuse.

The temptation to accept a seemingly irresistible offer can be tempered if the outlook for the business is sound and good business practices are followed. As we move through this book it becomes evident that the return on a successful family business is almost always greater than the after-tax return of an estate produced by the sale of such a business.

2

Participative Management Across Generations

I t isn't easy to change the way you manage your business when a child joins the family firm. But the reality of it is that change is necessary in order to develop a company culture that can be passed from generation to generation. The next three chapters delve into those issues that can make the transition meaningful. Many family business founders—especially those who worked their way up from humble beginnings—feel that the only way to learn how a business works is from the ground up. They may resent their children enjoying advantages they didn't enjoy, or think that the only way to earn the privilege of inheriting a family business is the hard way. These founders believe that their children should start at the bottom of the business ladder like any other employee, receiving no special favors, no privileged access to the higher realms of power in the company, and no "fast-track" or accelerated promotions.

You might expect me to agree with these hard-liners, but in fact I don't. I also don't believe that family members should waltz out of college straight into top management jobs. I take a more middle-of-the-road approach.

Bringing Children into the Business

If a family business is to survive a change in leadership, the business's employees must respect the work of any family members who may eventually be their bosses. For this reason, as John Ward suggests persuasively in *Keeping the Family Business Healthy*,[1] it helps to establish a few rules governing entry into the business by family members. These rules should stipulate appropriate educational requirements (at minimum a college degree for most businesses), some outside work experience, and a responsible attitude toward their work from the moment the family member joins the company. Working for the family business should never be regarded as the easy road or as a layover before they make up their minds about what they really want to do.

Most experts agree that outside work experience is helpful to family members joining their family business; I think it's essential. If the family business is manufacturing, family members who want to join the business should try working for a time in a manufacturing plant similar to that run by the family. If the family business is retailing, they should find a job in a large retailing operation. The benefits are manifold. Outside work experience gives future leaders some background in dealing with the world outside the family business and helps them gauge their ability to function in a nonprivileged environment. They can learn how to get along with people in the workplace—their subordinates, peers, and supervisors—and see that they can do good work and fit in on their own terms, without special advantages. They can test themselves and learn how to behave on the job without the added pressure of being the boss's kid. This will build their self-esteem and make them more confident and effective when they do join the family business. They will also come aboard with a more objective, informed view of the business that can only contribute to their success. And rather than entering the firm at the bottom, they can move laterally from their last job outside the firm. If it later becomes necessary for them to learn a particular step performed at a lower level, they can easily learn that process as part of the job they are performing.

While working in an allied field, young family members may also chance on opportunities to learn about specialized areas of the business that could be useful to their parents' company. They may observe alternate manufacturing protocols or work processes, or study how certain tasks are approached differently, and decide for themselves which methods work better. They may even become fascinated by something new—such as emerging technology, alternative business models, or unconventional marketing methods—and bring back valuable information and ideas. This will build their credibility when they join the family business, lead to greater acceptance by their colleagues—family and nonfamily alike—and set them on the road to becoming key players within the company. In addition, it will increase their pleasure in their work and their commitment to the family business. There's nothing like a little success to heighten the enjoyment we take in our work.

Frequently, the outside knowledge younger family members bring to a family business has a dramatic effect on the future of the business. Knight Kiplinger spent thirteen years working outside his family company, the Kiplinger publishing business, before he returned to work with his father. From his experience outside the company, he gained the expertise and the confidence to expand the business into videotapes, computer software, and other new media ventures. He entered the business as a vice president when he was in his mid-thirties. Nine years later, he succeeded his father as editor of the *Kiplinger Washington Letter*.[2]

Compare this with the experience of youngsters who are forced to start at the bottom of the ladder and learn each job in the company, one at a time. These potential company leaders start out their careers at an automatic disadvantage because they are "the boss's kid" and consequently are frequently regarded with disdain by other employees. This is not a minor irritant; it's a common phenomenon, genuinely discomfiting for most young people. Sometimes a potential star will overcome this problem, earn their stripes at the bottom of the business, and gain valuable knowledge about how the company works as they slog their way upward. The odds are, however, that most newly minted adults, thrust into an atmosphere of suspicion and ill feeling, will run into difficulties and end up disliking what they're doing. If this is their introduction to the family business, they may choose another career. Even those who don't bail out will not have gained any new knowledge that could benefit the family company and help boost their own self-confidence. They may in fact be hindered by training that is limited to the status quo. Under these circumstances, it is easy to lose interest, ambition, and the desire to excel.

Family members entering the business usually don't *need* to start at the bottom of the ladder in any case, because typically during their high school and college years they worked summers or weekends for their parents and already have a basic understanding of how the business works. So in addition to encouraging children to take up work projects in order to build good values and a strong work ethic, let them know that doing so will give them a head start on learning about their family business culture (I discuss different types of business cultures, and what I think works best for family businesses, below). They will quickly pick up on the culture's basic organizational model, its strengths and stresses, and how the company treats its customers and employees. This will help them decide whether they want to join the business later or pursue something else.

Hal Lancaster, in a 1996 article in the *Wall Street Journal*,[3] surveyed a number of family businesses and came up with some advice to children considering entering them. "Don't expect a red carpet," Lancaster wrote. This applies especially to family members who go directly into the business, whom he felt should be prepared to come in earlier every day and work later. To maintain credibility, he contended, family members have to work harder than nonfamily members. His advice, like mine, was to build a track record elsewhere, earn a reputation and expertise in an allied industry, and then come into the family business. He also suggested that each individual create their own training and development plan, which should include attending industry conferences and taking outside management courses. Lastly, he contends (and I totally agree) that a sure way to promote success in the family business is for each family member to establish him or herself as an adult with a distinctive identity and ideas. A great way for a family member to do this is to pick a weakness within the company and become an expert on that subject, with the goal of coming into the business to strengthen this area.

This approach produced excellent results in our family. From the beginning, Elaine and I made it clear to our children that they were free to follow any career they wished. We would welcome them into the family business if they chose to join us, but they should do so only if they decided that working at ScrubaDub would be the most rewarding course they could follow. All three worked at the car washes while they were teenagers, so they had a pretty good idea of what a career at ScrubaDub would entail. Our daughter, Carol, became a teacher and went on to get her master's degree in education. Our oldest son, Bob, was sure he would make a fine dentist until some science courses changed his mind. Our youngest son decided early to come into the family business and never wavered in his intention.

Bob was the first to come aboard. He was in graduate school working on an MBA when a key management position opened up at ScrubaDub. Bob felt that he could handle the job and complete his graduate degree at night. He and I discussed how other employees would feel about his coming right out of college and into a management position and decided that they would not be pleased. As a solution, I agreed to hold the position open if he would agree to go to work for some other car washes first. Excited by the prospect, Bob set off traveling around the country, working for several car wash companies that we agreed were the best in our industry. He even journeyed to Germany and worked for an industry leader there.

At the time (the early 1980s), most car washes, including ScrubaDub, used electromechanical switches to turn equipment—chemicals, hoses, brushes, drying systems—off and on as the car proceeded down the tunnel. Bob noticed that a few companies were trying to adapt low-voltage computer-controlled devices to work in place of the electromechanical switches. Computer technology was in its infancy, and no one had developed a control system that would work in the extremes of wet and dry, hot and cold that characterize the car wash environment. When Bob joined the business, he set to work with a local engineering company to develop the first control system for our industry. His knowledge and expertise in low-voltage controls eventually led to the elimination of all switching devices and allowed us to turn detergent, waxes, and water on and off automatically for each car. Besides being more efficient and cutting down on waste (we used as much as 40 percent more of these resources than we do today), this innovation saved the company thousands of dollars in utility costs each year. Our employees embraced Bob, clearly indicating that they felt he had earned his place as a key executive in our company.

Our younger son, Dan, shared a similar experience. After college, Dan took a sales job for a wholesale distributing company that supplies the car wash industry. He spent a year calling on car washes up and down the eastern seaboard. Over and over, he observed lapses in both market positioning and customer service. He decided that a more professional, aggressive approach to marketing and the training of employees could set ScrubaDub apart. When he joined the company, he had already developed several ideas for improving both our marketing and our employee-training program. Shortly after coming aboard, Dan set out to market our differentiation by creating a brochure that named ten ways in which ScrubaDub was better than our competition. For example, we used custom-made car wash detergent manufactured according to our specifications because it was common in the industry for suppliers to reduce the concentration of their detergents in order to lower their prices and beat the competition. Dan marketed this fact by explaining in the brochure that we use a secret formula containing a blend of eight solutions. This secret formula is so effective, Dan wrote, it creates a glow on your car. In the brochure, Dan also promoted the fact that our detergent is environmentally safe, that the water we use comes from our own wells, and that we soften and heat the water for a spotless wash and reclaim it for undercarriage washes. The brochure went on to explain about our robotic washing machines, selected from the best manufacturers around the world and made to our specifications. It was also Dan's idea for us to offer a "bumper to bumper" guarantee that allows the customer to go through the car wash as often as they wish for total satisfaction. He dreamed up the idea of giving customers a free wash on their birthdays. These and other marketing innovations helped us expand our image and brand identity, achieve greater market share, and move into double-digit growth.

Dan also created a program that took all new employees through three phases of classroom training using the latest teaching devices. Before that time, we had always trained new employees on the job. For the first phase of training, Dan created an employee guide to answer most questions a new employee might ask and explain our policies for our government-mandated hazard communication training as well as for dealing with discrimination and harassment. In this first phase, employees learn about their employment status, hours, wages, and benefits, as well as how to communicate within the company. We explain our expectations for their general conduct and teach them our procedures for safeguarding their health and safety. We also explain our emergency procedures. New employees then go to first-phase training for their specific jobs. This includes a video overview of the job and a description of the company's values, including our dedication to customer service. Only after this introduction do new employees begin their jobs. They later return for phase two of their training, which goes into more detail about their specific role in the company. Here we use role-playing and written examinations. Only those employees whose workmates vote to have them join their teams move on to the final phase of training. The final phase of classes goes into advanced skills and commends employees for their achievement, aiming to arm them with a sense of pride in their ability to work well as part of the ScrubaDub team.

By specializing and improving this area of our business, Dan benefited both our customers and our employees. Better-trained employees are able to answer questions and service customer needs more effectively. These employees project our company's values and meet our quality objectives.

Worker satisfaction is also higher. In a survey we take semiannually, we have seen continued improvement in employee attitudes about the company. For example, 65 percent of our employees said in 1993 that they had a positive attitude about top management. In 1997 this had risen to 80 percent. In response to the statement "I am pleased to tell others where I work," only 70 percent concurred in 1993. In 1997, 92 percent said they were pleased to tell others where they worked. In response to the statement "Frequently I am sorry that I work here," 58 percent concurred prior to 1993 and by 1997 only 28 percent concurred. In response to the statement "I would recommend employment in ScrubaDub to my friends," 71 percent agreed in 1993; this rose to 92 percent in 1997.

The work experiences both boys pursued before joining ScrubaDub helped them enter the business with a positive attitude, plenty of self-confidence, and special skills. In addition, they each brought a unique viewpoint about where the business could be improved. As a result, they were quickly able to make substantial contributions to the company's growth, and just as quickly earned the respect of other employees. They had demonstrated their capacity to lead from their very first days on the job, and I'm convinced that this smoothed the way for them and made their entry into the business far easier than it might have been otherwise.

Relaxing Your Hold on the Reins

For an article in the *Family Business Review*,[4] W. Gibb Dyer Jr. studied forty successful family businesses to see if they functioned in similar ways and what, if anything, they had in common. He concluded that there were four basic types of family business culture:

- paternalistic
- laissez-faire
- participative
- professional

Paternalistic

The founder or leader retains full power and authority and makes all key decisions. He or she gives family members preferential treatment in terms of both job opportunities and compensation, does not believe in consulting outsiders, closely supervises employees, and expects them to do as they are told without questions or arguments. Often, this leader is a charismatic person whose personality inspires employees to carry on his or her vision. If he or she has the expertise, the business might be capable of moving quickly to respond to competitive threats or take a proactive approach to developing new products and markets. Paternalistic businesses often move slowly in response to changing market conditions, however. They tend to stick to the market niche developed by the founder and perpetuate traditional ways of doing business.

When it comes to succession planning, paternalistic business cultures usually run into trouble. Since these companies depend so much on the leader's direction, and members of the next generation usually receive little or no preparation to take over, paternalistic firms often go into a tailspin when the leader dies or becomes incapacitated. Even if the leader doesn't die, the business or its market sometimes outgrows his or her capabilities. But since the leader has made all the decisions, other executives and family members are left feeling unequipped and unprepared to save the business in a time of crisis. For these businesses to survive, a change in business culture must take place.

Laissez-faire

The leader holds the reins, the family receives preferential treatment, and employees are expected to obediently pursue the family's goals, but in this culture employees are considered trustworthy and given responsibility to make important decisions. So while the leader still establishes the mission and goals of the company, employees enjoy the freedom to reach those goals through their own direction. The downside is that since employees hold so much responsibility and the family does not deal with day-to-day operations, companies run on the laissez-faire model sometimes run out of control or pull themselves apart.

Participative

More group-oriented than individually directed, participative cultures rely on team management and de-emphasize the status of the family and its power. Rather than operating through hierarchical power structures, these cultures focus on giving employees a chance to develop their talents while empowering them to act in the best interests of the company and its customers. Because employees share in critical decision making, they are more likely to understand and endorse the values of the company.

Although these businesses suffer the least when a family leader dies or becomes incapacitated, team management is also the cause of their biggest weakness—too much time spent making decisions. The primary challenge faced by businesses run on the participative model is to effectively manage time-critical decisions.

Professional

Family business owners turn over the running of their companies to nonfamily professionals. These professional managers draw on their training and experience to bring in programs that improve efficiency and cut costs. Management is more impersonal, with employees measured on their ability to contribute to the profits of the company. Job success depends on each individual's performance and his or her career goals. This culture has the advantage of reinvigorating family firms with new ideas and techniques they might not have embraced through other management styles. The disadvantage, however, is that this management style tends to cultivate bad morale and create unhealthy competition among individuals and departments.

In his study of family business culture, Dyer maintained that it is difficult to change the culture of any business, since the leader creates and shapes the cultural pattern and most leaders don't possess sufficient understanding of their own behavior to make the kinds of changes necessary for the business to thrive and grow. It is my opinion that the most successful family business cultures are participative cultures with a little of the professional mixed in. Combining these two management styles creates a family business culture that I believe can be passed down from one generation to the next.

Like many family business owners, I started out making most of the decisions about my business and holding tightly to my authority. I only began to move toward consensus management after my children joined the business. With my sons in two key positions within the company, I found myself reluctant to make unilateral business decisions that might affect one of their departments adversely or displease one of them. Some of my friends and business peers considered this reluctance a cop-out and a weakness. I didn't care. If my love for my children was preventing me from being what some people might consider a great boss, I could live with that. And I think that parents who believe they can make independent decisions for the betterment of their companies without putting their relationship with their children at risk are kidding themselves.

Our move toward a more participative culture, brought on by my unwillingness to continue making key decisions myself, turned out to be a great boon for ScrubaDub. I discovered that leading the future managers of the company into making key decisions was far more satisfying than making them all myself. And I found that the decisions we made together were often better than the ones I would have made myself. Excited by this discovery, I tried expanding our meetings from just the four of us (Elaine, Bob, Dan, and myself) to include ten or twelve key managers. The enthusiasm became infectious, and the results could not have been more positive. Together with all our managers, we agreed that what made us different was our commitment to quality service in every aspect of the business. This recognition prompted us to introduce several added service features to emphasize that commitment. We began offering free gourmet coffee to interior cleaning customers and made it a policy to always welcome customers when they arrived and thank them when they left. We also decided to expand our database so that we could recognize our best customers immediately, address them by name, and look at a record of their last visit and the services they purchased.

The Magic of Empowerment

These early fumbling attempts at shared decision making led me to research team or consensus management and the concept of employee empowerment—the philosophy and practice of giving frontline workers opportunities to make decisions about their work processes, schedules, and objectives.

Empowerment is a wonderful philosophy, easy to talk about, difficult to execute. Under the old system, where decisions were made at the top and handed down through all the levels of a company, people merely had to listen to orders and execute them to the best of their ability. It didn't matter if they agreed with what they'd been told to do or thought it was the best possible course of action. They were paid to obey. In stark contrast, the aim of empowerment is to get every worker to feel involved in the decisions that govern their job. The expectation—well borne out in my experience—is that workers who take part in planning and who help set their own productivity targets will be more likely to meet or exceed those goals, if only to prove that what they said could be done can be done. Their attitude toward their work will differ radically from the attitudes of workers who are simply told what to do.

But a paternalistic, authoritarian entrepreneur can't just say "What do you think?" to a few lower-level employees and expect the workforce to feel empowered. For empowerment to work, all employees must be convinced that their company's leaders recognize their importance to the firm, genuinely want to know what they have to say, and will take their ideas and suggestions seriously. A CEO truly committed to empowering their workforce typically presents his or her views—about priorities, short- and long-term goals, process or quality improvements, and major policy shifts—to a management committee. The CEO and the members of the committee discuss these ideas as well as other critical issues facing the company. Ideas and opinions are welcomed from any quarter, and the CEO's main function is to listen, facilitate open debate, and guide the discussion to fruitful conclusions. Eventually, the managers on the committee vote on the issues discussed, and the decisions of the majority set the company's policies. Although the CEO can have some influence over how these policies are shaped, the real decisions are made by a group of people rather than by just one person.

Empowerment and consensus management do not detract from the authority and responsibility of the CEO. His or her ideas will always shape the vision of the company. But those ideas must first be presented to a management committee, their pros and cons debated, and the best ways to implement them discussed. Having been given the opportunity to approve and shape major policy decisions, the members of the management committee will feel empowered; feeling empowered will increase their commitment to making the policies work. And since input has been solicited from many people who do not serve on the management committee but possess specialized knowledge that committee members do not possess, the end result is a better-thought-out policy as well as a broader-based commitment to see that policy realized. If, on the other hand, a majority feels that a policy change or a new idea cannot work, it will be doomed from the outset and is best abandoned.

Empowerment Through Teams

There are many models for combining consensus management with empowerment. The one I find most compelling involves reorganizing the company from a pyramid-based structure into a team-based structure. This means transforming a typical department, with a department manager, an assistant, and a group of lower-level employees, into a team made up of a leader and team members. The team leader is responsible for communicating the company's vision, values, and goals. He or she organizes team meetings, sets agendas, acts as moderator, and keeps records of team decisions. It is also the team leader's job to develop an open and trusting environment that encourages new ideas and allows for constructive criticism. Teams are part of a whole new counterculture business-management movement. Whole Foods, the retail leader in organic- and natural-food markets, grew 900 percent in the 1990s. Whole Foods' employee teams vote on hires and all receive financial statements, including sales and profit figures for their departments. They even evaluate the salaries and performance of their bosses.[5] Most team-based organizations also establish cross-functional teams made up of members from different functional areas who have been assigned to address a particular issue or problem.

When the people who will implement a project are the same people who design, plan, and organize that project and set its goals, that's when empowerment begins. Many ideas that sound practical at the management level turn out to be unworkable at the operations level. Similarly, what appears to be a roadblock to one team may be easily detoured around by another. Team management is great at anticipating problems and solving them when they arise, because it draws fully on the entire knowledge base of the company—that is, the experience, talents, and skills of every employee. Some critics argue that consensus management does not always produce strong decisions at difficult times in the growth of a company, and although this is sometimes true, one of the benefits of consensus management is that it tends to be more conservative and therefore less likely to produce drastic mistakes.

Reflecting on these trends, I was inspired to overhaul ScrubaDub's management structure and move to a team-based system with all managers becoming team leaders. We also organized cross-functional and ad hoc teams to address special issues and problems. One of the first cross-functional teams was a quality-improvement team made up of a representative from each of our locations. No managers were included; everyone on the team worked hands-on in one of our car washes. This team's mandate was to devise ways to exceed customer expectations in everything we do. One of the ideas produced by this team has been a big winner with customers. During a New England winter, many people inadvertently scratch the hoods or trunks of their cars while removing snow and ice. Frequently, they don't even see the damage until the car is washed and the dirt removed. The improvement team suggested that ScrubaDub associates make it part of their standard service to buff the scratches out of cars at no charge. Talk about building customer loyalty! At a later time, we needed to add another person to our office staff. Questions arose about the duties of this new person. Bob formed an ad hoc improvement team made up of the four existing office staff members to reorganize our office procedures. The office staff's responsibilities included normal bookkeeping as well as auditing the daily sales from each location—an arduous and complicated job. The improvement team took only a few weeks to develop new, streamlined procedures that made the entire office more efficient and detailed the duties of the incoming employee.

This first quality-improvement team produced such great results that we immediately adopted the concept of employee empowerment as a central tenet of our business culture. The payoff has been amazing. From the very first, we found that when employees are given responsibility for their actions and for the impact on the business of everything they do, they uniformly rise to the occasion. For example, a customer recently stopped at one of our locations and asked for help changing a flat tire. The associate he asked recognized the customer and proceeded to help him. The customer was distraught because he was late for a meeting and had to leave for a business trip early the next morning. The associate offered to take the damaged tire to be repaired after he finished his shift; once the tire was fixed the associate delivered it to the customer's home. Needless to say, this far exceeded the customer's expectations, but it also exceeded anything the young man would have considered part of his job prior to his empowerment training.

Since converting to team-based management, we have used special teams from time to time to tackle individual projects that were being discussed at management meetings but needed input from those closer to the issue. These special teams routinely report back to the management group with dozens of valuable ideas from the people who will be charged with making the project work. Many times these insights helped prevent a disaster. I am constantly amazed by the ideas empowerment brings out from unexpected sources; I am also impressed by the degree of dedication team members bring to the projects they help design and direct.

Watching these wonderful changes improve our service quality and our bottom line, I became convinced that a consensus approach to decision making could solve the problems of a lot of family businesses. Remember, I originally ventured into team management because of my fear of hurting one or the other of my sons by making autocratic decisions. If nothing else, I learned to follow my instincts when it comes to mixing family with business. Team management has made both Bob and Dan far better leaders of the company than I ever was, and far better, I'm convinced, than they would have been if our business culture had not changed. As a result, ScrubaDub is doing better than at any other time in its history. Sales have grown an average of 12 to 15 percent a year since we adopted team management and in 1998 that growth exceeded 20 percent.

I feel sure that most family businesses could avoid interfamilial squabbles and enjoy similar success by making the switch to consensus management. With few exceptions, every family business thrives in part by building a loyal customer base, offering a high-quality product or service, and developing a cadre of experienced, loyal employees. Empowerment and consensus management teach everyone to respect these three basic elements of good business practice. If the employees charged with implementing a decision made by their CEO think that decision is a bad one, they will help it fail. But when everyone knows their input is welcome and that their ideas will be listened to—when you have the full organization working together toward the same goal—the chances for success are much greater. Empowering others is a process of turning followers into leaders.

Making the Shift to Consensus Management

Assuming that you subscribe to the principles of team- and consensus-based management, the process of nurturing future generations while achieving widespread empowerment at all levels of the organization will take time, resources, and the unflagging commitment of the CEO to lead and champion the cause—in word and in deed. As with any major change initiative, instituting team management can take three or four years to take hold, resulting in fundamental changes in the way the company is organized, decisions are carried out, and performance is measured.

Perhaps the most important component is the degree to which the CEO, as leader, sets an example for the rest of the company. *The Leader-*

ship Challenge, by James Kouzes and Barry Posner,[6] provides terrific suggestions for behavioral changes CEOs can make when adapting to a consensus-management culture. I found five of them particularly useful:

- get to know the people who work for you;
- develop your interpersonal competence;
- use your power in the service of others;
- keep people informed;
- make heroes of other people.

Get to know the people who work for you

Sensitivity to others is a prerequisite for being a good leader. You can't isolate yourself in your office. An open-door policy and a regular practice of getting around to talk to people on nonbusiness subjects reminds everyone that you're human and lets them know you care about them as people, not just as cogs on a wheel. Voice mail and e-mail can be very useful for encouraging your associates to communicate anything on their minds (good or bad) directly to you. In addition, when people talk, show a sincere interest in their ideas as well as their lives; this will earn their respect and loyalty. The worst thing you can do is come across as insensitive, aloof, or arrogant. I've found that setting time aside each day to walk around and talk to people is an excellent way to make sure that no one feels taken for granted.

Develop your interpersonal competence

Leaders need to know how to paraphrase and summarize complex business concepts and financial data to make them clear to everyone. They also need to know how to disclose personal information, express their feelings, admit mistakes, respond nondefensively, ask for clarification, and solicit different views. A command of these interpersonal skills will make you far more adept at responding effectively to any situation that arises. If these face-to-face communication skills do not come easily to you, interpersonal-skills training programs can be found in any city.

Use your power in the service of others

There are two parts to this idea. The first involves not drawing attention to your power by surrounding yourself with prestigious ornaments, thick carpets, a fancy desk, and so on. Ostentatiously proclaiming your power and position in this way demonstrates insecurity more than anything else and can antagonize associates and subordinates. Successful leaders don't trumpet their importance so much as use their power to help others become more effective in their work. In other words, instead of keeping their leadership power to themselves, they pass it down through the ranks of their company by empowering others. Enlarging other people's spheres of influence through delegating responsibility and granting subordinates the autonomy to fulfill their responsibilities according to their best judgment is another way of imparting power. By forming teams, you put in the hands of others the right to make key decisions.

Keep people informed

The more people know about what is happening in an organization, the better they can perform. This means providing accurate, up-to-date financial information, not fudging the figures for promotional reasons or to influence the market. There is nothing more counterproductive than working on a project with the wrong assumptions. Information empowers people by strengthening their resolve and providing them with the resources they need to be successful.

Make connections for the people you empower. Help staff members get to know the people above them who may have influence over their work and may be able to contribute to its success. Find ways to connect individuals with important information sources and contacts outside the company by taking or sending them to conferences where they can meet their peers. If necessary, create strategic alliances with outside companies to open avenues of communication and access to resources that can help your employees do better work.

Make heroes of other people

Great leaders find ways to shine the spotlight on others. Not only does this give credit where credit is due, but it increases the loyalty and gratitude of the people being credited. In my experience, crediting everyone connected to a project in some visible way—similar to the way everyone is included in a movie's credits—makes people happier in their jobs and more eager to get on to the next challenge. You can use plaques, newsletters, and even personal letters to acknowledge individual effort. All forms of acknowledgment, whether public or private, strengthen feelings of empowerment and build job commitment.

In addition to these behavioral strategies for promoting empowerment and team management, instituting a few new systems can do a lot to make team management work. Formalizing four systems, to my mind, is essential. They are:

- meeting protocols
- measurement systems
- training requirements
- feedback and reward systems

Meeting protocols

Well-run, productive meetings are the foundation of consensus management. Regular meetings that focus on real issues and produce clear decisions reinforce the values of the business for employees. They also renew their purpose, allow ongoing projects to make midcourse corrections, and provide a forum for the airing of ideas, questions, and grievances. They are a major forum for brainstorming as well as for the constant review of received ideas and unchallenged paradigms. Asking the same questions in different ways and in different groups often produces diametrically different answers; this can lead to a third dimension or an alternative previously unthought of by any group.

To make meetings more effective, be sure to follow these simple, but often ignored, guidelines: Try to ensure that everyone who is invited is in attendance, distribute agendas that clearly outline goals, and follow up each meeting with a detailed, written account of the proceedings. All of these activities help to reinforce a participative culture; for example, meeting notes recording ideas that have been accepted and approved help build empowerment, since one of the great motivators is seeing your ideas recognized and accepted by the group.

Measurement systems

Without clearly articulated measurement criteria, employees in a consensus-management environment may be confused about how to judge the quality of their work. Team leaders must help their teams establish deadlines, performance standards, and productivity goals for their functional areas or for whatever tasks the teams were organized to complete. This contributes enormously to empowerment because employees agree to goals they believe are reasonable and attainable; it also makes it easier for them to pace themselves, anticipate problems, and take corrective action as soon as they suspect a goal may be out of reach or likely to be delayed.

Training requirements

As I discuss in a later chapter, ongoing training is central to business renewal and competitiveness. In a team-based system, training is, if anything, more important than in a more traditional system, because employees are asked to take so much more responsibility for their work and its impact on the company. In this type of environment, every staff member, in addition to needing adequate training to perform the job they are hired to do, must be well trained in problem-solving techniques and in the parameters of the business systems they must work with, such as measurement criteria and feedback and reward programs (see below). Refresher courses in the principles of consensus management and empowerment keep everyone focused and reinforce the values of your business culture.

Feedback and reward systems

A regular feedback system to inform employees and teams about their progress helps grease the wheels of consensus management. Not only does it help all employees keep track of the programs they have designed and approved, it notes milestones as they are reached, signals problems, and celebrates accomplishments.

Rewards must be part of any feedback system. Rewards can achieve many things. They can create an incentive for individual employees to come up with improvement suggestions. They can inspire teams to excel if their performance is linked to a compensation plan. They can also help raise the performance levels of underperforming staff members, since the ability of every team to perform well is dependent on the performance of each individual member. If one person is not performing up to team standards, it never takes long for everybody to become aware of it. With the incentive of a bonus or a raise urging them on, team members often put in extra hours helping to raise the level of those lagging behind, sometimes retraining them, other times helping them catch up on work if they've fallen behind. Pay for performance is a powerful motivator for team involvement. When feedback systems include team and individual performance reviews, teams typically achieve higher levels of productivity.

In addition to formal reward systems, team leaders at every level should be encouraged to take the time for individual recognition. Nothing increases an employee's inclination to go beyond the call of duty and truly excel than being recognized and rewarded for doing so. In an environment dedicated to empowerment, top management should be on the lookout at all times for individuals to recognize.

Creating Opportunities and Rewards for Nonfamily Members

For consensus management to work, it is essential, in a culture that combines participative and professional management styles, for nonfamily employees to be full participants. If all the top positions in a company are held aside for family members, gifted, ambitious people will look elsewhere for a job. Similarly, if the family hangs on to all the tangible rewards of success, even the most empowered and dedicated employees will begin to feel aggrieved. By sharing their success with their employees, family business owners can increase their loyalty, motivate their future performance, and create a workforce that turns a contented, positive face toward the public—the business's clients and customers. Creating opportunities and rewards for nonfamily members raises the level of everyone at the firm by attracting and keeping the best people and making sure they enjoy their jobs and strive to do their best at all times.

Kiplinger Washington Editors, a third-generation family business, has thrived on this policy. Willard H. Kiplinger began publishing the *Washington Letter* in 1923, and it took over ten years before it turned a profit. Since then it has become a highly influential source of business commentary, read by presidents and bureaucrats. Willard was succeeded in 1959 by his son Austin, who continued to expand the business. Because they depended upon a small staff, the Kiplingers considered every employee crucial to their success and paid them above the industry average and offered many perks. They also valued employee input and developed a consensus management style.

Austin's son, Knight, who joined the business in 1983 as a vice president, brought with him many new ideas he'd developed while working outside the company. Knight expanded Kiplinger into other media and ancillary products. By this time a family culture had developed. It included management by consensus, a close relationship with employees, a dedication to the highest standards of customer service, a belief that family leaders are stewards of the business, and a commitment to remain privately owned.

To put these ideas into practice, the Kiplingers divided ownership into three groups. The family members actually working in the business own less then one-third of the stock, employees as a group own 35 percent, and fifteen other family members spanning three generations own the remaining third. Kiplinger family members who work in the company view themselves as salaried employees responsible to a large group of owners. Family members receive no special privileges. Senior management sets new policy but builds consensus for it through strong communication with employees. The work environment is collegial rather than cutthroat. In addition, all employees share in a deferred profit-sharing plan that sets aside 10 percent of pretax earnings to be distributed on a proportionate basis to all eligible employees. Kiplinger also matches employee charitable contributions at a two-to-one ratio and maintains an employee resort in Florida that all employees may use free for two weeks every year. Kiplinger also offers real job security—employees know that when the business cycle turns down, the family will tighten its belt and wait out the cycle until the inevitable upturn.

Although Kiplinger has had many opportunities to sell out and spread wealth to all of its limited stockholders, the family has chosen to pass on their family values to the next generation by trying to manage the business through proper estate planning. On the subject of going public, Knight Kiplinger has said, "I think going public is greatly overrated. . . . It is much easier to run a closely held private company in terms of being able to make bold decisions that are valuable to the future of the company without outside shareholders looking over your shoulder." He believes that outside shareholders have an expectation of steadily rising earnings and that this is unnatural. In private companies, earnings might not be as important as investing in new opportunities or reinvesting in capital improvements for long-term results.[7]

The Kiplinger story is a wonderful model of a family business in the best sense—one that takes great pride in the quality of its product, and equal pride in its commitment to employees. Despite the high prices the company could command on the open market, this family has decided that there is more value—to the family, the business, and the employees—to be gained by retaining private ownership and passing on a successful business to their heirs.

Family Business Plans and Family Meetings

An essential tool for successfully managing across generations in a family business is a good family business plan. In most companies, developing a well-thought-out company strategic plan is sufficient to prepare for the future and ensure the survival of the business. In a family business, the company's strategic plan takes a backseat to the family business plan. It is in this document that you lay out the principal values of your family business. The family business plan then becomes the foundation for every decision concerning the future of the business and the family's role in safeguarding that future. The family business plan also becomes the basis—the originating text and reference document—for building the family culture that will enable the business to remain in family hands and continue to thrive. The main features of that family culture are formulated in the family plan. Just as the freedom to take a long-range view of market and economic conditions separates family businesses from public companies, a long-range view of the family's values and goals makes it possible for family business owners to hang on to their businesses and retain a competitive edge for many generations.

A family business plan differs from a company strategic plan in that it articulates the family's overall intentions for the business instead of stating strictly business goals and outlining how those goals will be achieved. A family business plan spells out the family's conception of the business as a trust for which each generation acts as a temporary guardian, preserving it to pass on to later generations.

A useful family business plan should make several key points. Since, as I said above, most family businesses owe their success to a quality product or service, a strong customer base, and experienced, loyal employees, the family plan should address all of these subjects. Let's start with having a great product or service. The family plan should discuss the founder's pride in the business's product or service, and charge future generations with carrying on that tradition by committing themselves to constantly improving that product. Here, the family plan can also introduce the principle of constant change, noting that change is a given and that the business must continue to innovate to stay in business.

The second element contributing to the success of most family businesses is outstanding customer service. Declaring this to be a family commitment in the family business plan draws attention to the importance of customer service and sets up excellence in customer service as a primary goal for each generation of owners. It guarantees that future leaders of the company will know that outstanding customer service is a hallmark of the family and that falling short in this area will destroy a proudly held tradition.

The third key factor ensuring the success of most family businesses is a dedicated workforce. Austin Kiplinger emphasized this point in a 1996 article in the *Washington Letter:* "We urge our leaders in management to value their employees, who should be considered an organization's most important asset."[8] Although there are many ways to assemble teams of highly skilled and committed employees—and many variations on the types of compensation that will keep these people happy and working hard—at the very least, any family plan should announce the family's intention to treat all employees with fairness and dignity. It is here that the family plan can demonstrate the family's desire to be the very best employer it can be. Since I am a strong believer in the value of ongoing training, I think that this part of the family plan should also include support of continuing training and education for all employees. In addition, it can record a general family desire to provide generous benefits, which may include standard items such as health and life insurance, holidays, vacation time, and retirement programs, as well as elective programs such as profit sharing, stock options, and even company-subsidized vacations.

In addition, to promote the family's commitment to the community it serves and profits from, the family plan should encourage generosity to charitable causes and a creative approach to supporting the needy. The plan should also encourage family members to take part in local community affairs and play an active role in industry associations, sharing information in noncompeting markets and doing what they can to raise the standards of the industry as a whole.

The family business plan should also include a section of work-ethic and personal-habit guidelines for family members who work in the business. The rationale for this is simple: The business can create a superior product, provide excellent customer service, and maintain a dedicated workforce, but if the firm's employees do not respect family members, the business is doomed.

Running a family business by consensus acknowledges that since all family members are not born geniuses, no one should automatically be anointed ruler just because they happen to be part of the family. It is appropriate to include an expression of family love and respect for one another along with an agreement that the most competent family or non-family member—for the betterment of the business—should rise to lead the company. The plan should declare the family's intention to abide by majority decisions as a conservative way to avoid mistakes and admit that family members may not always be right. The plan can reserve the last word for the family because the family carries the obligation of protecting its inheritance and legacy, but the plan should state in no uncertain terms that this "last word" should be used with great caution.

To help create and regulate a culture that all family members can support, the plan should spell out the requirements for family members to enter the company and set the rules for settling conflict. These can include the use of an outside board of directors or advisers, the appointing of a deadlock trustee, preestablishing the stock value among family members, and clarifying the family's stock-redemption agreement—the conditions under which a stockholder can sell out if he or she is unable to resolve a dispute. (I explore these conflict-resolution techniques in detail in Chapter 4.)

The plan is also a good place to make the point that the inherited asset is only a loan to be protected and nourished for future generations. The principle of stewardship should be explained, as well as the idea of the family business as a legacy of temporary guardianship left to each generation.

The family plan should also include instructions for the handling of perquisites, or "perks," among family members. Some people believe that extras should be completely equivalent: If one person gets something, everyone else should get the same thing or something of equal value. I think that this approach can cause problems. Perks should take into consideration accountability and fairness. They should be distributed based on job requirements, performance achievements, or special needs. They should also be subjected to the same scrutiny as any company policy and freely discussed.

I should also say that the family plan can be a fluid document to be changed by each generation as changing times require. But as long as everyone proceeds in good faith and adheres to the basic principles laid out by the founder or the founding generation, the family plan can continue to function as a constant reminder of the family's values as the business passes from generation to generation. To give you an idea of what a family plan looks like, here is the Paisner Family Plan for the ScrubaDub car wash chain:

> How fortunate we are to be involved in a family business. All members of our family share one way or another in our success or failure. Our business gives us financial independence, an opportunity to excel in our industry, and a sense of pride in our accomplishments. Since the business gives each of us involved a chance to build our estate, it also helps those in our family not directly involved in the business. It is, therefore, in all our best interests to resolve any problems and commit ourselves to give this opportunity to future generations. Let them share not only in its financial rewards from productive work, but also in community and family commitment. To protect our equity position, we should agree to let the most capable associate of the company rise to the presidency. To this end the business must be run as a business. Salaries must be based on responsibility and performance. Constant growth, reinvestment, and prudent personal living styles will demonstrate to our associates long-term commitment by our family.
>
> In order to ensure that our business will pass on to another generation, we must be diligent in our effort to respect each other and be willing to accept majority rule. To assist us in the wisdom of our decisions, our family Board of Directors should always include three nonfamily members. We therefore are responsible to each other as a family but must also pass the test of our competence by our full Board of Directors. We should be able to convince the outside directors of the rightness of our business plans and goals. Hopefully the discipline of preparing for our board meetings will also prepare us as better managers of our business.
>
> We must see that our stock remains in the hands of family members in the business. We therefore agree to a stock redemption plan that presets the price of our stock to book value payable over time for anyone who wishes to leave the company. To prevent dilution among family members, we must make entry into our company limited to highly motivated, well-educated (BA or MBA) children of family members. Our CEO must be a family

member, elected by our Board of Directors, who will ensure by example the work ethic of our family. To help decide difficult issues, control over expansion, or dilution of assets, a special vote of our third outside voting trustee is required. This adds a neutral vote on issues when our family members cannot agree.

At best, this plan, which tries to project the benefits of our business to future generations by ensuring that the most competent family members rise to the role of leadership, is no stronger than the will and love that we have for each other. Together with the understanding of our spouses, we provide great opportunity for ourselves and our children and even their children. Some families have managed to do it. Why not us!

In his study of successful family businesses, *Keeping the Family Business Healthy,* John Ward found that three principles appeared to guide such companies.[9] The first is a commitment to the future. Everyone in the family, whether a part of the business or not, agrees that future generations should benefit from the family business. The second principle is a system of extensive communication. This involves informing the entire family of major business decisions, strategy shifts, and general progress, as well as communicating successes and accomplishments so that everyone can take pride in the company's performance. The third common guiding principle is conscientious planning. Tools used to ensure good planning include the family business plan as well as the company's strategic plan. The vehicle used to establish the principles behind these plans is the family meeting.

Most successful family businesses, Ward discovered, bring all family members, including spouses, together at least once a year to discuss the company's mission, its strategic plan, and changes in the family plan. Without exception, every professional adviser to family businesses endorses the concept of a family meeting or council.[10] These meetings enable all family members to express their views and concerns. The reasoning is that, directly or indirectly, all family members feel the effects of what happens within the company. Spouses hear the news at home; family members who don't work in the business get the information thirdhand. By hearing about changes, unfortunate developments, and good news firsthand, everyone has an opportunity to express their reaction, and a lot of controversy can be avoided.

Although some people worry about so much frankness (first-generation parents, in particular, often fear that simmering dislikes or disagreements would be better left unexplored), research indicates that ignoring these issues only creates more tension in family relationships. Ward contends that extensive communication is actually necessary to preserve family relationships.[11]

The family meeting can take the form of a retreat in a vacation environment or it can be a one-day meeting in a local hotel. A facilitator—a professional business adviser or psychologist—should be present to provide an objective view of the discussions, provide structure to the meeting, and keep arguments from getting out of hand. Every meeting should follow a preset agenda that includes a time for open-ended discussion. During this time, all family members should feel encouraged to speak out on any issue that bothers them. Although this seems risky, experience has shown that dealing forthrightly with hidden issues helps build a stronger foundation for future understanding.

In addition to setting out goals and guidelines for the running of the business, family council meetings offer the added benefit of bringing out issues that might have remained unaddressed otherwise. This can head off more serious conflicts and build stronger bonds within the family down the road. There will be spouses who feel their other halves are underpaid or work too many hours, children not in the business who feel they should be reaping more benefits from the company's success. Less-divisive issues will emerge, too. In one family business, a daughter not in the business felt that the family was not doing enough for those less fortunate. Prodded by her concern, the family formed a charitable foundation and donated a percentage of the firm's profits for several years. Eventually, the annual interest represented a meaningful donation and the daughter who had suggested the idea took over administration of the foundation.

Perhaps the most important element in making a smooth transition between generations—something that will inform and underpin all these other changes and techniques—is communication, open and ample communication throughout the family and the business at every stage. The family meeting is a great place to start, but communication among family members should not be restricted to once or twice a year. Family members in business together need to talk to one another, which, while helping the business run smoothly, will also bring the family closer together.

Key Messages from This Chapter

❖ Encourage outside work experience before bringing children into the business.

There is no question that the lessons learned in working outside the family business prepare potential successors in fundamental ways. Developing self-assurance and learning skills that might be helpful in the family business is more likely to result in a family member being successful. Encouraging this move early gives children a motivation to choose their direction carefully.

❖ Develop a participative family business culture.

The participative culture remains the best model for family business succession. Without this organization, we as parents are too often put in difficult positions with respect to our children. They can easily misinterpret a business decision we make on our own as a lack of love or respect for them. Decisions that come through consensus leave no question about their intent.

❖ Introduce the principles of empowerment through team-based management.

It may seem that we are giving up authority and responsibility as owners of our business when we turn to consensus management. However, the opposite happens. Our vision of the company becomes the goal of all subordinates, who now have a vested interest in our objectives. Empowerment adds to their feeling of being respected and they become much more active in striving to reach our goals.

❖ Create a family business plan.

By creating a road map of our values, we enable others to follow its path. Since this document spells out the seriousness by which we conduct our business, it sets the pace for those wanting to be a part of it. It is our vision for our business, the things we stand for, the source of family pride.

3

Building a Resilient Business Culture

The most careful succession planning is worthless if the business you
pass on to your heirs cannot survive. In other words, passing on stock
without passing on an effective business philosophy won't sustain your
heirs or your beloved business through all the changes the future will
surely throw at them.

Research suggests that family-controlled businesses do so well because
they are oriented toward long-term goals.[1] Rather than leaping at short-
cuts or rushing expansion, these businesses focus on managed, slow
growth with a premium placed on satisfying customer expectations. They
care deeply about the quality of their product or service and about the
general welfare and job satisfaction of their employees. They also benefit
from leadership that has developed a tradition of excellence.

I have already discussed many of the elements that go into building a
family business culture with these attributes. But there are a few other
important ideas that I believe family businesses must understand if they
are to thrive.

The Importance of Renewing the Business

The first and perhaps most important tenet of a sustainable business philosophy is recognition that change is inevitable. Business practices, regional, national, and global economic conditions, and social trends that
affect niche markets (where most family businesses function) are all in a
constant state of flux. Therefore, remaining competitive requires continual
renewal of the business. Especially if a family business aims to distinguish

itself from its more impersonal corporate competitors, the culture of that family business must embrace change rather than resist it. This involves assuming that every product and/or service can be improved, no matter how successful it appears to be. It involves creating mechanisms for constantly tracking and analyzing change—in manufacturing processes, in technology, in management techniques, in economic conditions, and in the business's market. Most important, perhaps, it involves creating a culture that encourages experimentation and the development of new ideas.

In this regard, family businesses can learn a lot about dealing with change from the most successful large corporations. 3M, for example, a famed master of innovation, is renowned as a company in which the eleventh commandment is "Thou shalt not kill an idea." By treating people who develop new products as heroes and rewarding patience and follow-through, the leadership at 3M has built an environment that encourages receptivity to even the most modest suggestion about change or improvement. The company nurtures every idea and pursues it to a conclusion. Most important, there is little stigma if an idea fails to pan out. This is because 3M recognizes that "failure" is a predictable and even useful result of active experimentation. Other famous innovators reinforce this approach. Soichiro Honda, the founder of Honda, says: "Many people dream of success. To me success can only be achieved through repeated failure and introspection. In fact success represents the one percent of your work which results only from the 99 percent that is called failure."[2] Winston Churchill put it differently: "Success consists of going from failure to failure without loss of enthusiasm."[3]

For a family business to survive, business owners must accept failures as essential paving stones on the road to success. And rather than penalizing employees for proposing ideas that don't work out, we must teach them not only that we welcome their ideas but that we allow for a learning curve and that initiative will always be rewarded. At ScrubaDub, we incorporated Total Quality Management (TQM) ideas into our business culture—and wrote them into our strategic and five-year plans—to promote and enhance our commitment to constantly improving everything we do.

Reinvestment, Managed Growth, and New Technology

Once a family business has recognized that change is inevitable, the next step is preparation. The most important element of a change-ready policy, to my mind, is a strong reinvestment program. This program should not only fund the making of necessary changes (i.e., buying new equipment, upgrading the physical plant, etc.), but it should fund research. I'm a strong believer that every business with long-range ambitions should include a research department, not only to monitor changes external to the business that will have an impact on the business, but to regularly poll customers about their wishes, expectations, and satisfaction with the service and/or product being provided. Ideally, a research department will also drive change by developing new technologies to improve product or service quality and by pioneering new types of products or services that build on and extend the business's core expertise. I think family businesses need to recruit an imaginative, paradigm-busting research staff and arm it with the motto "If it ain't broke, break it." Researchers should be urged to question received wisdom and never settle for "We've always done it that way" as a sufficient explanation for how things operate.

Of course, having a strong reinvestment program makes it necessary to budget and allocate funds each year (research and development can be funded with pretax dollars). I recommend building a research allotment into an operating budget and treating it as an operating expense. When someone in your company discovers or develops something that looks promising, it has to be funded as a capital investment from after-tax profits. I also think that every business, large or small, can benefit from regularly scheduled brainstorming sessions that produce wish lists of potential improvements in the company's product or service. Later, during the budgeting process, you can allocate funds to investigate the feasibility of one or two of these items. Even if some of these investigations turn out to be dead-ends and produce no substantial positive results, the mere fact that you support this type of exploration will transform your company culture. The important thing to remember is that nothing comes easy and most projects will end in failure—but it only takes one good success to place your company ahead of the competition. Let me give you an example. For years, we allowed our managers a small budget for making our car wash tunnels more friendly to children. They have always used these funds in imaginative ways, often displaying well-known cartoon characters on our equipment for kids to spot as they go through the tunnels. In one of our brainstorming sessions for a new unit, Bob suggested that we try to make the tunnel as entertaining for adults as we do for children. This led us to research using lasers to create a light show during the drying portion of the car wash. Although we were very excited about this idea, the initial tests failed. The cost was too high and the area too restrictive. But the experiment drew our attention to other light and projection devices that could create a similar effect. We are not completely satisfied with the results yet, but we will continue to improve this feature and expect it to eventually become a distinguishing characteristic of our business.

The most important advice I can give regarding reinvestment is to do it imaginatively. Don't put all your money into expanding if you are simply replicating a formula that worked pretty well when the business was started and has never been reevaluated or adapted. Not only do you risk getting left behind by a competitor with a new idea, you lose out on a lot of the fun of owning a business. To my mind, brainstorming, hatching new ideas, and trying them out go a long way toward making the drudgery of owning a business worthwhile. Every year at ScrubaDub, we allocate a certain portion of our reinvestment funds for expansion; another portion is earmarked for the acquiring of new sites; some goes for remodeling existing sites; and a small amount is set aside for developing new ideas.

There is no fixed formula for how much you should allocate to improvements, but there are better and worse ways to approach this issue. Many family business owners take a small salary during the year and then distribute profits to themselves at the end of each year. The problem with this approach is that it encourages owners to see their success in terms of their total earnings each year. If something extraordinary goes wrong, requiring an investment to correct it, they may resist doing what's necessary because it will decrease their earnings for that year. This is guaranteed to limit growth and may even threaten the survival of the company. Other family business owners pay themselves exorbitant salaries in order to beat Uncle Sam out of profit taxes. This thinking also tends to limit growth and produce a business culture in which employees and future generations feel unable to pursue innovations because the funds are not available—the opposite of how a family business should operate.

My opinion is that, in this respect, family businesses should operate like public corporations. Salaries, from the CEO down, should be determined by the market value for the work performed. Profits should be allocated to reinvestment or distribution, with the proportions to each dependent on the nature of the business and the state of its market. Most companies need capital to expand. In times when interest rates are low, some family business owners prefer to use debt rather than after-tax dollars, and that can make sense when the situation is right. My formula has always been to reinvest 80 percent of our profits and distribute 20 percent. The success of this method has been proven by steady growth in the dollar amount of that 20 percent distribution. Every business needs reinvestment, if not for growth then at least for upkeep of facilities or updating to new technology.

Of course, there are wrongheaded ways to reinvest profits, and I'm not ashamed to give you an example from our experience to illustrate the mistakes we made. As ScrubaDub grew and established a strong image in our community, we encountered a lot of pressure to expand more rapidly than we were ready to on our own. Investment bankers suggested that we consider using outside investors to fund expansion; we aligned ourselves with a company that specializes in franchising to help successful businesses grow. Flattered by the attention and by the admiring things these people said about my business skills, I ignored my misgivings and let temptation take over. Our prospectus for a limited-partnership car wash venture sold out in short order. We received more than enough money to build a new car wash and set out to find a location. As is typical, negotiations for site selection took over a year. But the investment bankers wanted faster results, forcing us to choose a location in which we later admitted we would not have invested our own money. After three years of operation with the bankers looking over my shoulder and the investors questioning our slow progress, I realized that this was not going to work.

This experience taught me that investors usually have exceedingly high expectations and when these are not met they can force you to make bad business decisions that you would not have made on your own. They wanted high short-term profits to push growth. I wanted slow growth built on the momentum of small accomplishments. We finally decided to buy out the limited partners.

Our venture into franchising led me to the same conclusion. Franchises did not share my belief in managed slow growth built on satisfying customers. We sold four franchises for a quick-lube and tune-up facility that we had built at one of our car wash locations to add another profit center to our sites. At all four franchises, the owners thought they knew more about running the business than we did. Since they invariably turned out to be wrong, I found myself spending most of my time putting out fires. When the venture capital people wanted to roll out a full franchise program before I thought we were ready, I finally balked. After some long nights of soul searching, I released the franchisees, returned the venture capital money, and went back to concentrating on our core business.

These two experiences convinced me that too often family businesses are tempted to speed up the process of being successful. I came away convinced that the only route to long-term success is to pay attention to your core business and continually renew the business through reinvestment and improvement. In the five years that I spent trying to use other people's money, my own locations grew shabby and neglected. The next five years were spent reinvesting every dollar of profit back into the company. It became clear to me that reinvestment must be a continual policy, and that research and renewal—rather than rapid expansion or courting outside funding—provide the best protection for the future.

Let me say a few words about new technology. We live in a very exciting time, when technological breakthroughs are speeding up all sorts of processes and allowing for the performing of many functions more efficiently than ever before. It is hard to name a business that has not benefited from the introduction of new technology in the past two decades. For this reason, any family business that wants to survive must stay on top of new technology, because in many cases whoever gets there first grabs market share from the businesses that lag behind. I also believe, as I've said above, in developing new technology yourself if you see a need and can muster the capabilities within your own organization, or in partnering with an enterprising engineering or computer design firm (or anyone who possesses the expertise you need). But one word of caution. More than one business has failed by overinvesting in untested technology or by sinking too much money into systems that quickly became obsolete or were not adapted to the scale of the business. Once again, managed slow growth usually beats rushing blind into a new area before carefully studying the ramifications of the changes you make. Every time I saw a new technology that I thought could be useful for our business, I looked at it as an investment. When computer-controlled systems were first introduced, I approached a supplier in this new industry and offered to fund the development of a system for our business application. The only thing I asked in return was the rights to improved versions at their cost. This approach has always given ScrubaDub an edge on our competition because we have always had the newest technology first.

ScrubaDub's Internet presence provides another example of using technology to develop new markets. At scrubadub.com, we offer free, helpful information about caring for your car. To make going to the site fun, we also developed a game that potential and current customers can play to win free car washes. Anyone who plays wins at least a fifty-cent discount coupon that can be printed out and used at once. Incentives like these have increased activity on our home page every month; we are convinced that the Internet will eventually become a substantial source of business for us.

Inspiring a Shared Vision

One of the most important parts of any business philosophy you pass on to your heirs must be ideas about leadership. What makes a leader effective? What qualities in particular should the leader of a family business possess, especially if he or she is to continually renew the business?

A survey conducted by James Kouzes and Barry Posner, reported in their book *The Leadership Challenge*, asked more than 550 business leaders to describe their best leadership traits. Kouzes and Posner concluded that "a clear vision is a powerful force. . . . When leaders clearly articulated their vision for the organization, people reported significantly higher levels of job satisfaction, commitment, loyalty, esprit de corps, clarity of direction, pride, and productivity. It is quite evident that clearly articulated visions make a difference."[4] I agree. In fact, I think that for a family business to survive succession, its leaders must be capable of rejuvenating or reinventing a vision for the company in each generation. Simply repeating a tired-out formula that worked years ago has been the death of many a stalwart family firm. Don't let yours be one of them.

When I first started out, my vision was to wash cars at higher speeds by separating labor and machinery. As the business grew, I wanted to expand our services to include total care of a customer's automobile (that's why we went into the quick-lube and tune-up business). My vision then changed again to adapt new technology to our business in order to increase efficiency. The vision that has lasted the longest and given us our biggest growth spurt is that of "exceeding every customer's expectations." Visions get developed as you reinvent your business. One of the advantages to consensus management is that having your key people involved in the process of understanding your vision facilitates its translation into the concrete details needed to make the vision a reality. This process adds

excitement and commitment to management. I have never met an entrepreneur who didn't have a clear vision of what their company stood for.
I've met many, however, who have never taken the time to articulate their
vision so that others could understand and buy into it.

So let's say you have a strong vision for your company. How do you communicate it to your employees and see that it drives their labors every day?
If a loyal, happy, and skilled workforce is one of the family business's greatest assets, how is this workforce created? To begin with, loyal workers must
have faith in their company's management and trust management's business judgment as well as its commitment to employees. Without the trust
of their employees, no leader will be able to communicate their vision for
the company and motivate employees to give their very best. Without
trust, no company can hope for excellence. This is not just my opinion. The
Wall Street Journal reported that "more than 78 percent of American workers are suspicious of management and develop an 'us against them' syndrome that interferes with their performance."[5]

Frank Sonnenberg, in his book *Managing with a Conscience,* compares
trust to rings piled on a rod. The first ring, he feels, is integrity, which
encompasses honesty, openness, and reliability. The integrity ring represents the leader's intention and willingness to act honorably and respon-
sibly. The second ring is consistency. Employees are quick to notice if a
policy is applied selectively, if exceptions are made for family members,
and if nonfamily employees are held to a higher standard. They also lose
their trust in a leader if what he or she does differs noticeably from what
he or she says—if the leader doesn't carry through on policies adopted or
promises made, or announces a certain course for the company and then
strays from it. The third ring is faith. When it is added to the other two
rings, everything that came before it is strengthened. This ring, which
does not adhere to the others, but rather encompasses them, is the stage
at which actions are so predictable that we don't consciously have to think
about the relationship.[6]

I have expounded in Chapter 2 on the approach to management that I
think best creates this kind of environment: an approach that embraces
consensus management and employee empowerment. It has been my experience that employees trust a decision that has been made by consensus
and commit their best efforts to seeing it realized. They also trust their
leaders if empowerment allows everyone's voice to be heard and everyone's
ideas to be respected.

As it happens, smaller businesses seem to have a knack for creating this kind of trust. A recent Gallup poll conducted for *Inc.* magazine found that worker satisfaction tends to be much higher in smaller businesses. Of eight hundred people polled, 44 percent of those working in companies with fewer than fifty employees said that they were extremely satisfied with their jobs because they feel they have some impact on what the company does. This, compared with a satisfaction rate of only 28 percent for those working in companies with over one thousand employees.[7] This poll tells me that the leader of a family business starts out with an automatic advantage in his or her efforts to build trust among their workforce. By making a point of being open to new ideas and recognizing the value of every worker's contribution, he or she can establish solid, trusting relationships with employees. And once employees trust their leader, they will be primed to follow his or her vision for the company's future.

W. Gibb Dyer Jr., in his book *Cultural Change in Family Firms,*[8] explored trust-building in each of the four types of family business cultures he identified (as outlined in Chapter 2). In a paternalistic culture, replicating the patterns of a patriarchal family, the founder shows little trust in the ability of others to perform up to his or her standards. The patriarchal leader limits the amount of information dispensed, makes all of the decisions, and gives employees minimal discretion in the performance of their tasks. If they follow the leader's rules of behavior, they are welcomed into the "family." They are rewarded with lifetime job security and assistance with family emergencies. If a patriarchal leader possesses charisma, they may inspire their workforce with the power of their vision for the company, and under their leadership the company may achieve significant success. The problem arises when the leader tries to pass the business on to their children. Charisma cannot be willed to another person and it can't be taught. Second-generation leaders in this type of culture often run into trouble earning the trust of the workers, who begin to resent their lack of independence, and the new leaders may find themselves unable to inspire the kind of loyalty their fathers or mothers enjoyed.

Leaders of a laissez-faire business culture offer a higher level of trust to their employees by giving them more latitude in the performance of their work. The founder determines the ends, but employees are given the power to determine many of the means. But even though the family leader trusts employees, because he or she does not consult employees in determining the company's goals, he or she may not enjoy *their* trust.

They may think the leader's judgment is poor, that he or she is too disengaged from the business to know how it really works, or that his or her ambitions for the business are unrealistic or misconstrued. These employees may therefore not "sign on" to pursue the leader's vision, or their efforts to realize the leadership's goals may be halfhearted.

The participative culture, on the other hand, is based on a high degree of trust on both sides. Family leaders of this type of culture share all decision making with their staff. Although they may formulate the overarching vision that motivates this group-oriented culture, they indulge in very little overt flexing of their own power and influence.

The professional culture relies on management methods associated with nonfamily businesses. In this culture, the leadership emphasizes individual motivation and achievement, rewards talent, and for the most part recognizes only contributions that can be quantitatively measured. In a responsibly-run professional culture, in which the criteria for judging performance are clear, the company's mission is in fact achievable, and promotions, compensation, and other rewards are doled out fairly, employees may feel a cautious kind of trust in their leaders. In this type of culture, however, there is little sense of real loyalty—either of leadership to workforce or workforce to leadership. The suspicion always exists that if the company's situation changes, management will do whatever it takes to adapt, even if it means firing long-term, hardworking, and productive employees. And since employees feel that their employers have made no commitment to them and they enjoy no real job security, they have no qualms about leaving the company if a better opportunity comes along. Few workers join a professionally managed company these days with the idea that they will spend the rest of their careers working there. It is important to note, however, that because a professional culture often promotes competition among employees and ties rewards to performance, this type of culture can be very effective at getting workers to implement a leader's vision—in the short-term, at least.

You will recall that I believe the most effective type of culture for family businesses is a cross between the participative and professional. This combination, in my experience, is ideal for constantly renewing the business. Employee empowerment makes the entire staff feel committed to the future of the company and it encourages them to propose improvements that will keep the company fresh in its response to social changes, technological advances, and competition. Employee empowerment also makes employees feel that they have some control over the company and their destiny, which increases their loyalty and their trust in management. The addition of professional managers in this type of culture ensures that the family business doesn't become too insular. It helps keep the company current with new management practices, and brings in specialized expertise that the family leadership may not possess. That the family is humble enough to recognize that it needs the help of outside managers also helps build employee trust. Inspiring your workforce to pursue your vision for the company involves not only convincing them that you know what you're doing but that you can admit to it when you don't know something.

In the UMass Family Business Center *Related Matters* newsletter, I found an interesting story titled "Rugg Lumber—Stewardship of a Five-Generation Family Business."[9] For four generations, this 153-year-old business was passed on to each upcoming generation by borrowing against the net worth of the company to fund the retirement of the previous generation. The risks of this system became apparent in 1987, when a business slump forced over 40 percent of the business's net worth to be collateralized for the previous generation's retirement fund. When the current president, Mike Fritz, who was fifty-seven at the time, realized that this threatened his own retirement and the business itself, he made some major changes. Under the old system, no one wanted to expand because the company was already supporting such a heavy debt. The family feared that incurring more debt might jeopardize the retirement plans of the generation running the business at any given time.

Fritz's solution was to restructure the company, making a rapid transition to active employee involvement based on "trust, honesty, and communication." This included team-building, strengthening employee benefits, and disseminating a philosophy that made Rugg's employees see themselves as stakeholders. Fritz also adopted profit sharing, gain sharing, and an open-book operating style to ensure that employees understood the cost of doing business. The results have been extraordinary. Fritz and his staff grew the business by 30 percent in seven years while reducing their operating costs to 3 percent below the industry average. Since the business has grown so substantially, funding for his own generation's retirement is secure. Fritz says: "If you do what is necessary to make the business more profitable, your retirement will be taken care of and you won't have to worry about collapsing a five-generation business."

This is only one example of how preserving family businesses from one generation to the next relies on leadership skill—the skill to formulate a strong vision for your company and put it into practice, even if that means radically revamping the company from top to bottom.

Giving People More Reasons to Work

Why do people work? To pay the bills, put their children through college, live the good life—in other words, because almost everyone needs money. But is financial compensation the only reason people work? Or, put another way, are people who work only because they need a paycheck the best employees you can possibly hire? I don't think so. To develop a high-quality workforce that will help make your family business thrive, I firmly believe that you must give employees more reasons for doing good work than just the promise of regular pay.

But let's not kid ourselves: How employees are paid lays the groundwork for their feelings about the company. Faith and trust between employer and employee start here. For many years, businesses operated on the principle that employees expected an annual raise. At a minimum, this raise had to keep up with the consumer price index (CPI) so that wages kept pace with inflation. This system was so ingrained that any company failing to make this minimum annual increase heard about it loud and clear. And rather than increasing employee trust in management, this system created an adversarial relationship between management and workers. If all signs indicated that the company had had a good year but the annual raises only matched the CPI, employers felt aggrieved. If the company had had a tough year and raises were below the CPI, employees felt aggrieved. And since giving ample raises across the board every year would very soon drive labor costs sky-high, employees were rarely delighted with their increases. There was almost no way for this system not to have a debilitating effect on morale. Spirits were regularly raised and lowered by the size of this required annual increase, with a corresponding impact on production, worker commitment, and the personal feelings between management and the company. In many cases, management's desire to please its workforce resulted in increased labor costs that hindered the company's ability to compete. As a result, especially in the 1970s and 1980s, much of our manufacturing base moved to foreign countries in search of lower labor costs. So the annual wage increase—designed to ensure worker security—ended up costing thousands of American jobs.

These days, to be competitive in the fast-changing global market, many companies are changing to a system of "pay by performance." This system rewards those who produce results. Employees understand when they are hired that there will be no automatic annual wage increase. If the company has a good year, employees will earn more. If the company has a bad year, everyone shares in the necessary sacrifices. Under this system, success in each job must be measurable by objective criteria, and these criteria and the methods for measuring them must be approved by the employee. This is but one more extension of empowerment. If management only decides on the performance or productivity factors to be measured and dictates how to measure them, this will be construed as a carrot-and-stick approach, which is not conducive to building good faith. When the employee or team share in discussing which criteria are relevant, this helps lay the building blocks of trust. A consensus agreement about pay practices may include a cost-of-living provision if the employees view the lack of an annual increase as unfair. But if employees have agreed that this cost-of-living adjustment will be tied to a particular index and that it will pertain only to base wages, they will feel as though they control the policy and trust management to do what it has agreed to do.

If, however, everything beyond that cost-of-living adjustment depends on the results of each employee's personal contribution to the success of the company, employees are likely to feel more committed to seeing that the company thrives. They will feel that they have control over their fate to a far greater degree than workers in other types of business cultures, and they will more closely identify their own fate with the fate of the company. Many companies emphasize this subtle shift in the relationship between workers and company leadership by changing the term they use for their nonmanagement staff. Some companies call their workers "associates." Others refer to them as "partners." Disney calls them "cast members." This change from employee to empowered associate helps build a culture with the capacity to fulfill a shared vision of the company's future.

The results can only have a positive effect on the bottom line. A person who is now an associate of the company, compensated by his or her own actions, feels greater motivation to achieve excellence in the product or service provided to customers. After all, it is the customer who ultimately controls that associate's wages. Consistently dedicated service will also earn the trust of the consumer. Consumers want to do business with companies that project integrity in their product or service. They want to have confidence that the product or service is safe, the attendant competent, and the pricing fair. They want consistency and reliability. By providing this predictability of service, the associate can win a repeat customer for the business who has complete faith in whatever the business provides.

So even though every employee would like to be guaranteed an annual raise, looked at objectively this system is not in the best interest of the employee or the company. No annual raise can ensure the success and survival of the company. If you can make your workforce identify its own interests with those of the company—instead of regarding the company as an ill-intentioned monolith whose goal is to squeeze the most out of workers and reward them as little as possible—you will have gone a long way toward giving your employees a greater investment in their jobs, and more reasons to do their best.

At your first meeting with a prospective employee, communicate to him or her that working for you offers more than a paycheck. Too often at these interviews the most important part of the discussion focuses on wages and benefits. But consider what happens if you take a completely different approach. Instead of presenting the wages and benefits as the most enticing thing your firm can offer, present your vision of an exciting company whose goals are inspired by the people who work in it. I guarantee that something different will happen. Prospective employees will get a different message, a message that this company is special—it's a company in which respect for employees is high on management's agenda, where everyone works to exceed customer expectations, and where slogans are backed up with programs that help achieve the company's lofty goals. Suddenly, the whole character of your discussion will change. Instead of slogging through the nuts-and-bolts of compensation, vacation days, sick time, and retirement plans, the discussion will address ways to achieve the company vision. At this moment, you will be able to tell the difference between a person who is interested in a challenge and one who is interested only in a wage for work performed. I am convinced that those people who become the best employees—in terms of performance and productivity—are the people who are interested in working for a company with dynamic goals.

Explaining your vision for the company and for every employee's experience at the company in the initial interview helps you identify people who are more responsive to high ideals and whose temperament and values will fit into the culture you are building. Explaining your vision at the first interview will also help you to attract the right kind of people—people who are impressed with the advantages that working for you offers, and who want to get more out of their work lives than simply wages and benefits. When you consider that people spend more than twice the number of waking hours at work than they do at home, you can appreciate how important it is that your workers care about what they do. Building the systems that help create this good feeling into the culture of your family business is an important part of making that business sturdy enough to survive.

Kouzes and Posner became convinced by their research that leadership is an observable, learnable set of practices.[10] In their study of "personal best" leadership cases, they identified five behavioral commitments necessary to become a strong leader:

- challenge the process;
- inspire a shared vision;
- enable others to act;
- model the way;
- encourage the heart.

Challenging the process

This is the same as our "if it ain't broke, break it" philosophy. A good leader can inspire people to strive for excellence in everything they do by creating a company culture that gives people the freedom to question everything. Rather than a passive concession on the part of the leader ("I'll listen if anyone happens to have an idea"), this should involve an active injunction to staff at all levels. In other words, you must train new employees to challenge the way things are done and give them the latitude to experiment with change. This of course contains risk—resources may be wasted on fruitless efforts and some changes may not represent improvement after all. But the risk will be well worth the rewards when one change turns out to be a winner.

Like everything else, however, experimenting with change requires follow-up and control. If you promote the idea that suggested changes will be tested, then you must have a system in place to put that promise into action. This system should recommend trying new ideas on a limited basis at first, determine the length of trial periods to give each change a realistic chance of proving out, regulate how many changes and what kinds of change can be attempted at the same time, measure costs and benefits, and study consumer responses. And remember, under consensus management, if a change has been approved by a team, the idea probably has merit. Embracing change will go a long way toward giving your employees more reasons to work beyond that paycheck. The average person hates routine. Being asked to reorganize a task to make it less monotonous (on the principle that monotony has a detrimental impact on quality), or to take out unnecessary steps, or to improve quality control adds a creative element to any job.

Inspiring a shared vision

We have already discussed the concept of vision at length, but let me make a few more comments here. To inspire, a vision must be presented with confidence and energy, and it must elicit excitement and promote empowerment. Good leaders listen carefully to employee assessments and respond strongly—but not defensively—when presented with negative criticism. Whether a leader's vision for his or her company is grand and ambitious or modest and small in scale, if it inspires employees and enhances the pride they take in their work, it adds another level of value to their jobs.

Enabling others to act

When you bring people together and challenge them to work on a problem, the mere fact that they have the authority to act independently to solve the problem is a powerful motivator. A good leader not only expresses the desire for people to be empowered, he or she removes roadblocks in their way. When workers realize that they not only have the power to act but the power to collaborate with others in the company in order to act in the most effective way possible, your vision is well on its way toward being realized.

Modeling the way

The ways in which leaders reveal their personal values can have a significant impact on their organizations. This is particularly true of family businesses. If a family member is perceived as lazy, careless, or lackadaisical but holds other managers to a different standard, then the staff will lose respect for their leader, and some of their zeal to excel—and their pleasure in doing so—will be destroyed. If, however, employees respect the values of their leaders, they are more likely to adhere to those values in their own work habits. According to Kouzes and Posner, shared values "foster strong feelings of personal effectiveness, promote high levels of company loyalty, facilitate consensus about key organization goals, encourage ethical behavior, promote strong norms about working hard and caring, [and] reduce levels of job stress and tension." Clearly, the leadership of a family business can earn big dividends by modeling high standards in their personal behavior. This is so important that I suggest including a version of the following statement in every family business plan: "Salaries (of family members) must be based on responsibility and performance. Constant growth, reinvestment, and prudent personal living styles will demonstrate to our associates long-term commitment by our family." The values your company abides by also set standards for your employees. If you adopt ethical policies in your manufacturing methods and treatment of customers, then you will be respected by your employees. They in turn through empowerment will see that these values are executed at every level of the organization. And, again, this gives people pride in what they are doing and more reasons to work and work well.

Encouraging the heart

Rewards systems are a great way to instill pride in employees. Everyone's self-esteem is heightened by recognition, and the best leaders know how important it is to celebrate individual accomplishments. Many companies try to do this with an "employee of the month" program. Unfortunately, these often fail because too often the same employee wins the award. Many other workers may have done great things during a given month but because the program can only recognize the best one, other contributions go unnoticed. Good intentions can lead to a demoralizing program. Once again, organizing into teams provides a lot of advantages. In our program, team members vote every month for an individual who did something extraordinary. This kind of recognition by one's peers can be a powerful incentive to work harder and better—and it can greatly enhance the enjoyment people take in their work. Every month, ScrubaDub management also recognizes teams with above-average performance records, and management can give an award to any employee who exceeds expectations at any time. Part of what makes our program effective is that we link rewards to performance recognition. And to prevent the program from getting stale, we give our awards in points that when accumulated can be redeemed for a variety of prizes.

Another important part of "encouraging the heart" is celebrating major accomplishments. These can be milestone events in the growth of the company or unusual accomplishments by individuals. When everyone has pushed hard for a deadline—a new product rollout, a systems redesign, or a productivity target—nothing makes people want to go back and do it again more than praise, thanks, and some form of celebration. The making of heroes is another important part of business culture. By singling out someone for exemplary work, you not only encourage that employee to keep doing their best, you inspire everyone else and give them a new goal or standard to measure themselves against.

Training—The Heart and Soul of a Business

Once you have hired a talented, ambitious group of workers who like working in teams and share your vision for the kind of company you want to be, you need to train them. You could just throw them onto the job and let them learn as they go—it's a tried-and-true method and it works pretty well, eventually. But if excellence is really your goal, and you want to create a workforce that can help pilot your firm to the top of your field and keep it there, one of the obvious ways to make your company stand out from the competition is through aggressive training. When you shop at a store such as Wal-Mart and an employee greets you at the entrance, you know that this company takes employee training seriously. Visit a Disney theme park and again witness the results of exhaustive training. Look at the impact of Total Quality Management on dozens of manufacturing firms. Where quality used to be narrowly conceived as pertaining to the end product or service, progressive companies have found that getting people to think about excellence in every department, work process, and independent function produces better results throughout the service or production chain. Take any industry and compare those companies with formal training programs to those without them and I guarantee that the firms with training programs will be the growth leaders.

A good training program isn't merely a means to become an industry leader, however; for family firms I believe that training is a matter of survival. Companies that do not get involved in some form of organized training will eventually lose out to the competition. You need to train your employees to adhere to the best standards in their field; you need to train them in team building and team decision-making; you need to train them in consensus management; and you need to train them in the principles of constant change. You also need to train every employee in customer service. It's simple: People want to do business with companies that produce a top-quality product or service for a good price. But if several companies produce an equally good product for a comparable price, the customer will choose the company that makes doing business with them most pleasant and efficient. In one way or another, doing business is showmanship. Many of us are not born with a winning smile or a pleasing personality. However, to beat the competition and truly excel, we must demand these two attributes in addition to specific job-related knowledge and teach people how to use their interpersonal skills to best effect.

Good training starts at the job screening interview. Define the personal attributes necessary for employees in your business and then strive to hire people with these qualities. Molding their behavior to your vision of how you want your customers treated should then become a primary goal of your training program.

Let me list some of the fundamental elements necessary in a good training program. To begin with, it must start the first day of the job. Many companies, including Wal-Mart, keep new employees in training for two to three weeks before they ever face a customer. Your goal should be for your business to present a consistent front at all levels, from top to bottom. This means not letting any new employees start working until they have passed at least one level of basic training and acquired a good understanding of the company culture. I recommend standardized tests at each level. These set consistent expectations and allow you to weed out people who are unable to meet your criteria.

If your training program is to succeed, your training must also be interactive. Experience has taught me that you cannot lecture to people if you want them to leave the classroom fully equipped to fulfill all your requirements. Learning works best when people actually experience the types of situations they will encounter and see for themselves the results of different responses. Interactive personal experiences illustrate the points made in your written materials and make them memorable. Let's take one excellent customer-service training technique as an example. Stating repeatedly that you expect your employees to be polite to customers will have far less impact than asking the members of a training class to describe their very worst service experiences. If you then ask the class to speculate about why the retail clerk or sales representative behaved the way he or she did, and then ask the class to recommend alternative methods for handling the same situation, they will understand the difference between good and bad service far better. If you then ask members of the class to describe their very best service experience and discuss what made this service so exceptional, they will better understand what makes for excellent customer service. Explaining how excellent customer service works in your environment will now have more meaning. Training must also be fun. Creating skits or using role-playing not only makes the experience of learning more pleasurable, it emphasizes from the beginning that you want your employees to enjoy their jobs. You can use a variety of games—those modeled on the television game show *Jeopardy* are popular and effective—to help illustrate your points and make learning an interesting experience.

The third element of good training is that it must be goal oriented and measurable. A class, whether it lasts one day or one week, must have a specific goal. Let's say you are teaching the basic philosophy of the company, including rules and regulations. You may do this through an interactive dialogue, and everyone may participate and seem to understand, but at some point you need to test the class on what they have learned. Developing a written syllabus to guide both instructors and students accomplishes two things. First, it ensures some degree of consistency in the material being taught. Second, it signals that a certain level of competency must be attained before a new employee is sent onto the job. Testing for results also sends a message of how important training is to the company's future.

An effective training program should also tie training to compensation. Rewarding employees with predetermined pay increases for attaining certain skill levels makes an important statement about the importance of training and the company's readiness to recognize and reward individual performance. Naturally, it also provides extra incentive for employees to develop their abilities and make a greater contribution to the company. As an extra benefit, by moving from one skill level to the next, employees not only increase their wages, they gain self-esteem and added pride in their accomplishments. Your acknowledgment of employee achievement will be even more effective if you formalize the process with certificates, graduation ceremonies, or some other type of recognition program.

If you do not have a training program and you're not sure where to start, you have a number of good alternatives. The Internet is an excellent resource. Use any search engine and type in the keywords you are interested in. With very little effort, you can find generic videos and training material on almost every subject. There are also many companies listed on the Internet that will help you develop your own training program. Your suppliers may be another good resource. Many companies will provide material explaining their products to businesses that use those products. You may discover unexpected resources in-house as well. As you begin building a training program, you may discover one outstanding employee who excels at both understanding your vision and explaining it well. This employee, with a little training in how to train, may be just the person to lead your program.

Since training, like everything else in the family business environment, should be designed for long-term results, it should be ongoing. This may mean not only sending employees back for additional training periodically, but occasionally featuring a guest speaker on a subject of importance to your company. You can also benefit by subsidizing outside training that enhances individual skills or teaches specialized subjects that may be needed by only a few members of your staff.

A strong training program should include training for the company leadership as well as for its frontline workers. To move from one generation to another, a company must develop strong leaders, and as we discussed above, leadership skills *can* be learned.

Lastly, it is essential that dedication to training involve all levels of management. Who better to explain the vision of a company than its CEO or president? In a family business, it is even more important for a family member to express excitement about the vision of the company and communicate a sense of esprit de corps. Let's put it another way. If you thought that each new employee was the person who would make or break your firm, you would give each one special attention, wouldn't you? So why not do it?

Building a Customer Franchise

We all know the importance of building a customer franchise. After all, family businesses practically invented the concept of a customer franchise because they traditionally provided the kind of service that earns customer loyalty: friendly, personalized service. But with the growth of our cities, the sprawling of suburban America, and the increase in commuting and telecommuting, we can't rely on old friends in the neighborhood to keep our businesses going. Never mind that our old friends may be long gone—the neighborhood itself may have disappeared or become unrecognizable. Still, I'm convinced that the ideas discussed in this chapter can help any family business find and win that solid customer base it needs, as long as the business is providing a product or service that people continue to need.

Let me give you an example of how we at ScrubaDub used all of the ideas discussed in this chapter to renew our business, expand in a sensible way, and build a strong customer franchise. In 1983 I read the book *In Search of Excellence: Lessons from America's Best-Run Companies,* by Thomas J. Peters and Robert H. Waterman Jr. I immediately decided that our business could reap big rewards by making it a policy goal to exceed customer expectations. At about the same time, American Airlines announced its frequent flyer program, the first in the industry. At a brainstorming session, we hatched the idea of creating our own frequent wash program to reward our best customers. Our first step was to identify which of our customers gave us most of our business. We did this by forming a car care club that offered special benefits, such as a two-day clean-car guarantee. If bad weather or even a bird dirties your car within two days after we've cleaned it, you can return for a free wash. Another benefit was a coupon for a free "works wash" (our best wash) after ten paid washes. By tracking our car club members using bar code technology, we were able to learn who our best customers were, what kind of cars they drove, where they resided, and which service options they preferred. It turned out that about 20 percent of our customers were responsible for 80 percent of our revenue! We created a database containing all the information we had collected. From then on, the bar codes we affixed to our club members' cars enabled us to recognize these customers as soon as they drove onto one of our lots, and the database allowed us to treat them like very special people. This gave us a competitive edge and helped us build a very loyal customer franchise of people who will bypass other car washes to come to us.

Another family business that exemplifies a sustainable business culture of the type we have been discussing is Rosenbluth International.[11] This company was founded in 1892 to provide transportation for immigrants from Europe to the United States. After three generations, Rosenbluth had grown into an established full-service travel agent in the Philadelphia area employing a few dozen people and doing about $20 million in business annually. When Hal Rosenbluth, a member of the fourth generation, entered the business, he was asked to start a corporate division catering to the travel needs of large companies. This coincided with airline deregulation, which created new opportunities for corporations to save on corporate travel expenses. The early days of getting the corporate division off the ground were pressured and hectic, and Hal Rosenbluth was impressed with the dedication, spirit of cooperation, and friendly good nature displayed by his staff. He became convinced that by placing employees first, he would end up providing his customers with excellent service. From this basic idea of placing employees first, Rosenbluth Travel grew in under fifteen years into a business with 2,350 employees and 350 offices doing over $2.5 billion in sales a year.

Hal Rosenbluth's system starts with the interview process in which potential associates are screened. In 1996 the firm received twenty-one thousand job applicants and hired only eight hundred from that pool.[12] Rosenbluth makes no bones about looking for employees who fit into the firm's culture and will respond with excellent customer service. The number one characteristic he is looking for, he says, is niceness. Kindness, caring, compassion, and unselfishness rank far higher among the firm's selection criteria than a potential employee's past work history. Rosenbluth also seeks out people who will inspire those around them. Once hired, the firm's staff members are never referred to as employees; they are all called associates. Every new hire goes to the firm's main office in Philadelphia for two days of orientation. During the first day, they learn about the company's philosophy and values. They study teamwork and listening skills. They spend the second day in role-playing, using skits that ask the new recruits to act out their worst and best service experiences. Before the day is over, the officers of the company serve the new associates tea, and the associates experience both the open-door policy of the CEO and management's belief in their importance to the success of the company. After this orientation, new associates attend an extensive six-to-eight-week training program. By the time they start serving clients, they are fully trained in their jobs, fully immersed in the company culture, and fully empowered to make their own decisions.[13]

Rosenbluth believes that in order for people to give their best, they must be happy in what they are doing. The company monitors this regularly through a "happiness barometer," a systematic approach to measuring associate morale. Management also makes a concerted effort to show concern for their employees' welfare and encourages them to use voice mail and e-mail to put forward any criticisms they may have.

Rosenbluth has also created an environment that inspires creativity. The company is team-based, with both quality and cross-functional teams meeting monthly. A large in-house training staff regularly introduces new programs to improve the skills of all employees. Brainstorming techniques are taught in their training sessions, and Hal Rosenbluth sponsors a special week every year during which employees are urged to come up with new ideas to improve service quality.

Because Rosenbluth's management listens so intently to the needs of employees, they demand outstanding performance in return. Through investment in new technology, the firm has developed its own software that monitors the speed and accuracy of its agents. Compensation is linked directly to performance, and every associate receives a review by his or her immediate superior as well as subordinate. Before any merit increase, associates also receive a written performance appraisal that includes a variety of objective measures. These methods have been so effective in inspiring employees and giving them every reason to work at the top of their abilities that Rosenbluth's associates earn the highest average wage in their industry.

The firm's success and huge market share—as well as proprietary software Rosenbluth has developed that gives it direct access to all airline reservation systems—has enabled management to negotiate advantageous deals with all the airlines serving the U.S. market. This gives the firm a competitive advantage in servicing its corporate clients. Information in the database gives every associate extensive information about the preferences of individual clients, enabling them to routinely exceed their customers' expectations and provide the highest quality of service. The information in the database also helps with future strategic planning.

Let's look at how many of the ideas discussed in this book Rosenbluth used to fuel its tremendous growth. Hal Rosenbluth did not start at the bottom of the ladder to work his way up. He entered the family company in a management position and brought along a few ideas about managing people. He started a new division. He recognized early that pay-for-performance would keep a well-trained, motivated staff attentive to customer needs. By providing a "fun" work atmosphere and displaying genuine concern for his employees, he proved that people do not work only for money. By using technology in a creative way, Rosenbluth collected and analyzed information about the travel habits of his best customers, which gave him a competitive edge in winning and keeping their business. An early believer in TQM, he trained his people to be quality conscious in everything they do. His "idea week" and constant quest to change for the better demonstrate the value of challenging paradigms and remaking old ways of doing things. For these efforts, Rosenbluth International was recognized as Service Company of the Year by author and business excellence expert Tom Peters and named one of the ten best companies to work for in America by Robert Levering and Milton Moskowitz.[14]

The Rosenbluth family were able to change the culture of their business in order to survive and grow. In their quest to renew the business for another generation, they reinvested substantial funds into new technology, employee training, and exceptional customer service. The new CEO inspired a shared vision and through a participative culture gained the trust and dedication of his employees.

Key Messages from This Chapter

❖ Encourage experimentation and the developing of new ideas.

Passing on an effective business philosophy is critical for long-term competitiveness and survival. Renewing the business is one proven way of keeping up with the times. This will happen only if resources are allocated to developing new products and services. The lifeblood of future generations will be their ability to continue to come up with new and timely ideas.

❖ Create a strong reinvestment program.

Too often I see second-generation businesses in which the profits are evenly split at the end of each year. Their culture did not include constant reinvestment for continuous improvements. It doesn't matter if the funds are used for remodeling older facilities or research into new technology. The key is a model that makes a commitment to the future.

❖ Inspire a shared vision.

People prefer to work for a company that has a clear, identifiable vision. When you can articulate this in an exciting format, remarkable things happen. Your associates will find other reasons besides their paycheck to work for the company. Pay by performance will be accepted as both reasonable and challenging. There will be a greater motivation to achieve excellence, and everyone in the business, including your children, will be proud of what they do.

❖ Formalize a training program.

Every company has some form of training program. How serious you become with employee instruction differentiates you from the competition. Customers react positively to well-trained personnel. This is but one more step in building a business culture that will help the next generation survive.

4

Managing
Family Conflict

There is no family business story that doesn't involve some degree of conflict. Fathers who favor one child over another, brothers who don't get along, spouses who think their mates are overworked and underpaid. Conflict among family members is so prevalent in family businesses that we must assume it is inevitable. Understanding and accepting conflict as natural will ease the burden of trying to avoid it. Recognizing that conflict can also be helpful—to the business as well as the family—will make dealing with it easier.

Psychologists say that conflict in family businesses typically starts early on, at the entrepreneurial stage.[1] Many people who start their own businesses do so, apparently, because of unresolved conflicts with their own parents. They feel driven to go into business by themselves in order to escape the authority of a more powerful figure or figures. The business becomes their domain, where they can exercise their wills without being challenged. Those who work for these founders learn quickly not to question their authority or try to struggle out from under their dominance. Then along comes a child and two forces collide. The founder's desire to create a dynasty, even on a small scale, clashes with his or her realization that some of the power must be yielded. At the same time, the son or daughter tries to gain their independence and take on increased responsibility, but the parent resists loosening his or her hold on the reins. Eventually, the child rebels against the constant intrusions and broken promises of retirement on the part of the parents. And this is only the beginning!

If conflict between generations is not enough, sibling rivalry can be almost as disastrous. Put two or more siblings in the succession order, and conflict becomes a given. The rivalry among children for their parents' approval often begins early and only escalates when the children reach adulthood and enter the business. If the oldest child is chosen as successor, the younger child (or children) becomes convinced that the oldest was the favorite all along and that merit and fair play never entered into the decision. The pot begins to simmer. Once the children marry and their spouses join the fray, the business becomes a battleground, with each family fighting to protect its turf.

The large-scale entry of women into the business world in the past few decades and their demonstrated competence in every area of management have created other sources of conflict. A father, for example, may be more protective of his daughter and more critical of his son.[2] Or, he may feel that women belong at home, and subtly undermine his daughter's attempts to build a career for herself beyond motherhood. Then there is the question of bringing in a son-in-law as a possible successor. I have encountered many businesses where this has worked very well. In most successful instances, the son-in-law brought with him particular expertise that helped the business grow. Even in those cases, though, conflict has arisen over whether the son-in-law should be given stock.

My family was not exempt from problems. Conflict between our sons arose early in their careers. I took the position that their salaries should be based on their job performance. My older son, Bob, felt that he should have a higher salary because he'd been part of the business longer and therefore had seniority. Dan felt that they should have equal salaries if they were going to be equal partners someday. Holding to my own point of view, I challenged them to defend their salaries on the basis of their job performance. They did this very well. Bob, who supervised operations for the entire chain, argued that if he didn't satisfy customer quality expectations, all his brother's efforts to train employees and market our services wouldn't mean anything. Dan responded that well-trained employees perform to higher standards, and therefore make a significant contribution to satisfying customer quality expectations. He also pointed out that without his marketing and advertising skills, we wouldn't have many customers in the first place.

This conflict came to a head around the question of work habits. Bob, who was married without children, spent many more hours on the job. Dan, who had gone through a divorce and had an infant son whom he saw on a limited basis, was sensitive to his parental obligations and was able to spend less time at work than Bob chose to spend. He felt that he was capable of doing adequate work in fewer hours. Bob thought the bottom line was that he worked harder than his brother. Their mother and I were caught in the middle.

Is Family Conflict Healthy?

At about this time, I attended a conference on conflict given by Bobby Gordon, a well-respected family business consultant.[3] Gordon declared that conflict was the number one reason family-owned businesses fail to survive into the next generation. She defined conflict as "the inability to understand the other person's issue and unwillingness to compromise your position." To my surprise, though, Gordon didn't believe conflict was a bad thing. She said that it was simply a fact of life in a family business. Other experts support her point of view. In a study of family businesses by Paul Rosenblatt and his associates, 90 percent of the families surveyed reported ongoing tension or stress in their relationships because the business was a family one.[4] An article about family businesses in the *Wall Street Journal*[5] went even further, noting that squabbles abound and warning children who want to join their family businesses that this decision will probably lead to bitterness and bad feeling. The article cited several examples, including one of a bank CEO and his children who ousted their father, convinced he could no longer cope with the complexities of running a modern bank. The *Journal* article also mentioned several well-publicized cases in which brothers who were partners in large businesses fought over seemingly trivial things.

But Gordon made another point that really got my attention. Conflict in and of itself isn't bad, she said; what causes trouble are an excessive fear of conflict and the inability to deal with it constructively. To make this point, she gave the audience at the conference two tests. One asked us to rate ourselves on a "conflict comfort" scale whose responses to conflict ranged from "Sorry, gotta run. I'll get back to you about that later" to "Oh yeah?!!! Well, I don't want to do it that way!!!!" The audience was evenly distributed between those who preferred to dodge potentially inflammatory issues and those whose reflex was to "go at it." The second test asked us to pick what we thought was the ideal combination of conflict and cohesion for effective problem solving. The choices were:

- high conflict/low cohesion
- high conflict/high cohesion
- low conflict/low cohesion
- low conflict/high cohesion

The majority of as picked low conflict/high cohesion, reasoning that business would proceed most smoothly if the family got along well enough to avoid conflict most of the time and had high enough cohesion to deal with it on those rare occasions when it arose. In fact, Gordon contended, the ideal combination is really high conflict/high cohesion. Her studies had shown that businesses owned by families able to tolerate and work through a lot of conflict tended to be aggressive, innovative companies that continued to grow. She said that the persistence of change—in business and in families—necessarily creates conflict. That gives families in business together a clear choice between destructive or constructive solutions.

Most family business owners don't approach conflict in this way, unfortunately, as Gordon's test demonstrates. Most of us clearly prefer to avoid conflict. But a business and family culture that practices conflict-avoidance will also be a culture in which people are afraid to point out problems, will decide they don't care enough to challenge decisions they disagree with because the risk of conflict is too great, or will conclude that discussing differences of opinion will only make things worse.

The question then is how do we turn conflict into a constructive force for our families and our businesses? The first step is to accept the notion that conflict is a natural phenomenon that is always present. The nature and personalities of the parties involved will determine whether it is brought out. When people harbor grievances and avoid confrontation, their concealed resentment influences their own work and their interactions with the people around them, whether they want it to or not. Eventually, despite the most strenuous efforts to avoid it, conflict will raise its ugly head. By then, the grievance will have festered, and a happy resolution may be impossible. The alternative is to accept that at one point or another, in one generation or another, conflict will develop. We can keep it from destroying our businesses and our families if we build ways to deal with it into our family culture.

How do we do this? Conflict resolution is as old as the hills, and the library is full of books written about the subject. John Ward, in *Keeping the Family Business Healthy,* proposes that each family develop a code of understanding or a code of conduct. This code might proscribe arguing or criticizing a family member in public, passing judgment on the private lives or parenting practices of other family members, or spending company money on personal needs without the full knowledge and/or approval of others in the business. The code could also urge family members to work toward consensus whenever faced with difficult decisions. Most important, it should advise family members to treat one another with respect no matter how much they disagree.[6]

David Bork in *Family Business, Risky Business,* discusses a number of things families should not do.[7] Bork especially recommends against trying to manage conflict between two people or two factions by bringing in a third. To explain how and why people do this, Bork refers to Murray Bowen's theories of "differentiation of self." Bowen calls this conflict-resolution strategy "triangulating." Rather than dealing directly with the source of conflict, Bork says, families often try to resolve difficulties through triangulation. He makes the point that only when triangles are eliminated can two people resolve their conflict with each other. For example, if one person has a problem with someone and goes to another person to discuss it, that is triangulation. This is different from two people in a conflict agreeing to go to a third person for mediation.

John Ward and Craig Aronoff, in volume 5 of their leadership series, propose some useful techniques for dealing with conflict over compensation—a classic problem that can be damaging and divisive if not handled properly.[8] As Ward and Aronoff point out, compensation problems rarely arise during a family business's first, entrepreneurial stage, because the parents remain firmly in control and determine all questions of compensation. But during the second stage (Ward and Aronoff call this the sibling stage), problems frequently develop. The causes are predictable: Either the parents haven't taught their children that salaries must be based on market conditions, or the children don't appreciate the difference between salary for a job performed and dividends for equity as owners. Misunderstanding their own role, children often enter the business with high salary expectations. They may have the same expectations for perks.

To avoid these problems, parents not only need to teach their children about basic economic principles and the concept of pay for performance, they need to establish a fair policy for paying family members. They should also make clear that this policy and its application can be discussed at any time. Ward and Aronoff believe that younger family members confronted with the powerful will of their parents often do not feel free to express their confusion over salary decisions. While establishing an equitable pay policy, parents should also spell out rules dealing with work habits, lifestyle choices, and other issues that arise among siblings. Having these rules in place can help clarify the real problem when, for example, one child works very hard and holds a responsible position and another works only a few hours and shoulders little responsibility. Rules can also take emotion out of the mix when hard truths surface, such as the inescapable fact that we are not all born with the same talents, ambition, or stamina.

But how to set a standard that applies equally to everyone and that everyone can agree with? Business consultants recommend copying corporate America. Make the difference between job performance and company ownership clear from the start. Hew to a policy that pays every employee, even your favorite child, for current performance of the job he or she has been assigned to do—not for expected future performance, not for potential performance, but for proven performance. Develop objective and clearly defined job descriptions for every post. Make sure that compensation stays competitive with pay for similar jobs in similar industries. Insist that the most qualified—not the most closely related—people fill open positions within the company, and require annual peer reviews to ensure that everyone continues to perform to the highest standards. All of these policies will help head off conflict and provide a basis for settling disputes when they do arise.

My sons' dispute about compensation was a classic second-stage conflict. One partner, Bob, was a workaholic; the other, Dan, wanted every other weekend off to be with his infant son. This difference in their working styles not only had an impact on the relationship between them, it had an impact on their wives and families. I tried giving them both performance reviews on a quarterly basis, but I found it difficult to excessively criticize them, and in any case I was pleased with their performance. As I puzzled about the problem, I realized that the best solution would be for someone other than me to do their performance appraisals. Exploring ways to make this happen led to a companywide system in which someone below each employee being appraised rates that person's performance. This worked beautifully. Not only did the new system move us further into management by consensus, but it actually improved performance at all managerial levels. Human nature is a powerful force, and no one wants to think that their subordinate does not think much of the boss.

Bob and Dan were pleased with this solution, since it seemed entirely fair and unbiased; their wives were satisfied; my wife, who had feared a rupture in the family, was delighted; and our nonfamily employees were happy. I was relieved, since I was convinced that if we hadn't found a way to bring the conflict to the surface and resolve it, this issue would have begun to intrude on our business. Whichever of my sons was more unhappy would have continued fretting over a situation that he felt was unfair. At some point, his feelings would have interfered with his work; this would have created a new problem, masking the original problem. The relationship between the brothers would have begun to deteriorate, they might have lost respect for each other, and eventually they could have been forced into a major confrontation. The performance review procedure helped us resolve the compensation discussion.

My family also held the potential for another common second-stage conflict. As I noted, my two sons joined my business but my daughter did not. If, in a desire to be evenhanded and fair with all my children, whom I love equally, I had given my daughter the same amounts of stock that I gave to her brothers, the following scenario might have developed. Since she became a schoolteacher and teachers are notoriously underpaid, my daughter at some point might have wanted to sell her stock in order to make a major purchase—a house, for example. Needing to make as much money as possible, she could have chosen to sell her stock on the open market, to the highest bidder. This would have threatened her brothers' future control of the company, and changed ScrubaDub from a business wholly owned by the family to one owned in part by investors with little long-term commitment to the business. Hoping to avoid this change, her brothers might have decided to buy her shares themselves. This would have necessitated borrowing against their own shares; if this debt later became burdensome, it could have forced them to sell the business even if they didn't want to.

Protecting second and future generations from these scenarios and others like them starts with a family culture that encourages all family members to bring problems relating to the business to the table as soon as possible. In my experience, a great format for this is a weekly meeting for all members of the family working in the business. Instituting a time and place for the family to meet each week creates a regular forum for the airing of grievances and the working out of disagreements. Unlike a typical corporate meeting, at a family meeting both family and business issues can be discussed. Everyone has a chance to express concern for other's troubles and enthusiasm for the successes. After the CEO presents an update on current activities, each person can report on the progress of their work or special projects. In this way, everyone knows who is doing what, no one feels shut out of the loop, and everyone has a chance to debate policy changes. When debate does not lead to consensus, majority rules.

I know of one family business employing over a thousand people, Massachusetts Envelope Company, in which three generations meet not just every week but every day. Although a member of the third generation is running this business very successfully, he told a large group of family business owners that his day would not be complete without the daily ritual of meeting his grandfather and father for morning coffee in the conference room.

A second useful device for constructively dealing with conflict, as I discussed in Chapter 2, is an annual family council meeting. This meeting, which should be run by a professional facilitator and include spouses and family members not in the business, gives all members of the family a chance to voice their ideas and express their feelings. At this meeting, some issues will come out that matter to different people for different reasons or only matter to some members of the family, but nevertheless need to be heard. Only through this kind of open communication will the people who do need to know become aware that these issues even exist.

In addition to these standard family business practices, I recommend instituting four other formal provisions to deal with conflict: (1) assembling a board of outside directors or advisers to provide an objective analysis of how the business is being run; (2) developing a system for limiting ownership of the business to family members working in the business; (3) appointing a deadlock trustee to settle disputes that can't be resolved through other means; and (4) writing up a standard stock redemption agreement controlling the sale of stock by family members. These last three techniques are discussed in detail in Chapters 5 and 6. Here I will discuss the importance of outside directors.

Using Outside Directors

The founder of an old-line Massachusetts manufacturing company announces his retirement and relinquishes day-to-day control of the company to his son-in-law.[9] But he hedges his bets, holding on to 51 percent of the company's stock. He also expects to continue controlling the company's direction. "Just keep doing what I've been doing," he advises his successor. "It's always worked fine. I don't want to risk my retirement income on a too-aggressive growth plan." Although committed to seeing his father-in-law enjoy a comfortable retirement, the younger man protests that the status quo won't work. "Our products are gradually being replaced by entirely new technology," he explains. "If we don't redefine our business, we're dead." Dad remains unconvinced.

Here again we have a situation in which two members of a family business, both acting in good faith, honestly disagree. On the one hand, the retiring founder's concern for his future may be influencing his business judgment. On the other, the younger man may be dazzled by the promise of new, untested technology and ready to jump into new markets without adequately studying the implications of this move. Rather than tussling over who has the authority to make the decision, these two men must figure out the best strategy for the future of the company. If the company continues to thrive, the retiring founder's final years will be secure.

In this situation, one of the best resources a family business can have is an outside board of directors. An outside board can help clarify the issues to be studied, provide an objective analysis of alternative scenarios, and help refine future strategy.

Here's another example. Two brothers serve as copresidents of a medical technology company whose proprietary process once afforded them comfortable margins and steady growth. Now a competitor's R and D department has developed a faster, cheaper alternative and the brothers' company is losing market share. One brother wants to diversify beyond the medical market, adapting their proven technology for new applications. The other brother feels that they should invest aggressively in new process improvements and defend their traditional market position. Both men are lobbying the rest of the management team and pushing their senior managers into choosing sides.

Once again, an outside board could help defuse this situation and point the company in the right direction. Since more and more businesses are being reinvented in today's fast-moving competitive economy, the odds are high that an outside board member will have already gone through a similar decision-making process. Even if none of them have, a board can help a family business get past gut feelings and emotional judgments to design a process that will systematically weigh alternatives and study their ramifications.

Let's look at one more common family business conflict. Having succeeded their father, three siblings share leadership of a fourth-generation family business selling luxury goods. As they approach the new century, each has a different vision of what the company should be. The oldest is committed to keeping the original U.S. factory open at practically any cost. "This is our heritage and our identity," he explains. "We're an American company manufacturing American goods with American labor. I believe it's why people buy our product." The youngest, concerned about staying cost-competitive, is pushing to move manufacturing overseas. "We can't afford to be sentimental," he says. "Our name brand will carry us. But if we don't lower our costs, our products won't be around at all." The middle brother worries about the gulf opening up between his siblings. His strongest feeling is that the three of them must find a way to agree. Over four generations, it has been a central part of his family culture that everyone in the family at least respect everyone else's point of view. What was not part of the culture was a process for achieving agreement. Once again, the ideas and insights of an outside board of directors could help ease the tension in this situation and help these brothers assess their options and agree on a solution.

An outside board can also be helpful in resolving conflict over compensation, job performance, and interpretations of policy decisions. Most of the time, these issues can be resolved without turning to an outside board. But the existence of the board provides a strong incentive for disagreeing partners to work things out. An effective board can even prevent the sale of a family businesses if one generation is ready to retire and the next generation isn't ready to take over completely. An outside board can help find a mentor for a relatively green CEO or even bring in professional management to run the company for the family until a new generation of family leaders is in place.

It's also important to note that the existence of an outside board need not have a dehumanizing effect on the business, making it a place in which compassion for family members in need plays no part. Obviously, decisions cannot be made to satisfy the needs of a family member if the business will suffer as a result. But balancing the needs of the family with those of the business can be difficult, especially if the CEO also happens to be the parent of the family member in need. Here again, a board can be useful, sometimes taking delicate decisions out of the hands of the CEO, making the right course more obvious, or simply refereeing a debate about the best course of action. Numerous research studies have shown that an outside board of directors can keep a company focused and help the CEO separate family and business issues.[10]

My own search to find better ways to handle conflict between my sons persuaded me that an outside board would be helpful. Every book I read about family businesses supported this conclusion. Experts in the field unanimously agree that family businesses can only benefit from establishing an outside board of directors to advise on major decisions. Benjamin Benson, a highly regarded family business consultant, believes that independent boards of directors can provide valuable advice and constitute a check and balance to owners who are willing to submit themselves to their review. He feels that an outside board can bring new dimensions of objectivity, experience, and candor to a family business, as well as provide valuable networking connections.[11] A study of 322 family businesses reported in *Family Business Review* concluded that companies with outside board members were more satisfied than firms with no input from outside the family. Outside directors were perceived as being more helpful than boards made up entirely of family members in providing unbiased views, forcing accountability, and establishing networks of contacts.[12] John Ward, in *Keeping the Family Business Healthy,* writes: "When the company and its owners become complacent, these advisers can help the organization focus on fresh potential in the market and give it new, more exciting visions of the future. They can also lobby for and help develop new standards of performance."[13] An article John Ward and Craig Aronoff wrote for *Nation's Business* lists ten myths that make family business owners resist outside boards. Ward and Aronoff conclude that the real obstacles are usually family politics or one partner's lack of enthusiasm for the idea. They recommend creating an advisory council first, to demonstrate the value of outside opinions and ideas.[14]

Although I was fully persuaded of the value an outside board could bring to our business, my own family didn't agree. For two years I proposed creating a board, and each time the rest of the family rejected the idea. My wife was afraid that outside board members would not be sympathetic to family issues. Although I assured her that boards do not get involved in family disputes except to recommend processes for resolving conflict, she was not convinced. My sons, I presume, did not want outsiders judging their performance. I argued that if we were going to build a family culture that would allow our business to survive from one generation to the next, we had to accept that we couldn't do it all ourselves. Our family was too small to possess all the capabilities and knowledge that would make this possible. In addition, I said, like most family cultures, ours was too insulated, too informal, and too influenced by our feelings for one another. With only family members making business decisions, I feared we would agree on a strategy for reasons that were not always in the best interests of the business. I suggested that outside board members could help us bridge the gap between family concerns and business realities. Everyone listened to me talk, but they remained skeptical. Since I had committed myself to consensus management, I resisted imposing my will on the others, but eventually I realized that I had to force the issue.

Finally, as a compromise, the family let me follow Ward and Aronoff's suggestion and set up an outside board of advisers rather than a board of voting members with decision-making power. At the request of my sons, I agreed that the board members would not be friends of mine. Since it is generally agreed that board members should not include professionals retained by the company, we chose people we respected in the business community but did not know. We began by making a list of people possessing expertise we thought we needed. Since we wanted people who would question our marketing and finance strategies and since we were also interested in what large public companies were paying consultants to study, this list included a marketing person, a financial person, and a consultant to large corporations. Each of the three people we asked to become members of our board of advisers accepted. They were intrigued that a closed family business was interested in outside input.

The results turned out to be a surprise for each of us. From the beginning, members of the ScrubaDub board of directors made it clear that they did not want to deal with family issues. They believed that they should stay focused on business issues. This allayed Elaine's concerns. Also, rather than evaluating the individual performance of my two sons, they were interested in looking at the success of the business overall. After a few meetings and some probing questions, they became very knowledgeable about our industry, our problems, and our operations.[15] They have helped us stay focused on our core business, introduced new ideas in their areas of expertise, and encouraged us to face issues that many family businesses postpone addressing. One of their recommendations was that we change accountants. Our accountant at the time was a personal friend who had worked for me from my first day in business. Our board felt that because of the size of his firm and its limited resources, we were not getting the services we needed at that stage in our development. It was extremely difficult for me to end a long-term business relationship and I was sure that doing so would damage the friendship. It took me a few years to realize that the board was absolutely right, however, and I finally made the change. Without their prodding I never would have done it. Sadly, however, the friendship did not survive.

Here is just one example of how a member of our board of advisers helped our business. Richard Valintine was the CEO of the Jiffy Lube franchise for the Boston market. His franchise ranked in the top 5 percent nationally out of all the franchises in the Jiffy Lube chain. We chose him because we admired his company's marketing efforts and were impressed with its growth. Once he joined our board, we learned that he'd achieved this remarkable growth because of a deep commitment to target marketing. During one of the first meetings he attended, our marketing plans for the coming year were on the agenda. Until then, we had favored saturation-by-zip-code direct-mail promotions because we assumed every home would have a car. Dick suggested that even if every car owner was a potential customer, some owners were likely to wash their cars more frequently than others. This observation prompted us to explore how we might learn to distinguish the buying habits of our customers. We had developed a program using bar code technology to track over fifty thousand of our customers by the year, color, and model of their cars as well as the communities they lived in. With Dick's prodding, we identified our most frequent customers and were able to target special programs, incentives, and service options to their needs and tastes. As a result, we substantially raised the effectiveness of our marketing program and—more to the point—increased our revenues by 20 percent.

The ways in which the board members shaped their own roles gave me a few ideas for making the best use of an outside board. To start with, new members of your board need to understand your company. You must introduce them to your family culture, explain the high standards you have set for your family business, and help them understand your long-term vision for the company. Three key documents can help you do this: a family business plan, a company strategic plan, and a current five-year plan.

I described the importance of a comprehensive and carefully considered family business plan in Chapter 2. This document guides the family in every aspect of running the business. It distinguishes the goals and values of the family business from those of a public company and articulates the ethical standards that will underpin all dealings with employees, vendors, competitors, and customers.

The second document that helps outside board members understand your company is the company strategic plan. Many books have been written about developing effective strategic plans, so I will not go into great detail here except to note a few features that I consider essential for family businesses. For a family business, composing a strategic plan requires a thorough analysis of your market and the position you play in it as well as thorough research into the long-term requirements of staying competitive in your industry. Family members and key managers must study economic projections, new technology breakthroughs, and changing regional conditions in order to evaluate what changes are necessary for you to remain a leader in your industry. In a study of two hundred family firms, the common traits of those able to survive into another generation included re-generating the business strategy in each generation, regularly pruning family ownership, and installing the most competent leaders.[16] A strategic business plan should commit the business to each of these goals.

I also think a strategic plan should announce the business's commitment to empowering all employees and encouraging them to take responsibility for their own job performance as well as for the overall excellence of the company. Lastly, a strategic plan should detail the company leadership's expectations for the company's performance and require management to meet these goals. This part of the strategic plan acts as a road map for everyone in the company to follow and gives the board of directors or advisers a concrete standard to measure management results against. (Note: The performance expectations in a strategic plan should be reviewed on an annual basis in order that they remain responsive to changing conditions.) The broad range of goals set out in a strategic plan should also be summarized in a mission statement. This brief paragraph of expectations, by capturing the mission of the company, will help the board you select understand the main thrust of the family's ambitions for the business.

The third document you should provide to a board of advisers or directors is a five-year plan. A five-year plan lays out a comprehensive set of short-term goals that have been developed to lead the company toward the longer-term goals in the strategic plan. A five-year plan also provides a yardstick for measuring the accomplishments of management on a year-to-year basis. It should be updated annually in case some goals are not met or conditions change, requiring adjustments in both the five-year plan and the strategic plan. To your board, five-year plans will serve as an invaluable document for assessing the efforts of managers—whether they are family members or not—in achieving the goals that the family has set for the business. Taken together, family business plans, company strategic plans, and five-year plans make board meetings active and valuable and provide family members who have been cloistered within your family business environment a useful and often refreshing peer review of their efforts.

When you have decided that you want to establish an outside board, I recommend that you do as we did and start off with a board of advisers. I suggest this because most founders are reluctant to form an outside board of directors that may question their direction and strategy. If other family members are involved, it becomes even more difficult to sell the idea of a board of directors that includes anyone besides stockholders. Research shows, however, that boards containing only stockholders are far less effective than boards containing outsiders. A Harvard Business School study, which asked CEOs to rate their boards, found that those containing only family members received the lowest value rating, while those with outside members received the highest.[17] In their study, Ward and Aronoff found that because of the difficulty of agreeing on the need for an outside board, less then 10 percent of medium-size family firms have them.

Setting up a board of advisers provides a good compromise move that will be perceived as less threatening by those family members opposed to an outside board of directors. A board of advisers closely resembles a board of directors but its decisions are not legally binding. I suspect you will find, however, that if the meetings are properly structured, most of the decisions suggested by your board of advisers will be followed. In creating your board, think small. According to the Harvard study, most boards consist of five to eight outside members. Like the ScrubaDub board, the boards of most small companies typically include the CEO, another equity partner, and three outside members. You should limit the outside members to CEOs of other businesses that share something in common with your business. Although advisers are paid for their time, they should not be people who work full-time as professional advisers or consultants; you are looking for hands-on expertise from someone actively working in an industry with issues and challenges similar to yours. You do not want CEOs of firms that work for you, or retired executives of your own company.

To find the best people for your board, start by compiling a list of experts whom you would hire to help you run your business or plan long-range strategy if you had an unlimited budget. They can be marketing specialists, managers famous for their effectiveness, or experts in employee empowerment, customer service improvement, or research methods: anything that you think will help your company. Next, add the names of CEOs at companies that have accomplished things you admire. When done, your list of prospects will include people with specialized knowledge in areas where you need help and people with experience from which you can benefit. Next, put together a prospectus giving an overview of your market, number of employees, sales volume, and company strengths and weaknesses. This prospectus should introduce your company and give the candidate a sense of its strategic goals and challenges, competition, and market share. Then rank your list, putting the people you'd most like to serve at the top, and start making telephone calls. To help your candidates decide, describe the experience and skills you think the position requires, explain why you've chosen them, and estimate the time commitment they will have to make. Most company boards meet four times a year for three to four hours. Annual compensation ranges from $2,000 to $4,000 depending on the number of hours involved and whether board members are expected to serve on any outside committees. Terms of office vary but average eight years (few boards dictate a specific term). If you are setting up a board of advisers, your advisers will bear no legal responsibility for the actions of your company and therefore no liability insurance is required. If you eventually move on to a board of directors, company indemnification is all that is normally needed, usually provided in some form of insurance paid for by the company.

Once you have created your board of advisers, what should you plan to do at each meeting with them? Obviously, these meetings require some preparation. The CEO should schedule internal planning meetings to set an agenda. The agenda should highlight new challenges facing the company as well as pick up on items discussed at previous meetings. Time should be set aside to review the minutes of the last meeting. This will help the board focus on the issues and recommendations made at the last meeting and make sure that an action plan has been put in place to address them. Since board members are paid between $50 and $150 per hour for their time, they are expected to do some preparation as well. They should review the agenda and backup documents in advance and if necessary do some homework on the new business concepts to be introduced or evaluated. They are expected to come to the meeting fully prepared to discuss all the issues on the agenda. It is up to the CEO to keep discussion focused on the agenda and specific issues. Since the board meets only a few times a year and time is limited, the CEO must exercise strong control or discussions may wander and the meeting will not be productive.

After each meeting, the CEO should assign people in the organization to take charge of implementing ideas suggested by the board. Throughout the next quarter, the CEO should then monitor their progress. Outside boards of advisers expect to see some action taken on their recommendations. Otherwise, they feel as though their time is being wasted. In addition, the process of discussing ideas, planning appropriate action, and then reporting on results is exactly what makes board meetings so valuable. If the system is working properly, the people responsible for pursuing each idea will take pride in their efforts, work hard to prepare a presentation to the board, and look forward to the comments and feedback they receive from board members. In this way, the board provides an outside peer review of management's ability to move forward. Although any company could institute a similar process without an outside board, in practice this rarely happens. Without an outside board, family managers who are also owners can make up excuses for why a project is not complete. This is much more difficult to do with outside board members, who have different expectations. So you can see how the mere presence of outsiders can help strengthen the performance of family managers.

Another way to make the most of board meetings is to include younger family members in the planning sessions for the meetings. Encouraging everyone to develop new ideas for discussion gets people thinking creatively. Often, this results in presenting issues for discussion that might never have been suggested without the push to plan interesting board meetings. No one wants to waste the time of these busy people; consequently, exciting ideas have a good chance of making it onto the agenda. This can boost the self-confidence of younger family members, increase their excitement about their jobs, and produce original ideas and business innovation.

At ScrubaDub, we invite a nonfamily manager to attend each meeting unless a topic will be discussed that may be inappropriate for outside

s. This gives nonfamily managers a look at the issues discussed
ard and the quality of the discussion. It also gives the board a
o see that the actions we have taken actually reach down through
anization to the people intended. I also recommend giving nonfamily managers the opportunity to suggest items for the agenda. Because
you listen to them, take their advice, and report back about the response
to their ideas, they will garner more respect from all levels of management and take more satisfaction in their jobs. Nonfamily managers know
when they join a family company that their upward movement will be
limited. When they are made to feel like active partners in determining
the future of the business and see that the business is professionally managed, their loyalty to the firm will increase.

Katharine Graham, in her book *Personal History*, gave credit to the
Washington Post's outside board of directors for some of that paper's enormous success. When Graham's father bought the *Post* at auction in 1933,
the D.C. market was dominated by the *Washington Star*, a family-owned
paper without an outside board. When Graham took over management of
the *Post* in 1964, a second-generation owner, she shared leadership with a
professional manager, Richard Simmons. At the time, the *Post* was still
the number two paper in D.C. and nothing like the world-class paper it
is today. Since 1964, the Washington Post Company, a public company
controlled by the Graham family, has grown 3,150 percent. Its annual
compound earning rate is 22.5 percent and its return on equity averages
26 percent. During the same period, the top six publicly-owned media
companies posted only half that growth. Graham attributes much of that
transformation to her shared stewardship with Richard Simmons and
compares it to the fate of the *Star*, now defunct, at which she believes
"family involvement got out of hand. Too many families, for one thing."[18]
The business is currently led by a third-generation member of the
Graham family and a team of professional managers. It is an example of a
family business that has been able to grow with professional guidance and
has managed to stay family controlled.

An Act of Good Faith

Now let's look at another common cause of family conflict: a spouse's feeling that their mate is being unfairly treated. Suppose we have two
brother/partners who work together in a family-owned manufacturing

company. One partner works exclusively on the inside, directing the production, quality control, and shipping of finished goods to customers. The other partner directs the sales staff. The salesman brother must travel extensively, flying all over the country and sometimes even going overseas. He has a substantial expense account for entertaining customers, and enjoys the many luxuries of high-class business travel. He stays in expensive hotels, eats at fine restaurants, and maintains box seats at professional sporting events. Occasionally he takes his wife with him on a business trip to Europe and pays for her expenses out of his own pocket. Nevertheless, his brother's wife sees all of this high living and begins to compare it to her own. At some point, she will ask her husband whether this is fair. Initially, she may only make a small suggestion during a dinner conversation. But as the partnership matures and the differences between the brothers' lifestyles become pronounced, the complaints of the partner's spouse may grow louder. When they are out with friends, she'll solicit their opinions. The friends will probably agree that there's something unfair about one partner enjoying all this entertainment money while the other partner sweats away producing the goods. Now the partner's wife starts to look at everything the other partner does with a jaundiced eye.

Most of us have heard stories about family businesses with similar problems. Again, we must conclude that conflicts of this sort are probably inevitable. The sad part is that the two partners were probably very compatible before things started to go wrong—well-suited to the work they were doing, good at their jobs, and pretty satisfied with their lives day to day. Part of their problem stemmed from the perception that in an equal partnership everything should be equal. In practice, it's usually impossible for everything to be exactly equal. One partner sees high-level clients and needs a better company car, while another puts in a lot of late-night hours and likes to have dinner brought in by a fancy restaurant. In any case, most of the blame must be attributed to a failure to address suspicions of unfairness as soon as they arose. Once again, this goes back to early training and a family work ethic that is fully accepted by all members of the family. In such a culture, any jealousy that arises will be buffered by the strength of the partners' commitment to protect their family asset. This of course requires family members to act in a rational way. Since jealousy and conflict are more often emotional and irrational, it is necessary to establish agreed-upon systems that in effect enforce rational behavior.

But what if our two partners respect each other, understand the differing requirements of each job, and have settled between themselves that each feels appropriately compensated and happy with his situation? How then to handle the spouse who believes her husband is being taken advantage of? The answer lies in a willingness to bring spouses into family conferences and teach them the principles the family has adopted for working together to safeguard the valuable business asset they all share. This is a long-term process and should begin very early in a young couple's marriage. If done correctly, this process will help make the spouse feel embraced by the family and part of the family culture. She will share the pride in the business that her mate feels and honor the values underpinning his commitment to make the business a success. When properly managed, family conferences can be great places for letting one's hair down and talking about troublesome issues. Even if an issue can't be resolved at the family conference, bringing it to everyone's attention will set in motion the process of finding a solution.

Issues of fairness can sometimes be difficult to address within the family conference when a family member is a poor communicator or feelings run too high. Finding a good solution may require outside assistance either from a psychologist or from advisory board members. But there's no way a solution can be found if the unhappy party never has a chance to make the family aware of his or her unhappiness. So it's vitally important to open family conferences to all family members and invite everyone to express dissatisfaction when it occurs. By the second or third generation of a family business, the young people should be brought up to understand that conflict is natural, that it will definitely occur, and that they should be prepared to deal with it according to the clearly defined rules the family has adopted. Over the years and through each generation, as the family repeatedly agrees to go along with the decisions of the majority, the idea of honoring consensus and working problems out together will become an integral part of the family culture. It may require a giant leap of faith to believe that family members can resolve problems by talking with one another, but I have seen it happen in my own family, and the alternative too often means the end of the business.

Our best hope is that the values we have embedded in our family culture might see the family and the business through this crisis. By imparting to each generation the belief that conflict is a normal and healthy part of being in business together, by agreeing to regard the business as a trust to be protected and passed on, and by resolving always to treat one another with respect no matter what our differences, we may be able to weather a severe storm. Some feelings may be bruised, and a few resentments may linger, but a wholesale rupture may be avoided.

The story of the Saunders family business,[19] which spanned over four generations, demonstrates the risks of not making systems for dealing with conflict an integral part of a family culture. Jacob Saunders arrived in America in 1875 at the age of fourteen. He became involved with real estate management and soon began to acquire commercial property. Two of his sons entered his business and worked with him. In the 1940s, they began taking over rundown hotels and restructuring them. During the 1950s, something caused a breach in the brothers' relationship and for many years they worked in the same office but communicated only through written notes. This was surely a sign that dealing with conflict was not central to this family culture. One of the brothers eventually managed to take control of the firm by buying out the other. This brother had two sons, Roger and Donald, both of whom joined him in the business. Roger managed the hotels and Donald managed the commercial property, but the father began passing ownership of all his assets equally to both sons.

The business got a big break when Hilton Hotels decided to close the Boston Statler Hilton. The story goes that without any investment, the brothers took over the hotel for the existing mortgage and borrowed the money to refurbish it. Although the brothers had always owned all properties equally, Roger, who managed the hotels, had the papers for the Statler drawn up giving himself 75 percent ownership and Donald only 25 percent. Donald went to his father, who was then seventy-five years old, and the father ruled to correct the ownership imbalance. This time, Roger presented papers at the closing giving each of them one-third, with the remaining third going to their children (the fourth generation). This was a clever idea, since Roger had four children and Donald only one, which meant Roger ended up controlling 56 percent of the company. Again Donald asked his father to intervene. He did, but this time he sided with Roger, whom he felt was the best choice as a businessman to run the hotels. From 1980 until 1996, the squabble proceeded from petty accusations to serious injustices, and a judge finally forced the sale of all the company's assets. No lawsuits, no mediators, and no court injunctions could bring these two siblings to a settlement. Had the first or even the

generation established a family culture in which differences could
discussed one on one and systems existed for resolving problems, this
might have had a happier ending.

How do we overcome the jealousy, the natural competitiveness, and
the jockeying for position that occur in every family business? We do it
by reminding ourselves and one another how fortunate we are to share the
life made possible by a successful family business. We do it by regarding
the job of enhancing the inherited value of our family business as a privilege and a challenge rather than as our entitlement. And we do it by the
love and respect that we have for one another.

If we decide that we want the inherited asset value of our family business
to pass from one generation to the next, then we must train each generation
to qualify for the role of growing this asset. As you will see when we develop estate strategies, gifting family business stock equally to all children
in a family, whether they work in the business or not, raises the odds that
within two generations the business will not survive. By keeping the stock
in the hands of the people who work in the company, who then become
stewards of the family heritage, we have a much greater chance of seeing the
business continue. Institutionalizing a number of methods for expressing
unhappiness, and making sure that no one feels ganged up on or trapped,
helps contain problems at a basic level where two people can deal directly
with each other to reach a solution. How we value family business stock and
how we distribute it is the subject of the next two chapters.

Key Messages from This Chapter

❖ Treat conflict as an opportunity.

Trying to avoid conflict is like sticking your head in the sand. It just
will not go away until the conflict is openly discussed and some ac-
commodation made to resolve it. Most conflict comes from someone
who wants to do something in a different way. It's possible that they
may have a better idea on dealing with the problem. This is why conflict can be healthy. There are many ideas in this book to help you create a system that resolves conflict.

❖ Take the conflict/cohesion test.

If your family believes that high cohesion and low conflict is desirable,
they need to be educated on why conflict can be healthy. You do not

want people around you to avoid conflict, because this inhibit
ideas and fosters feelings of resentment. Develop in your culture a system of open communication and a process of conflict management.

❖ Install an outside board of directors or advisers.

Many of the issues that cause family businesses to fail could be resolved using an outside board, which can separate family and business
issues and keep a company focused on its mission. There seems to be
an attitude in family businesses that children do not have to be ac-
countable. An outside board not only resolves this problem, it makes
children better managers in spite of themselves.

❖ Incorporate strategies that help resolve conflict.

In addition to an outside board, ScrubaDub's system includes limiting
stock ownership to those in the business, second-generation family
column trusts that hold most of the company stock, a deadlock trust
that has a few shares of voting nonequity stock, and a stock redemption agreement. Look for the details on these concepts in Chapters 5
and 6.

5

Developing
Tax Strategies

Tax policies—especially those concerning estate taxes—can distort the value of the company and put enormous pressure on first-generation owners to cash in. As I've argued strenuously already, I believe that the value of the family business as a way of life far exceeds the market value of the firm, and recommend that all owners consider a variety of options for building the investment across generations before taking the money and running.

Estate Taxes

Rather than encourage capital preservation, our government in its wisdom has created a form of "capital" punishment for being successful— estate tax laws that demand 55 percent of the fair market value of any business property when the owner dies and the property passes to his or her children and/or grandchildren. Few businesses, regardless of their size, can withstand paying out 55 percent of their fair market value over a short period. In effect the government is asking the inheritors, often a younger generation of family business owners, to purchase the business back from the federal government for 55 percent of its fair market value. To make matters worse, this repurchase cannot be timed to market conditions and may come at a time when the market value of the business is inflated. Even if the members of this younger generation have played a major role in the success of the business, they receive no legal recognition for their contributions as far as the tax laws are concerned.

The inheritors' primary relief under the current system is to defer paying the estate tax liability (principal only) that results from including the business interest in the decedent's estate (Internal Revenue Code section 6166). They can elect to defer and pay the tax in installments for up to fourteen years, paying the interest only for the first four years (at a special rate of 4 percent) and paying the balance (interest and estate tax liability) over the next ten years. However, an executor can elect this deferral only on the estate tax attributable to the value of a farm or other closely held business, and only if the value of the business exceeds 35 percent of the decedent's adjusted gross estate. So if the business owner was extremely wealthy and possessed a variety of assets besides the business, his or her heirs must immediately cash in a large portion of those assets—or use the business assets—to pay the taxes if they want to hang on to the business. As a result, servicing the estate tax debt can destroy the very framework of a family business by depleting the business's assets and thereby restricting the business's ability to reinvest for the future.

The Taxpayer Relief Act of 1997

The 1997 tax bill, called the Taxpayer Relief Act of 1997, tries to address some of the asset drain issue caused by the transfer of family-owned businesses, but the results are ambiguous at best. For example, under the new law, if the heirs to a family business decide to pay their huge tax obligation over time, the interest rate on the deferred liability is reduced to a special 2 percent rate on that portion of the estate tax attributable to the first $1 million in taxable value of the family business. This is a welcome change, but the benefit is offset by the fact that the 1997 Relief Act abolished the estate tax deduction for the interest paid.

The mixed messages do not end there. The new bill increases the unified estate and gift exemption amount from $600,000 to $1 million—a good move. But, because this increase will be phased in over a number of years, an average annual inflation rate during those years of only 4 percent will make it not much of a real increase at all. In another blow to the prospects of family businesses, the Relief Act reduces the capital gains tax rate from 28 percent to 20 percent. This clear and substantial income tax savings can only encourage family business owners to accept offers to sell out.

In addition to the items mentioned, the Taxpayer Relief Act of 1997 has already been updated by the IRS Restructuring and Reform Act of

1998, which simplifies the deduction process. This new law could provide estate planning opportunities for family-held businesses; however, it forces family business owners to follow a road that can be treacherous and costly with minimum results. The tax savings by planning ahead are still far greater then doing nothing and qualifying for this act.

Despite the good intentions of the Relief Act, it is estimated that very few businesses will in fact qualify for section 2033A and its revisions.[1] There are already additional pending changes proposed for the Relief Act to make it a little more friendly; however, it is more likely that the legatees of entrepreneurs who do not plan for succession will take advantage of the capital gains savings provided by the act and sell their parents' businesses.

A Proposal to Change the Tax Laws

The impulse behind our estate tax laws is a good one: to try to spread the wealth by making it difficult to pass assets from one generation to another. Considered in isolation, this is a worthy goal. But in practice the results go much further. Let's look at an example. The founder of a thirty-five-year-old family business dies, and leaves his estate to his only son, who has worked in the business for eighteen years and risen to become CEO. The business is in good shape, but many of its assets have depreciated. After recovering from the shock of his father's death, the young CEO experiences a second shock when he meets with his accountant. The accountant tells him that his potential tax liability may be as high as 70 percent of the book value of the business. Why? Because the market value of the business is much higher than its book value, and if the federal and state estate taxes approach 55 percent of the appraised market value of all the assets, they could exceed 70 percent of the business's book value. Faced with losing so much money, and convinced that the business can't survive loaded down with so much debt, the younger man decides to sell the business, pay the tax, and retire early. The government accomplished its goal of not allowing wealth to pass to another generation. Was this the best solution for this business and family?

By reinvesting profits and practicing a long-term growth strategy, the family business could have stayed innovative and aggressive, created a stable job base in the region, and helped shore up the local economy. Because the family owners recognized that the business was dependent on the community, they made generous contributions to local charities, beautified their business property, and took steps to minimize the business's impact on the environment. In addition, the business gave this relatively young man, the legatee, a purpose in life: It enabled him to be a productive member of society. However, the new owner, especially if it is a corporation based elsewhere, is not likely to feel the same commitment to the region felt by the founder's family. And although the young CEO may enjoy his early retirement for a while, is he better off because he has left the workforce? What about the local economy and the nation? Are they better off? As I have already pointed out, more than 70 percent of family businesses do not survive into the second generation, which means 10 million family businesses disappear every twenty-four years, or about 450,000 a year. Since family businesses make up 40 percent of the gross national product and pay 50 percent of all wages to the American workforce, for our economy to remain strong, 500,000 new businesses need to be created every year to replace the jobs, goods, and services from the family businesses that do not survive.[2]

The Consolidation Phenomenon

The consolidation problem is particularly pressing now, because fictitious market values are changing many industries, temporarily driving up prices and encouraging family businesses to sell out. The funeral industry provides an excellent example of this syndrome. Currently, 80 to 85 percent of the nation's funeral homes are still independently owned, but that percentage is shrinking rapidly. A few public, investor-owned chains are rapidly buying up independent facilities. These chains have large marketing budgets and cost-saving centralized facilities, giving the independents stiff competition. The *Wall Street Journal* reported in a recent article[3] that the small operators must also resist lucrative buyout offers from these powerful competitors. The article quoted a funeral home owner who was finding it hard to turn down a cash offer that was well over the current value of the business. To make the offer even more inviting, the corporate chains often keep the family name on the business and give lucrative consulting jobs to the retiring owners. And why not? The corporate executives are smart enough to know that customer loyalty took generations to develop—why start over again? From the seller's point of view, because of high demand and the appreciated value of the real estate, selling prices have soared to an average of $1.8 million per location.[4]

What has made this business so attractive to investors? First of all, the funeral home industry is not cyclical and has an assured customer base. Second, as the baby boom generation reaches old age, the death rate is expected to increase by over 1 percent a year. The consolidators believe that they can build on this growth and wring even higher profits from the industry. Their strategy is to buy as many businesses as possible, take advantage of economies of scale to lower prices, and encourage even more businesses to sell out. Their tactics don't always stop there. In February 1996, BBC-TV's documentary program *Public Eye* ran a segment about Service Corporation International, the largest funeral home consolidator in the world. The BBC's reporters had obtained internal documents describing the high-pressure tactics the company used to increase its revenues. One memo dealing with the selling of coffins gave the following instructions: "Direct the attention of the family to the highest quality item on display. Do not judge the ability of a family to afford a particular coffin or casket by their appearance. Prejudging could mean you talk yourself out of a higher item and your selling technique will reflect this."[5]

Another company active in the consolidation of the funeral home industry is the Loewen Group, a British concern listed on the New York Stock Exchange. The Loewen Group's mission statement claims that the company "facilitates the orderly transition of ownership and management of funeral homes and cemeteries from one generation to the next."[6] What this means in fact is that the firm encourages one generation of owners to sell their business and then lets the next generation manage it. In 1996 alone, the Loewen Group spent over $1 billion in new acquisitions of funeral homes in the United States. The company's revenues and stock price on the New York Stock Exchange increased over 50 percent during the same year. The company now operates over one thousand funeral homes, manages three hundred cemeteries, and employs over sixteen thousand people. All this might give the impression that the company is successful. On the contrary. In 1995 the Loewen Group reported a loss of $76 million. Although profitable in 1996, the firm spent $55 million on restructuring in a successful attempt to fend off an unwelcome $2.9 billion takeover bid from Service Corp. International, the industry leader. In addition, the company paid out $230 million to settle a breach-of-contract suit. If that's not enough, they also announced an $80 million charge from slashing fees in order to bring their costs in line with those of their major competitor.[7]

Unfortunately, this situation is far from unique. Consolidators in many other industries have demonstrated time and again that reducing labor and service costs may produce temporary profits but in the long run usually leads to losses. By that time, however, they have already dramatically changed the business culture and operation methods of these family businesses in order to accommodate the pressures of the stock market and the standardization necessary to manage so many businesses at once. They have also irreparably changed the market in which the remaining family businesses must operate.

Funeral home consolidators now control 15 to 20 percent of the market, and in some areas they have lowered prices by as much as 50 percent. You might think that this would be good for consumers, but it turns out that the lowered prices are heavily—and only temporarily—subsidized by the consolidating parent corporation as a way of driving independent operators out of business or encouraging them to sell out. Because of these tactics, in 1996 the Loewen Group agreed to sell funeral homes in three markets to settle Federal Trade Commission antitrust concerns. In other areas where a single consolidator has purchased all the funeral homes in a market, the government has stepped in to try to preserve competition.[8]

Industry consolidations are called "roll-ups." This practice really got started in 1995 when Browning-Ferris Industries began consolidating the trash industry. After observing the practice for three years, the *Houston Business Journal* described the recipe for a successful roll-up: "Take a group of mom-and-pop operations in a highly fragmented industry of more than $5 billion, add a professional management team with consolidation experience and mix together with an initial public offering of more than $40 million. Poof: You get a public company with national clout, deep pockets, a broader product line and a network of offices to service America's largest national concerns. Indeed some people on Wall Street call them 'poof!' companies."[9] The success of this recipe has created a rush among roll-up specialists to identify the potential in highly fragmented industries, reaching down to public offerings of under $20 million. In an equity market overview of the consolidation industry, Montgomery Securities reported that consolidations grew from $62 million in 1992 to over $3 billion in 1996, and the upward trend continues. Even if these new companies do extremely well trading in the market—and not all do—what does this mean for the entrepreneur who sold out? Since consolidators only want successful companies, the high prices they are willing to pay will probably do little to enhance the entrepreneur's standard of living (chances are, he or she is already living pretty well). The biggest impact of the increase in the business's value produced by the consolidators will probably be felt by Uncle Sam. Personally, I believe consolidations are a marketing whim. Hot today, but destined to cool off—leaving some very unhappy participants as well as plenty of opportunity for those patient enough to wait it out.

As the Federal Trade Commission has discovered, consolidators attempt to capture a market so that they can then increase prices to make greater profits for their investors and stockholders. Although this tactic has put an end to a lot of fine old businesses, it can create another opportunity for family businesses able to patiently wait out the low-price competition period. To compete with the consolidators, one member of a fourth-generation funeral home family has started a discount funeral home chain. Ren Newcomer charges $2,585 for an average funeral including all the basics. By comparison, the cost of traditional funerals industrywide has risen 17 percent from 1993 to $4,782. The April 1998 issue of *Inc.* magazine reported that the Newcomer Family Funeral Home company has built six new facilities from scratch and plans to have established fifty locations by the year 2003.[10] *Inc.* also reported that between 1993 and 1995, a period in which small companies felt plenty of competitive heat, payrolls in smaller drugstores with just one to four employees (the drugstore business is highly consolidated) actually increased by 8 percent more than the industry average.[11]

My proposal for changing the tax laws is to legalize the distinction I have made between the market value of a family business and what I have called its inherited value. Just as Section 2032A allows a "special use" valuation for some farms and business real estate, I think the tax code should recognize that family businesses belong in a "special use" category as well. The government could enable thousands of family businesses to remain in family hands by making the taxable value of a family business its inherited value, which would be calculated as the business's depreciated assets added to the after-tax profits that remain in the company less any debt (or the book value, assets minus liabilities). Following my suggestion, estate taxes would only be calculated on the book value rather than the market value if the business were passed on to another family member. I think the law should also decree that any family member who has inherited part or all of a business and enjoyed this tax break can sell part or all of the business to another family member at book value; if a legatee who has enjoyed the "inherited value" tax break wants to sell the business to a non-family member, he or she can sell it for whatever the business will bring on the open market but the government would be able to recapture the difference between the "inherited value" estate tax and the higher "market value" estate tax and he will also have to pay capital gains taxes based on the sale price. In this way, the government would only be postponing the expected estate tax revenue if the business is subsequently sold. If the next generation decides to sell out after a few years, the government will get its full tax bite as originally intended.

This acceptance by the government of a lower value for a family business passed on to another generation would accomplish several things. It would make it easier for families to plan for succession (and therefore to achieve it), knowing that their businesses will survive the payment of estate taxes. By encouraging families to hang on to their businesses, it could help start a tradition in this country of building and maintaining family businesses over many generations. This could only be a stabilizing influence in our society and a positive result for our economy.

The time is clearly right for this change in our legislation. The courts have already recognized that passing family business stock to the next generation at the lowest value is good tax planning. After a series of contentious court cases, the IRS issued a ruling in 1993 authorizing discounted values for minority interest, limited market, and nonvoting stock gifts.[12] The courts have gone even further than the general concept of a willing buyer and a willing seller to establish estate value if the following additional requirements are met:

- the agreement contains restrictions on disposition of the business interest that are binding during the owner's life as well as at death;
- the agreement obligates the owner's estate or beneficiaries following death to sell the interest at the price established under the agreement, either without any choice or at the option of the other parties to the agreement;
- the price set in the agreement is either fixed or determinable according to a formula, and was reasonable when the agreement was made.[13]

Studies have shown that these discounts average 40 percent, with some ranging as high as 78 percent (these studies were based on book value).[14] But be forewarned: You must document how the discount was established.

The Taxpayer Relief Act of 1997 also indicated the government's recognition that making it possible for families to pass on family business stock to succeeding generations is in everyone's best interest. But the 1997 legislation did not go far enough or high enough in its exclusion amounts. Following my suggestion, the government would legalize the process of passing on family business stock at the lowest value, enabling these businesses to remain financially strong without taking on tremendous debt in order to survive. Because family business owners can confidently plan to hand on their businesses to their children, they can make sure the next generation is prepared and ready to take over when the time comes. The business, by constantly renewing itself, will remain a pillar of its community, a steady source of jobs, and a reliable contributor of tax revenue to city, state, and federal coffers. Certainly, the government will earn more from the estate taxes on two or more generations combined with capital gains taxes if the business is sold than it would have earned from taxing the estate of the first generation at fair market value.

In 1998 it is expected that the treasury will collect $1.7 trillion in revenues. Estate taxes typically generate only about 1 percent of the federal government's total revenues each year. In 1998, however, the total collected from estate taxes is expected to be much greater. And this is just a scratch in the bucket of what's to come in the next ten years unless families take aggressive action to preserve their assets.[15]

The Legacy of Opportunity

Let's assume that the concept of two values for a family business is never adopted by our government. I propose that we as family business owners do it anyway. The Paisner family has agreed that the value of our stock between family members will always be at book value. We have done this by agreements that preset the stock price. We have taken steps to transfer our business from generation to generation in a way that enables it to survive, and that takes advantage of the government's limited recognition of the value of passing minority stock at discounted rates. As a family we have agreed that passing the business to another generation is not a transfer of wealth, but the loan of a family asset for one generation. It is a legacy of

Each generation may enjoy the benefits of business ownership,
st accept the obligation to keep the business viable and pass it
hildren. Liquidity of family stock is an essential element along
t exit route—by selling stock back to the family corporation at
—for anyone who no longer wants to participate. There is no
transfer of wealth. The transfer is of a means to a lifestyle.

For us, the key to ensuring the legacy of our investment while reducing the tax burden on future generations has been a policy of gifting stock to our children.

Tax Strategies

When my professional advisers suggested that I start gifting stock in ScrubaDub to my children, I began thinking about the consequences of this act. If I gifted the stock too early and it turned out they were unable to manage the business well, it could be the end of the business. Or, if I gifted the stock early and later wanted to sell the business, too large a proportion of the proceeds might go to them, and I might not net enough to guarantee a secure retirement for Elaine and me. But if I didn't gift the stock and instead sold the business to them, the heavy debt they might incur could also inhibit the business's survival. Since I am proud of the business and would like to see it survive, I decided that I would not gift stock until I was persuaded of my children's capabilities as well as their genuine desire to eventually own and run the business.

After they had worked in the business for a good ten years, were well entrenched, and had demonstrated their commitment to continuing the business, I decided that it was time to start giving my children stock. The value of the company had grown substantially, however, and the transfer of stock through annual gifting was not going to accomplish a great deal. I had read about discounted values in Mike Cohn's book *Passing the Torch.* My accountant helped me out by explaining the discounted value of nonvoting minority interest stock. He suggested I recapitalize ScrubaDub stock into voting and nonvoting shares, with approximately 10 percent of the shares designated as voting stock and the balance nonvoting. This solved two problems. By keeping the voting shares, I could continue to control the major decisions until I was ready to retire. By gifting the nonvoting shares at discounted value, I was able to pass along a larger proportion of the business each year and in this way show my sons that I intended for them to own the business eventually. As they progressed in their ability to run the company, I increased the size of my gifts using some of the $1.2 million unified credit exemption allowed to Elaine and me by the tax laws at that time.

While it made business sense to remove the business assets and the future appreciation from my estate and reduce the estate tax burden if I wanted the business to survive, my sons did not earn or pay for the stock I gave them. In my view, the stock was an advance on their inheritance. But whatever portion of the stock remained in my estate at my death—even if it was gifted in a will—would be valued at market value. Obviously, the difference between the market value and the discounted minority interest value of the stock I gave them was substantial. In keeping with the rest of my thinking on this subject, I dubbed the value of that discounted stock its inherited or family value, and estimated it as stretching far beyond dollars and cents. In addition, since the choice to gift the stock in this way was mine alone, and by doing so I was saving my sons and the business huge sums in future taxes, I felt that some strings could be attached to the gift. Those strings took the form of a moral commitment—detailed in our family strategic plan—to protect and enhance this inheritance for the use of future generations. I made no legal requirement that they keep the business. Once they have purchased the voting stock, they will have the right to do whatever they wish with it. But I have made it clear that I hope they will consider using the same technique to pass the business on to their own children. I do this not only because I would like to see the business survive, but because I believe the moral obligation I have imposed on them changes the psychological effect of inheriting a business for the better. Rather than seeing the business as belonging to them by right, they see it as a calling and a responsibility. And rather than regarding themselves simply as members of a wealthy elite, they see themselves as guardians of a precious trust, a trust with the power to take care of them and their families for generations to come.

Some loving parents might object to my reasoning and feel that I am ungenerous for not giving my business to my sons without restrictions and under the best financial arrangement possible. Others might say that my approach suggests distrust of my sons rather than the unconditional love parents should feel for their offspring. They may even feel that I risked undermining my sons' confidence in their ability to run the business by insisting on a testing period in which they demonstrated their ability, desire, and commitment to do so. My answer is that it was because I love them that I wanted to manage their inheritance with great care, fearful always of the negative power of money, which is surely as strong as its capacity for good. The alternative to giving them the opportunity to run our business in another generation is to let them inherit the after-tax wealth the business produces in a sale.

The Effects of Inherited Wealth

I am not alone in feeling that caution is necessary when dispersing family wealth, and that this is a murky area in which family business owners must proceed with care. There are great differences of opinion about the impact of leaving money to children. Warren Buffett, one of the most successful investors of this century, whose holding company, Berkshire Hathaway, is worth over $1.5 billion, does not believe in leaving wealth to children. He believes in leaving children enough money so that they can do something, but not enough for them to do nothing; Buffett plans to give most of his money to his charitable foundation. Of thirty multi-millionaires recently surveyed by *Fortune* magazine, six say their children will be better off with only a minimal inheritance, almost half plan to leave just as much to charity as they do to family, and the rest have no problem leaving their fortunes to their families.[16]

One innovative approach for parents and grandparents is to create incentive income trusts. These trusts encourage the beneficiaries to work and reward them for their efforts. Trusts can be set up to match or double the earnings of a beneficiary and/or to pay out some of the principal when a goal is reached. Other approaches include establishing trusts for limited purposes, such as education or the purchase of a home. Former secretary of the treasury William Simon, who has made tens of millions since leaving Washington, suggests that trusts be set up to start paying interest at age thirty-five and then allow access to principal in two installments at age forty and forty-five.[17] Of course, there are many other possible strategies. My point in discussing a few of them is to support my argument that it is vitally important to think carefully about how you will pass on your business and your wealth to your children, and to build a strong sense of values in them so that the wealth they inherit does not destroy their motivation to work. Central to that effort, I think, is making them appreciate the business's inherited or family value—the potential it possesses to take care of them and future generations and give them a solid grounding in worldly, as opposed to wealthy, verities.

Putting a Retirement Plan in Place

Once you have made the decision to pass your company to your children you must then consider your own exit strategy, which must include some form of retirement plan.

When it became evident that my sons shared my excitement for our business, I decided to plan for my retirement. Team management was in place. Decisions were made by consensus. Our system for handling conflict seemed to be working. Reinvestment had led to new developments in quality and marketing. Profits were financing slow but methodical growth. I was approaching sixty-five and they were ready to take over the business. They had already made major contributions to the company's success, and in response I had begun gifting nonvoting stock to them more aggressively. I wanted them to benefit from their hard work and good ideas just as my wife and I had enjoyed the fruits of our labors.

Before I turned over the voting stock, I wanted to be sure that Elaine and I could continue to maintain our standard of living. My goal was to take out of the business only enough money to fund the life we wanted to lead in our final years. At the same time, I didn't want to increase our taxable estate. I knew that whatever business assets remained in the estate of whoever died last would be taxed at 55 percent of their market value. My accountant pointed out that the value of ScrubaDub's depreciated real estate alone, when reassessed at market value, could double or triple the estate's value. If I didn't formulate a long-term plan to reduce this tax burden, taxes could force the estate to sell off some of our holdings to pay the tax.

A few of the pieces were already in place. In 1984 I had set up a defined benefit pension plan for ScrubaDub. Our goal was for the contribution determined by the plan's actuary to provide an appropriate retirement benefit at the appropriate time for each employee. By 1988 the cost of the plan became too great a burden and began to inhibit our growth. We then changed to a profit-sharing plan in which we based the company's contribution each year on our cash flow for the year. Our aim was to fund the program by contributing 10 percent of our earnings each year. This plan became such an important part of our business culture that we funded it every year even when we did not make a profit. Eventually, the program included a 401K plan that allowed employees to put in additional funds and take responsibility for their own investment decisions. Elaine's and my share of this retirement plan makes up a substantial portion of our retirement funds and contributes significantly to our ability to continue living as we like.

I believe that the creation of a program that encourages employees to save toward their retirement is an obligation of moral leadership. Retirement plans fall into two categories, qualified and nonqualified. Qualified plans must abide by strict rules and allow employers to make tax-deductible contributions; employees have no obligation to pay taxes on this money until the funds are withdrawn. The employer contribution can be based on profits of the company or calculated as an annual benefit tied to the employee's age or compensation. Strict rules govern how much employers can contribute as well as which employees must be covered under qualified plans.

The problem with many qualified plans is that they often do not give key employees retirement benefits in proportion to their working incomes. Nonqualified plans can add additional benefits but are less attractive to employers because the company's contributions are not tax deductible until the funds are withdrawn. Nonqualified plans can include:

- A supplemental executive retirement plan (SERP), which enhances postretirement income for key management people. SERPs can be informally funded or become an unfunded liability of the employer (in other words, the employer must come up with the promised funds even if he or she has not set aside sufficient funds in advance).
- Deferred compensation plans, in which you contract with a key employee to make a onetime payment when he or she retires. This can be combined with life insurance products purchased by the company to benefit a key employee's heirs if he or she dies prior to retirement.

Key employees frequently feel concern about the safety of deferred compensation arrangements during a transition between generations, since debt is almost always added to the balance sheet to finance a senior generation's deferred retirement arrangement. One way to safeguard employee retirement funds is to transfer them to a trust (often referred to as a rabbi trust). A rabbi trust is an irrevocable trust established by a corporation to fund its deferred-compensation arrangement for key employees. It is called a rabbi trust because the IRS first ruled on funds set aside in an irrevocable trust for a congregation that established the trust for the benefit of its rabbi.

If your business is small and you don't think it can support a full-fledged pension plan, at least consider establishing a 401K plan. This allows employees to set aside part of their salaries for retirement. Employers can encourage employee participation by matching employee contributions according to some preset ratio, and these employer contributions are also tax deductible. Once again, strict rules regulate the amounts that both employer and employee can set aside each year.

Because there are many variations and changing rules governing pension and retirement plans, always ask your lawyer, accountant, and insurance agent for recommendations and seek professional assistance in setting up your plan or plans. Obviously, also, consider your own needs as well as your employees' needs when establishing a retirement plan, and look at the retirement plan in the context of your overall tax and estate strategy.

As I discussed earlier in the book, many business owners also rely on rental income as part of their retirement plan. Elaine and I have in fact retained ownership of a few of our ScrubaDub properties so that we can continue to draw income from them. (This rental income combined with our share from the company retirement fund and the proceeds from the sale of our voting stock will fund our retirement very comfortably.) This strategy is fine as long as your retirement plan is not overly dependent on the rental income and the comfort of your later years doesn't depend on your getting top dollar from the real estate rentals. Ideally, you should rely on a combination of rental income at fair value, deferred income from a retirement plan, accumulated independent wealth, social security, and the proceeds from the sale of the voting stock. Together, these various sources of income should be sufficient to allow you to retire without changing your standard of living.

In any case, during the growth of a business I recommend independently acquiring and owning any real estate used by the business. In the early days, to help control the operating costs of the business, fair market rents may only cover the mortgage payments. As the business prospers, you can increase the rents to produce added personal income. By the time you are ready to retire, the mortgage should be paid off and the rental income can become a substantial part of your retirement plan.

In addition, if you expect the rental income to help support your spouse after your death, I recommend setting up a family limited partnership or limited liability company to control rent increases and keep charges within limits the business can afford. You can give an interest in the partnership to the children in the business so that they can participate in rent discussions, or you can lower your estate value by gifting real estate shares in the partnership to children not in the business. Just be sure that ownership of the real estate eventually reverts to the current owners of the business so that the process can be repeated.

If this combination of income sources does not reach your retirement income needs, you can add a supplemental retirement benefit to your plan. Through this vehicle, the business will be able to make deposits into a corporate-established grantor trust for a seven- to ten-year period. The purpose of these trusts is to increase your retirement fund. Deposits are not taxed until they are received and the employer cannot take a tax deduction until you are taxed on the income. The funds in these trusts can be invested in a variety of ways and while subject to a corporate tax on realized income, certain investments, including insurance products or growth equities, would permit these assets to continue growing tax-free within the trust.

Once you have a sound retirement plan and you have reached the point at which you can sit back and watch the next generation run the business, you still have a few more pitfalls to avoid. Management of the balance of your estate requires some attention, and once again, careful planning is needed. Even though a 55 percent maximum rate currently applies to both gifts and estate taxes, there are major differences in how that rate is applied. Apart from the allowable $10,000 maximum annual gift to any individual, every $100 gift requires a tax of $55 or a total cost to the donor of $155. Every gift of $100 while you are living thus reduces your estate by $155. But to give the same $100 through your estate after your death almost triples the cost of the gift. This is because you must will $222 for a recipient to receive $100, because a 55 percent tax on $222 ($122.10) leaves $100 in after-tax dollars. Obviously, whether you want your family to benefit from your generosity or some charitable organization, you should begin a gifting program as soon as possible to get the most money to your intended recipient and avoid turning the lion's share over to the government through estate taxes. One attractive method is to gift an income-producing asset to a grantor-retained annuity trust. The value of the gift can be discounted if it is a minority interest in a closely held family business. This type of gift to an irrevocable trust can pay a fixed annuity to the donor for a preset period of time; when the trust terminates, the asset passes to the beneficiaries. This could also be business real estate that you want to transfer to the generation running the business. Remember, however, that even with a grantor-retained annuity trust, you must pay a gift tax when you transfer the property to the trust.

Another tax burden on your estate that you may want to avoid is a tax on undistributed money in your retirement plan. Let's say that after your estate has been settled, $100,000 remains in your pension trust. If the beneficiary of your retirement plan is someone other than your spouse, this asset could be taxed at nearly 80 percent when you consider both estate and income taxes. That is, if the $100,000 is taxed at the 55 percent estate tax level, leaving a balance of $45,000, and then is inherited by a child in the 40 percent tax bracket, that child will receive only $20,600 from that $100,000. The Taxpayer Relief Act of 1997 offers some relief by repealing a 15 percent excise tax on excess accumulations.

Other Considerations for Retirement

Once you have a good retirement plan in place for yourself, you must move on to the question of how to leave the balance of your estate to your family. By this time, your children are, ideally, well established in the family business and doing well. If they are expanding the business and prospering, you may want to consider bypassing them and leaving some of your remaining assets to your grandchildren. One way to do this, as I have already mentioned, is through an incentive income trust, where the trust gives out principal only under certain conditions, such as for education, a new home, or meeting some other goal. Or you could set up a trust that matches your grandchildren's earnings every five years until the funds are used up. Then there is the dynasty trust concept. This technique was favored by wealthy families in the second half of the nineteenth century. Since an estate tax is levied at the death of each individual, money left to one generation gets taxed again when left to the next generation. Putting their wealth in trust enabled the very wealthy to avoid this double taxation. Eventually Congress caught on to this gambit and enacted the federal generation-skipping transfer (GST) tax. The GST is a tax imposed at the highest marginal estate rate on money passed down in trust. Some limited relief was later granted in code section 2632 (a), which provides a $1 million exemption from the GST per individual decedent (increasing for inflation beginning in 1999). To a lesser extent, this allows us to apply the same strategy used by the Rockefellers and the Vanderbilts. To do this, you need to establish an irrevocable perpetuities trust, or "dynasty trust." The first year the trust is subject to estate taxes above any use of the personal exemption that may be used. Any asset transferred into the trust to the extent of the exemption allowed will remain free from federal transfer taxation (not income tax) through the period of the rule of perpetuity, which is normally twenty-one years after the last living heir dies. At the end of this period, the trust will terminate and no transfer tax will be due until the beneficiaries who receive the assets die. So a wealthy man or woman can set up a trust that will provide income to their heirs. Typically the trustees are given discretion in determining when and if to distribute income or principal. The trust will continue to produce income for twenty-one years after the death of the last heir who was alive when the trust was created. Then the trust will terminate and whatever remains will be distributed to the remaining heir or heirs. This distribution normally falls into the estate of a great-grandchild. As an example, $1 million placed in a dynasty trust earning 5 percent and appreciating at 7 percent annually will produce an after-tax value of $488 million at the end of the perpetuity period (approximately eighty-five years).[18]

Clearly, the potential of dynasty trusts to create wealth for later generations is enormous, especially now when the equities market is producing such huge gains. Even more interesting, for our purposes, is the potential these trusts have to help family businesses. Let's assume you successfully pass on your business to your children. Under their administration, the business follows an average family business life cycle and enjoys a generation of significant growth. During this period, your children have no need to draw funds from the dynasty trust. Realizing that whatever they leave in the trust will grow Estate tax free and be available to their children, they don't touch it. Enter the third generation. Statistics show that this is the generation that often ends the family business. As backup, they can draw on the trust funds if the business gets into trouble. This fact alone may give them a greater feeling of security and inspire them to persist through difficult times. And realizing that whatever they take out will be taxed at a minimum of 55 percent in their estate, they may strive to leave the trust intact for their children. When the next generation pays the estate tax on the expired trust, it will have grown so much that there will be enough money left to start the dynasty trust again, providing the law still allows it. By educating your heirs at family council meetings about the potential of the dynasty trust, you could make understanding and stewardship of the trust another valuable part of your family heritage.

Key Messages from This Chapter

❖ Separate market value from inherited value
when considering financial strategies.

This concept is essential in developing a culture that believes in succession for a family business. If the next generation feels no obligation to the previous generation in the way they were able to pass their stock down to avoid estate taxes, the business will end. The market value will be so much greater than their inherited value, the temptation to cash it in and retire at an early age will be overwhelming. This theory must be developed in a family business plan and in all children entering the business if there is to be any chance for future generations.

❖ Establish an incentive income trust.

Here is a way for parents and grandparents to leave money to another generation without destroying their will to work. The obligations of the trust can be expanded to include education, new home, or new business ventures in addition to receiving an equal amount of their yearly earnings. Having a trustee as an intermediary gives some insurance that an inheritance will not be squandered.

❖ Plan your retirement early.

As obvious as this seems, too many owners of family businesses fail to execute a plan. When it comes time for them to retire, the only sensible exit strategy is to go public or sell out. If your goal is to live a certain lifestyle, you must make arrangements early on. This might require separating real estate from the business, having a retirement plan, and changing your stock to voting and nonvoting shares.

❖ Consider a dynasty trust in your estate plans.

By taking advantage of the $1 million exemption (increasing for inflation starting in 1999) in the federal generation-skipping transfer (GST) tax, you can put in place funds that will grow estate-tax-free and someday help save the family business. What is interesting in this concept is the valuable lesson for each generation to try and let this trust continue.

6

Developing Estate Strategies

How we plan to pass on our company stock affects our estate value and can help resolve issues that cause conflict.

Keeping Ownership in the Hands of Those Involved in the Business

As ScrubaDub grew and my income grew accordingly, my accountant suggested that I consider giving away stock to my children every year to take advantage of the $20,000-per-year-tax-free exclusion ($10,000 from each spouse in a married pair, meaning a total of $20,000 to each of my children). This would reduce the total value of the stock I held while transferring future appreciation in the stock I gave away to someone else. In addition, I was concerned about giving away control of my business prematurely; I was reluctant to do this because I'd heard horror stories about families in which children who worked outside the business owned stock. All these stories seemed to end the same way: The children who worked outside the business successfully forced the sale of the business. One of the most memorable and frightening stories involved the Steinberg family of Canada.

Founded in 1917 as a small local grocery store in Montreal, Steinberg's supermarket chain grew into one of the leading family businesses in Canada. Sam Steinberg, second son of the founder, was responsible for transforming the business into a market giant. During the Great Depression, when other stores were closing, Sam Steinberg doubled his locations from three to six stores. The chain subsequently grew to include 179 stores by the time Sam was ready to retire in 1969. Sam Steinberg believed the business should welcome any family member who wanted to join. This meant finding a place for four of his brothers, one sister, his mother, assorted aunts, uncles, cousins, nieces, and nephews, and later even sons-in-law and grandchildren. Although he made room for all these family members, Sam continued to make all major decisions himself. In addition, because he was old-fashioned about women in the business world, he isolated his four daughters from the complications of the business (he had no sons). When it came time to name his successor, Sam chose the most capable of his sons-in-law, who was married to his second daughter. His oldest daughter objected, so to pacify her he instead named as CEO someone poorly qualified to head the business—her husband.

When Sam Steinberg died, his four daughters inherited all the voting stock and his oldest daughter assumed control of the company. Under her supervision, the company took a nosedive, and eventually the board recommended that the company be sold. But the voting stock was held in a joint trust, and some of the sisters refused to vote for a sale. A long battle ensued and finally ended up in court. Steinberg's was eventually sold, but the family relationships were damaged beyond repair.[1] This was unfortunately a typical case. The entrepreneur meant to do the right things. He wanted all of his family to participate in the business. But when he gave the voting stock to his daughters not in the business and let family feeling dictate his choice of a successor, the business was doomed. Each daughter netted $112 million from the sale, but the company Sam Steinberg built with such care failed a few years later.

In addition to my fears about destroying both my family and my business if I gifted stock to all three of my children equally, it seemed to me that gifting stock to all family members created a system guaranteed to inhibit growth. And, as I've said, I was reluctant to give away voting stock at this stage of the game. Looking for a solution, I discussed the problem with many experts on succession and read pretty much everything written on the subject. This is when I hit on the solution of reissuing our stock in voting and nonvoting shares. But this didn't solve the problem of how to treat my daughter fairly (nonbusiness member of the family). If I was giving her brothers an advance on their inheritance, shouldn't I do the same for her? But more and more stories came to my attention of the ill-advised policy of gifting stock to family members not in the business. It wasn't that I didn't trust my daughter's judgment or thought she didn't understand what the company meant to me. I simply became convinced that the interests of any family member not working in the business differed fundamentally from the best interests of those who did work in the business. I considered gifting company real estate to my daughter, but then I heard stories of families fighting over rental payments on business property. In most of these stories, parents had gifted the operating company stock to their children in the business and left the business real estate to those not in the business. At some point, the children collecting the rental income would be advised by a lawyer or accountant that the rental income was not enough given the market value of the property. Their attempts to increase the rent would provoke a feud. The children in the business would claim that Dad never intended the real estate to be priced at market value and in any case the company couldn't afford it. The accountant would tell the land owners that value follows the property and that if their siblings can't afford the rent maybe they should move. You can guess the rest.

I saw this scene played out in what had been a very close family. The father, wanting to protect his daughter financially, left her the building that housed his business at his death. When someone suggested that the rent was too low, the mother sided with her daughter in raising it. The two brothers who ran the business were so upset with their mother and sister that they negotiated to purchase the building at higher than market value in order to get out of the rental agreement. From that day on, neither brother has spoken to his mother or sister. What was intended by well-meaning professional advisers as a sound plan to protect one child destroyed the family.

All these stories persuaded me that to prevent future family conflicts, all ScrubaDub business assets should remain in the hands of those running the business. I purchased life insurance to ensure a distribution of liquid assets as my daughter's share of our estate. This way, after my death, each of my children will have received gifts of equal monetary value from us, although my daughter will be getting cash while my sons will be getting the company. In addition, my wife and I gifted public securities to our daughter to make up for some of the benefits the boys were getting from the business while we were still alive. This done, I sat down to figure out the best way to pass the stock on to my sons. Convinced that the pyramid form of passing stock down had destroyed too many family businesses, I was determined to find an alternative.

Freezing the Company Stock Value

The object is to freeze the value of the family business stock in your estate. The most common way of doing this is to gift the stock to your children. This is how the pyramid system works. The first generation, as the sole originating stockholder, forms the peak of the pyramid. By gifting stock to the children, he or she begins to build the pyramid. Once the second generation begins gifting stock to its children, the pyramid starts expanding rapidly. Now a broad range of stockholders own stock, and many of them do not work in the business. Even if the company is extremely successful, produces ample dividends, and continues to grow, problems will still probably arise as a result of the number of personalities involved. Statistics show that in the majority of cases, this pyramid style of stock distribution ends in family disputes. The nature of family businesses, which rely on heavy reinvestment and long-term strategic thinking to maintain their market share, seems to make conflict inevitable. Those in management will eventually be outvoted in their desire to reinvest substantial amounts in growth or remodeling. As soon as pressure from stockholders not working in the business becomes great enough to force dividends, the die is cast. It is indeed a rare family, with extremely capable leadership, that can convince family members not working in the business to forgo a dividend in favor of investment in a new idea.

At this point, the managers of the business, also stockholders, usually try to buy out other family members to consolidate their position. This leads to the very thing the original founder was trying to avoid. A battle with high legal costs to establish fair market value for the stock. Eventually a settlement is reached that requires the working stockholders to put themselves and the company into great debt in order to buy out the nonworking stockholders. This creates a long-term debt position for the company, putting the long-term reinvestment strategy into further jeopardy. Not only can this limit the company's ability to stay ahead of larger competitors, it can eventually force the sale of the company. Making matters worse, members of the family who have become dependent on the dividend income may be reluctant to give it up even when sound financial judgment indicates that selling is the best option. This puts family votes up for grabs, and invariably ends with bitterness and heartbreak and family members no longer talking to one another.

Column Stock Distribution

With all these sad stories in my head, I worked with experts in the estate-planning field to develop what I call a "column" system for passing on stock. This involved creating family trusts representing the number of family working partners (in our case, two, one for each of my sons). All of the voting and nonvoting stock that I have given away or sold has gone into these trusts, which I call family columns. These column trusts stipulate that stock will be available only to family members working in the business through these family voting trusts. Owners of the stock in the trusts are given certificates for the number of shares they own (this makes it possible for them to gift stock in the trust to their own children when they enter the business). Holding the stock in the trusts simply provides a means to vote the stock. The owners of the underlying certificates retain all other incidents of ownership. The vote of each trust must be cast as a block. Therefore, if the family partnership is set up with two voting trusts representing the two family members who enter the business after the founder (as in my family), each family member serves as a trustee of the other's trust but votes only on behalf of his or her own trust. Each trust has only one vote. With two trusts, we have a fifty/fifty partnership.

When members of the third generation have entered the business, and have convinced their parents by their commitment and competence to begin gifting them stock, the members of the third generation will receive certificates representing their share of stock held by their family column trust. That means, of course, that after the first generation, for a long time parents and children will hold certificates for stock in the same trust. Since the trust has only one vote, the holder of the most certificates—the parent, in the beginning—will decide for that trust. Since the trust holds both voting and nonvoting certificates, while the parents remain active they only gift nonvoting shares to their children in the business. This prevents the children from "ganging up" on the parent once they as a group hold a larger block of shares than he or she does, and also prevents a "votes for sale" scenario in which family members try to recruit a majority of other family members to their point of view, with the usual relationship-damaging consequences. As the parents retire, they sell or gift the voting shares in the trust to their children, who then must agree on a way to vote their one vote.

Keeping the family business stock in trust also provides some protection against divorce by ensuring that a spouse leaving the family cannot be compensated out of family business holdings. I find this setup far preferable to prenuptial agreements, which are frequently used to ensure that stock gifted to a young couple will not become the property of the nonfamily partner if the couple splits. I think prenuptial agreements put a great burden on a young married couple and hold such negative connotations that they invariably leave the spouse who has married into the family with bad feelings even if he or she remains happily married to a member of the family and dividing the stock never becomes an issue.

It is important to note that once family column trusts have been established, no matter how many children subsequently enter the company, the structure remains the same: New columns should not be added, and each trust should never be granted more than one vote. If a voting member should die before his or her children are old enough to enter the business or take over his or her voting rights, the other trustee of the family trust (if there are only two participants, as is currently the case in my family) would vote the stock until the surviving children or grandchildren enter the business. If there are more than two column trusts, then the voting trustee of each column should indicate in a will which of the other participants he or she wants to vote the trust if he or she dies before the children reach maturity.

It must be a provision of the column trusts that the stock they hold can only be gifted to other family members who work in the business. Children who elect not to join the business and go on to other careers should be compensated by other nonbusiness assets in the family estate, such as cash gifts, residential real estate, stocks from a diversified portfolio, and so on. This may sound heartless, but it is vital to keep the control of the business in the hands of those working it. Any child who chooses not to come into the business and receives compensation in the form of other assets in the estate holds no claim on the business asset.

Children Outside the Business

For most successful family businesses, family members in the business will probably need to rely on life insurance to equalize the value of the business in their bequests to children not in the business. One common approach is for the company to fund insurance that provides a liquid distribution to family members outside the business. There are many ways of doing this, depending on individual circumstances. Split-dollar life insurance can be used to fund an insurance trust. With this type of insurance, the company gets back the premiums it has paid out at the death of the insured, and the beneficiaries of the trust can be the children not in the business. Parents can also buy survivor insurance, which pays only after both parents have passed away. This is probably the most affordable way to purchase life insurance, since the cost is reasonable and this type of policy may require no cash premiums after twelve to fifteen years.

If the size of the estate is such that it is necessary to give business real estate to children not in the business, I suggest you consider creating an entity such as a family limited partnership or limited liability company. This partnership can create a lease formula for establishing rental fees under all possible scenarios, and guarantee that the children not in the business will continue to earn an adequate income from the rental fees, while the children in the business retain control of the property. Another solution, if the business is large enough, is to create one column trust that holds nonvoting stock for family members not in the business. Or forget the trust and just give them nonvoting stock.

Another way of creating cash to equalize the value of business assets is through a charitable remainder trust. This involves donating an appreciated piece of income-producing property in trust to a charity of your choice. You collect the income from the property during your lifetime; the property passes to the charity at your death. You receive a tax deduction for the present value of the property at the time of the gift, and the income-producing asset is removed from your estate, saving substantial estate taxes. You can then use the income you receive from the trust to purchase survivor life insurance. This plan reduces your estate and therefore your estate taxes, makes a generous gift to a worthy cause, and creates cash to equalize stock gifts to children not in the business. Jacqueline Kennedy Onassis took interesting advantage of a similar method.[2] She made numerous specific bequests to friends and family and left the remainder of her estate to the C&J foundation, a charitable lead trust established in the will and designed to last for twenty-four years. The trustees, including her two children, were instructed to invest the money and disperse an amount equal to 8 percent of the fair market value of the trust to charities every year. At the end of the twenty-four years, the assets pass to her grandchildren. This is a great way to give money to family members and charities while saving on estate taxes—providing your heirs don't need income right away. The beneficiaries don't have to be grandchildren; they can be your children, as long as they have the discipline to give at least the applicable IRS-published percentage of the asset value of your gift to charity each year.

Let's continue using my own family as an example. Two of my children entered the business in the second generation. When the time came for me to gift stock, after recapitalizing into equity voting and nonvoting shares, I began transferring nonvoting shares into two column trusts, one for Bob's family and one for Dan's. For each trust, both sons serve as trustees, but each son votes his own trust. This enabled me to retain control of the company until my retirement, while reassuring my sons that they will eventually reap the fruits of their labor—ScrubaDub will be theirs. Bob and Dan are spared the anxiety of wondering whether I am really going to pass the business on to them. At the same time, the knowledge that they are building their own company motivates their work every day.

Since my sixty-fifth birthday three years ago, I have cut back significantly on my business activities and turned over a great deal of responsibility to Bob and Dan. I work fewer hours and spend much of the winter in Florida. They currently own 100 percent of the nonvoting shares in ScrubaDub, and are purchasing the voting stock as part of my retirement fund.

In addition, if I die unexpectedly, my will transfers all remaining voting and nonvoting stock to my sons' trusts. I think it is a great mistake for founders to pass on their stock to their surviving spouses, unless the spouse has participated in all aspects of running the business and indicated a willingness to take on full responsibility for the company after the founder dies. If this is not the case, leaving control of the company to a widow or widower places too great a burden on someone unequipped to make the wide range of decisions needed to run a business. In addition, friction between parent and children is guaranteed if children who are keeping the company alive must go to a parent not in the business for approval of capital improvements. Depending on when the will is being written (i.e., if the founder's children are still quite young), it can name an interim trustee to vote the stock that remains in the founder's estate until those in the business reach a certain age.

Since the widow or widower will not be inheriting the business, estate plans should provide for that spouse's welfare though life insurance or—as long as the necessary controls are in place—through rental income from the business real estate. As with making provisions to take care of

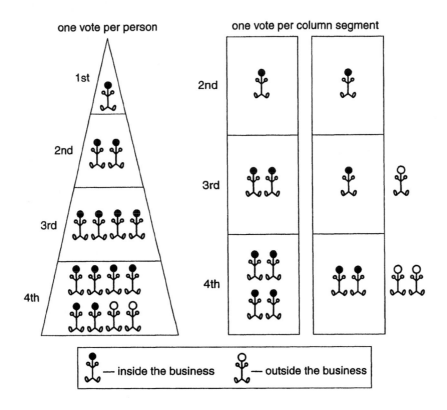

one vote per person

one vote per column segment

1st

2nd

3rd

4th

2nd

3rd

4th

— inside the business   — outside the business

FIGURE 6.1   Pyramid Versus Column Method of Gifting Stock

children not in the business, I recommend placing the business real estate in a family limited partnership that guarantees an adequate income for the spouse if the founder dies first, and passes both equity and control of the real estate to the founder's children in the business at the time of the spouse's death. By taking the burden of running the business off the shoulders of surviving spouses, they can go on with their lives, even if this includes remarriage, without disrupting their relationship with their children in the business. Even Elaine, who has worked with me at ScrubaDub since the beginning, has never wanted to take on the burden of running the business if I die.

Figure 6.1 illustrates a possible family column system extending over four generations and compares it with a pyramid system. The first generation, not represented in the column illustration, contains only the entrepreneur with his one and only vote. In the second generation, family column trusts are established for the entrepreneur's two children, both of

er the business. Each child gets only one vote. By the third gen-
e family has two children in the business, while the other has
d another in a different profession); each family trust still gets
ne vote. In the fourth generation, one family has four children in
the business while the other has only two, and two not in the business.
Again, each trust gets only one vote. Now compare this with the pyramid
style of gifting stock, where by the fourth generation there would be
eight voting stockholders, with only six in the business. The two stockholders not in the business would by definition have a different agenda
from that of the six stockholders in the business—with all the potential
conflicts that would inevitably result. In the column format, although
each column has only one vote, all six certificate holders share the same
purpose and goal—running a successful business.

The Deadlock Trustee

In a family with only two column trusts such as mine, you may ask, what
happens if the two trusts disagree—if votes on a strategic decision conflict? Another crisis in my family led me to a solution for this problem.
Bob and Dan strongly disagreed about a ScrubaDub strategy plan and
turned to me for the tiebreaking vote. The plan itself is not important, but
their disagreement about it made me realize that the worst situation for a
family business is a conflict that cannot be resolved. Finding myself forced
to vote for one son or the other, I balked. Would I be sending a message
that I loved one son more than the other by the way I voted? Would my
vote alienate the spouse of the other family who staunchly stood behind
her husband? Worse, I imagined a similar conflict arising once I was out
of the picture and my sons were equal partners in the business. How would
they reach an amicable agreement then? Puzzling over this problem, I
came to the conclusion that I needed to create a system that would lead the
parties in the conflict to a conclusion without my help.

I discussed the issue with my attorney, and together we came up with
the idea of a deadlock trustee. Under this plan, a few shares of voting nonequity stock would be placed in a deadlock trust. A trustee—someone all
parties believe to be fair and impartial—would be named by agreement
of the existing trustees of the family column trusts. In my family, this
means neither son will ever control more than 49 percent of the voting
stock in the company. Two percent has been assigned to the deadlock

trustee, although my sons retain all ownership rights except the right to vote the stock. The trustee of the deadlock trust functions as a built-in mediator for the family business, although he has full power to make a final decision if a disagreement can't be resolved. As it turns out, this does not happen very often. The fact that a deadlock trust exists is usually sufficient to resolve most problems before an outside opinion is required.

What about a situation in which three children of the founder have joined the business? In that case, after the death or buyout of the founder, each of the three column trusts would hold a full one-third of the equity but only 30 percent of the voting stock in their respective trusts. The deadlock trust would hold 10 percent of nonequity voting stock. Although I prefer to see decisions taken with the full agreement of the voting trusts, under this system, any vote would require at least 70 percent agreement before it could be approved. That is, if one trust (or one sibling or family member with the power to vote) disagreed with the other two, the disagreement would be brokered by the deadlock trustee. If he or she did not agree with the majority, the decision could not be passed. Without this provision, one voting trust would always be trying to get one of the other trusts to vote with it. This would impel brothers and sisters to compete for one another's votes, and in the end pit them against one another. There is no way that this can be a healthy situation; as the Steinberg case has demonstrated, it can lead to friction and disaster. If one voting trust disagrees with a decision, then the vote of the deadlock trustee is required. Since all the family members must agree on the appointment of the deadlock trustee, and the trustee has a fiduciary responsibility to perform in a fair and just manner, the trustee's decision, it is hoped, will be easier to accept by the "losing" parties. And, as I have said, the existence of the deadlock trust in itself creates a powerful incentive for the disagreeing parties to negotiate a compromise and move forward.

Let's consider a company run by three siblings, each holding a responsible position and earning a salary based on the importance of the job he or she performs. As stockholders, these three partners are entitled to disperse the profits generated by the company at the end of each year. When the time comes for them to decide how to do this, two of the three vote to distribute 80 percent as dividends to the stockholders. The third sibling, who happens to be the CEO, feels that to protect their market position only 20 percent should be given out as dividends and 80 percent should be reinvested in improvements. Since two votes in favor would

equal only a 60 percent majority, not enough to approve the dividend distribution, the three would have to find a compromise or take the issue to
the deadlock trustee. Since the deadlock trustee does not stand to benefit
in any way from either the distribution of dividends or greater investment
in improvements, he or she can be counted on to consider what is best for
the business. What would happen if this system were not in place? Let's
assume that the sibling with the lowest salary always votes for a large dividend distribution. Without a voting restriction of 70 percent to carry,
that person would invariably hold the controlling vote—guaranteeing a
power struggle among the siblings. One could argue based on this example that founders should leave voting control to the sibling they believe
to be most capable. The problem with this system is the impact on our
families. No matter how well-qualified the founder's choice may be, the
potential for anger and hurt feelings remains enormous. For generations,
family businesses in Europe have solved this problem by passing control
to the oldest son. But in today's competitive high-tech environment, even
this system may begin to fall apart. The use of a deadlock trustee makes
it possible to do what is best for the business without damaging our relations with our children. In this example, if the deadlock trustee voted
with the CEO, there would be no dividend distribution at all; this would
create an incentive to compromise.

I am not suggesting that all decisions must rest in the hands of the voting trusts—quite the opposite. Most decisions should be made by the officers in charge of running their divisions, with final approval reserved for
the CEO. For any company to function well, people holding responsible
positions must hold enough authority to perform to the best of their abilities. Officers of the company should report to the president, he or she
should report to the CEO, and the board of directors should conduct a final
review of the company's performance overall. A board of directors normally
votes on issues that affect an approved budget, such as the selling or buying of a major asset, the hiring of a key person, the creation of a compensation plan, a change in strategic planning, or the issuing of dividends.

A deadlock trustee tends to be most helpful in resolving conflicts over
issues of strategic importance, such as decisions regarding expansion.
Should growth come from the development of new products in the company's core business, or should it come from branching out into an allied
business? Should growth be financed exclusively by internally generated
funds combined with debt, or should it be asset-financed by venture capital? Should growth come from the acquisition of competitors or from

building new, more competitive facilities? All of these choices h[
plex ramifications, and can produce heated discussions with pers[
guments on both sides. Running a business is not an exact science, [...]
people of good will can honestly disagree. When those disagreements
seem unresolvable, then it is time to turn to the deadlock trustee.

Important decisions about building the culture of a family business
may also require a vote from the deadlock trustee. How do we protect and
build the image of our brand? If we are building a participative culture,
what programs and policies do we create to enhance our employee relations? Again, these are decisions with many possible answers, which
means many possible conflicts. On issues such as these, however, I recommend taking one important intermediate step before turning to the
deadlock trustee: Ask the advice of your business professionals or the outside members of your board. Their insight and experience can help clarify issues and focus problem-solving efforts, and the value of clarity and
focus can't be overrated when you are formulating policies and making
strategic decisions that will shape the future of a company.

Stock Redemption Agreement

The sad truth can't be ignored, however: Some issues cannot be resolved
even with the use of a deadlock trustee. The trustee may side with one
party, and the other party may be furious, convinced that this decision will
destroy the company. Or he or she may simply be fed up with struggling
unsuccessfully to see things done their way. If the person who lost the vote
feels bitter and resentful, he or she can turn to another fundamental element
in our conflict-resolution plan: the stock redemption agreement. A stock redemption agreement makes it possible for any unhappy working partner to
tender their stock and leave the company without disrupting the financial
integrity of the business. Any family business that wants to survive for
more than a few years after the death or retirement of the founder should
develop a stock redemption agreement and require everyone who buys or
inherits stock in the company to sign it. The stock redemption agreement
is the major device for keeping stock of the family business in the family.

A stock redemption agreement must do two things: establish the price
for which stock can be sold and regulate the circumstances under
which family stock can be bought and sold. Observing my distinction between the market value and the family or inherited value of family business stock, I believe that stock redemption agreements should state

unequivocally that the price for the redemption of stock—without exception—will be the current book or equivalent value at the time of the sale. It should also bind all owners of stock in the family business to sell their stock only to other family members or to the corporation. It should list situations in which the corporation will buy stock from individual family members, such as an inability to do one's job because of illness, a wish to leave the company for an extended period of time or permanently (this takes care of the unhappy sibling who has seen too many votes go against him- or herself), and the death of a family member active in the company who leaves no heirs who wish to take over his or her position.

Since it would be impossible for every happy part-owner of a family business to keep enough liquid capital on hand to buy out an unhappy or unhealthy member, the corporation should maintain life insurance policies for all stockholders that will cover the purchase costs of at least one-third the value of their stock in case of illness or death. The stock redemption agreement should indicate that if necessary the balance can be paid over time. This will keep the death of a partner holding a large proportion of the stock from threatening the financial viability of the company. If market value becomes much higher than book value, each partner can purchase term insurance on their own life. For partners between the ages of thirty and fifty this is an easy and reasonable way to protect their families in case of their untimely death. I also favor including a "survivor's benefit agreement" that continues the salary of a deceased partner to their spouse until the redemption agreement is effectuated. This kind of concern for one another—reaching beyond professional relationships to consider the fate of spouses and children—helps build trust and confidence into a partnership and strength into a family.

I recommend making each partner a nonvoting trustee of another family trust (or the other family trust, if there are only two trusts, as in my family) because of the stock redemption agreement. Let's say one working family partner suffers an untimely death or becomes incapacitated and cannot perform his business function. The redemption agreement would require the purchase of his stock by the corporation at book value payable over a specified period. If he has children who want to join the business someday, then the stock that has been redeemed may become available to them.

Of course, nothing is automatic. Children of a deceased partner must meet the entry requirements established in the family business plan and work in the company before they can purchase stock. They must also have the vote of the surviving trustee of their family trust. Having met all these conditions, they will be permitted to buy their family stock back from the corporation for the book value of the stock at the time they purchase. If they are denied the right to purchase their family stock because the existing trustee does not accept their qualifications, they can appeal to the deadlock trustee for mediation. The object here is to encourage a high performance standard and a strong work ethic, not to discourage young heirs from joining the business. To emphasize this point, your stock redemption agreement can even provide for loans to an eligible heir of a family member whose family has sold his or her stock back to the corporation by choice; this makes it possible for a child to purchase back the stock previously held by his or her family.

The Paisner Family Stock Redemption Agreement follows this general outline and meets the requirements set by the courts to go beyond the concept of a willing buyer and a willing seller. Our company stock cannot pass on to the spouse of a deceased partner. Instead, if any family partner dies or becomes incapacitated, his or her stock will be redeemed by the corporation through a buy-and-sell agreement. To make this possible, we maintain a minimum of one-third of the book value of each working partner's stock holdings in life insurance on that partner. Our stock redemption agreement stipulates that the balance can be paid over five years. This allows an orderly redemption of stock without threatening the financial integrity of the business. When I first presented this plan to my sons, they were somewhat reluctant to participate. After months of discussion—and, frankly, persistence on my part—we agreed on the total plan I have detailed. Since signing our stock redemption agreement, all our skills at conflict resolution seem to have improved, and I have seen numerous disagreements between Bob and Dan resolved through a compromise they have worked out together. I believe that neither thinks that any issue is worth the ultimate solution of one of them leaving the company.

In talking to other family business owners who have adopted similar agreements, I've learned that the mere existence of this type of agreement usually helps settle conflict. One has to be pretty desperate to give up one's stock in the company for oneself and future generations—and to give it up at book value—over an issue that has been fairly mediated through the accepted process. Nevertheless, the option exists for a partner who has become thoroughly disenchanted to leave the company with enough money to start over and change their life. But in practice, knowing that they can leave the company at the specified book value or work out their conflicts persuades most disgruntled partners and their spouses to work with the process. In these circumstances, most people want to be heard, to have an opportunity to express their feelings, and to feel that concrete steps are being taken to resolve differences. When another partner does not appear forthcoming with a compromise position, the existence of an outside mediator who will listen to arguments and offer an impartial opinion helps immeasurably. Many times compromise takes place and things again become normal.

Let's review the common ways of freezing the value of family business stock in your estate. The easiest technique is to gift stock over time using your annual $10,000-tax-free gift exclusion (or $20,000 for a married couple) and discount the value of the stocks you give because they are minority, nonvoting shares, because of their lack of marketability, or because of a combination of these factors (not many investors want to purchase small quantities of nonvoting shares of family business stock). You can also use your lifetime total allowable gift exclusion of $600,000, which will rise to $1 million over the next ten years. If you are keen to give larger amounts, you can certainly do so as long as you're prepared to pay the gift tax. Gifts in excess of the exclusion amount remove the appreciation of the stock value from your estate, but there is no step-up value at death.

Another popular method if your family business is not a sub-S corporation (in which the taxes on all profits must generally be paid by the shareholders) is to put all your family business stock into a family limited partnership or LLC. You can then transfer minority interest to other family members at the same discounted values but retain voting control through the general partnership interest, usually if you hang on to as little as 1 percent of the total shares.

Another common technique is to set up new entities for an expanding business with minimum capitalization. Use debt to fund the expansion from an S corporation or limited partnership distributions. Or you can use an installment sale, which also transfers the future growth of the stock. The sale has to be at fair value and the note must bear reasonable interest. The note can also provide cancellation at the time of the holder's death by paying a premium interest rate. For example, if you have a successful S corporation and distribute profits to the shareholders, that distribution can be loaned to a new corporation to start a new entity.

The grantor-retained annuity trust provides another method to freeze values. By placing S-corporation stock into this irrevocable trust, the grantor retains the right to receive annuity payments from the trust for a specific period of time. The grantor must outlive the set period of time; if he or she does, the remainder interest in the stock passes to the next generation. Greater estate tax savings take place when the company can produce greater profits than the annuity payments.

With changes in the tax code being proposed every year, you should consult with an estate specialist before you decide on any of these methods. If the major asset in your estate is the business and you feel that it is only fair to give stock to each family member, then consider the following. Give those working in the business an "option" that allows them to buy out other stockholders when and if they can refinance the business to do so. You might also consider building a reserve fund in the company to retire the stock of those who would rather have cash. Not making some arrangement for a pruning of stockholders is guaranteed to sooner or later produce problems for those running the business.

In my family, I have established the precedent of inherited value. I could more easily have sold the company to the highest bidder, but I have elected instead to pass it on to my family. My sons have been involved in the planning and execution of the system we have devised to keep the ownership of ScrubaDub in our family, a system that is easily repeatable for another generation if desired. They participated in the drafting of our family business plan and our stock redemption agreement; they chose our deadlock trustee and helped select our board of advisers. Our two family column trusts now hold all the stock of the company, and I believe that my sons' acceptance of this gift gives them the obligation to care for it through their generation. There is no guarantee that they will succeed, but arming them with strong values and sound training in handling conflict should go a long way toward helping them make the business thrive.

Key Messages from This Chapter

❖ Give stock only to those in the business.

As difficult as limiting stock to those in the business may seem, it is one of the basic techniques of preserving the future of the business. Almost as important is the way that stock is distributed. The earlier it is given away the lower the cost. Be sure, however, that you do not give away voting stock until your own exit strategy is secure.

the column trust technique.

concept is part of an effective conflict-resolution plan. Because
...yone must agree on major issues, it forces compromise and ac-
commodation. We know that beyond the first generation, it is likely
that there will be multiple stockholders. This system keeps one family from trying to convince another to vote with them on an issue,
which inevitably leads to conflict. Whenever there is more than one
equal stockholder in a business, the column trust is the answer.

❖ Utilize the deadlock trustee.

Since the column trustees do not have enough votes to pass on an issue
unless they all agree, the deadlock trustee becomes a mediator to help
resolve disagreements. If you build this into your culture, the idea becomes accepted as a fair and reasonable way to solve problems. When
trustees know that a mediator is in place, a resolution in the form of
compromise will most likely come about.

❖ Create a stock redemption agreement.

The stock redemption agreement establishes two very important principles. The first is an acceptance of a lower-than-market price for stock
passed between family members (I recommend book value). The second lays out the conditions by which stock can or must be redeemed.
The mere existence of this agreement helps keep conflict in check.

7

Who Should Name
the Next CEO?

You shall not hate your brother or sister in your heart. Rather, you must rea-
son with your kin, so that you do not incur guilt on their account. But you
must not seek vengeance, nor bear a grudge against your kin; you shall love
your neighbor as yourself; I am the Eternal One.

—Leviticus 19.17–18

Although we are clearly instructed by the Bible never to fight with
our siblings, it seems that when families go into business together,
no holds are barred. In the past two decades, the newspapers have been
full of stories about rivalry in family businesses. The Haft family, owners
of Crown Books and Trak Auto stores, pitted sons against their father in
a bitter court battle. The Steinberg grocery chain pitted sisters against
sisters and ultimately caused the demise of the company. In the Saunders
hotel chain, it was brother against brother; the courts ordered the sale of
all family holdings. One might think that all of these stories are about
greed, but a closer look reveals that these conflicts go much deeper than
money. The fight over dollars simply provides a way to keep score. What
all of these stories really have in common is a first-generation family that
did not build a strong foundation of love and respect into their family
culture. The founders of these companies may have been too busy growing their businesses to spend enough time with their children or, with the
best of intentions, they may simply have had more talent for business
than for parenting.

Preparing Heirs to Take the Reins

Dr. Steven Berglas, a consultant and psychologist on the faculty of Harvard Medical School, makes the following suggestions. First, raise your children to know the difference between your love for them as people and your respect for them as producers. In other words, even if they do not have your business ability, you must let them know that they are still lovable, valuable people—and loved and valued by you. Second, teach your children that there are many kinds of intelligence, many important and useful talents, and many ways of making a contribution. Let them know that not everyone possesses equal leadership potential, and that being CEO is not the only path to fulfillment. Show them that their aim, if they want to join your business, should be to find a position that suits their abilities and provides sufficient rewards to enable them to enjoy their jobs and their life. If you succeed at conveying this outlook to your children, you should also be able to teach them that finding the best person to serve as CEO will enhance the value of everyone's equity position. Let your children know, as well, that they are not alien beings if they don't love the business as much as you do. Some children require more distance between themselves and their parents to be happy and feel productive. If they seek new directions, encourage them and let them know that you love them regardless of the choices they make in their careers.[1]

In addition, don't make the mistake of thinking that your responsibility to bond with your children and build trusting, lasting relationships ends when your children become adults. If family love is not constantly nurtured and protected, small injuries can begin to fester. Sometimes, just one expression of anger can turn these minor abrasions into major wounds. This means that the parents and executives whose family members work in their companies must consider the impact on their families of every decision they make. Failing to do so can inflict terrible damage on the families that the parent-entrepreneur built their businesses to care for in the first place. The fate of the Legal Sea Foods business—a popular Boston-area chain with ten restaurant locations, five retail fish markets, a mail-order business, and a modern fish-processing center—provides a good example of this kind of damage. Legal Sea Foods was founded by George Berkowitz in the 1950s. Two of his sons eventually joined the business and worked together under their father's guidance, sharing various responsibilities, for over fifteen years. The chain experienced huge growth during this time and I'm sure both sons felt that they deserved credit for a substantial portion of that success.

To an outsider, the sons seemed unusually fortunate. George Berkowitz was not only a visionary in the fish-selling business, he was also far ahead of most of his peers in estate planning. One of the founders of the Northeastern University Center for Family Business, he had hired the best business consultants to help him plan his estate. As part of the plan they worked out, he'd gifted nonvoting equity stock to his sons at low values in preparation for his ultimate retirement. When the time neared to name a successor, George participated in a number of discussion groups at the Center for Family Business about the best process for doing so. Some participants felt that the current CEO had an obligation to name his successor. They felt that he should follow the corporate world's model and base his decision on an objective evaluation of each contender's historical performance. A minority group argued that family business owners needed to put their roles as parents before their roles as bosses and move cautiously if they wanted to avoid wounding or offending any family member who wasn't chosen. After listening to the conflicting arguments, George, feeling a moral obligation to his fourteen hundred employees and their families, named his oldest son to be his successor. At the same time, he offered his other son a job as CEO of a new division comprising all of the company's nonrestaurant activities. Under this plan, both sons would have the same title and earn the same amount of money.

On the surface, this seemed like a sensible, logical move. George had picked the person he felt was most capable to run the restaurants, which is certainly the prerogative of any corporate CEO. But this was not any corporate business. It was a family business with all kinds of excess baggage that have no place in the corporate world. The personal history, hard feelings, and relationship dynamics that caused George Berkowitz's younger son to not only reject the new position but to leave the company cannot be fathomed by outsiders. The father's simple act, which appeared to be a good faith decision, turned into a nightmare. Father and son have not seen each other for years except in court, where they battled over the value of the gifted stock.[2]

My point in recounting this story is not to illuminate exactly what tore apart the Berkowitz family; it's to demonstrate that children harbor strong personal feelings, and we as parents and bosses must contend with those feelings if we want both our families and our businesses to survive intact. Is there an alternative to decreeing who should become CEO? I think there is. If George had said to his two sons, "Look, I love you both. As your father, I can't bring myself to do anything that you might misinterpret and find hurtful. That's why I don't want to decide which of you is most capable of running the company. Since both of you must live with the decision for a long time, you decide."

As unorthodox as this approach may seem, I believe it makes a lot of sense. By handing the succession decision to your children, you begin a dialogue. The process of discussing and negotiating and disagreeing and compromising may take a long time, but when your children finally reach a decision among themselves, it will be far more secure than any decision that you might have forced upon them. Let's examine various scenarios that could result. First and least complicated, your offspring could agree that your oldest child is the most experienced and capable candidate for the job. If your children's current work responsibilities already differ significantly, and one child clearly shoulders more and does more, your children may conclude rather quickly that that child should be CEO. Your less capable or experienced children may realize quite quickly that the best way for them to protect their stock value is by appointing the most competent person to run the company.

If both (or all) your children feel that they contribute equally to the success of the company, they will undoubtedly express this feeling early in the discussions. If they agree, their next step would be to decide on their respective positions. This could lead to a copresidency, where two siblings have the same title but different responsibilities. If both or all feel equally competent but they don't all respect the competency of the others, each sibling will need to decide for him- or herself whether they want to point out the ways in which they think one or more siblings contribute less. Awkward and difficult, yes, but not the same as father versus child. Working out their differences and reaching an agreement that will enhance the running of the business over the long term will take time and effort. It may require the help of a family business consultant or psychologist. It could require canvassing the board of directors or advisers. At some point, if your children turn to objective criteria for measuring qualifications, this process may produce wonderful results—results that extend beyond the decision at hand. True, deep-rooted feelings may be exposed, discussed, and resolved. Your children may finally recognize qualities in themselves that annoy people or acknowledge behavior that is counterproductive. Driving them to deal with these issues will be their major interest in protecting their own futures. As the process unfolds, logical answers will present themselves.

Although it is impossible to know for sure, I suspect that the Berkowitz brothers would have found a solution they could have lived with if their father had made the choice of his successor their decision. You might argue that the Saunders brothers couldn't resolve their problems with each other, but remember that they kept going to their father to referee the dispute, and he sided with one son in the beginning and the other later. Theirs was an unhealthy family culture in which no one took a constructive problem-solving approach to disputes. Given enough time—with their parents' support rather than their interference—the Berkowitz brothers might even have come to the same conclusion that their father reached. And, having based their decision on sound, measurable criteria, they would presumably have been prepared to live with the decision.

Sometimes, a parent's personal experience interferes with his or her ability to effectively manage the leadership succession process for the children. Perhaps the company leader once fought with his or her own parent or siblings. In cases like these, to avoid any confrontation, founders often make their children co-CEOs. Cesare Mondavi was a first-generation wine maker in the early days of the developing California wine industry. When he passed on his business to his two sons, Peter and Robert, he gave them divided responsibility over the family winery. Peter ran the vineyard while Robert focused on sales and marketing. After Cesare's death, differences between the brothers developed into a battle for control. With only 27 percent of the stock, Robert was forced out of the family business because his mother sided with Peter on a major issue. As part of the settlement, Robert was awarded a small vineyard. This property, under his stewardship, became the foundation of a hugely successful wine-making business. Sadly, the pattern of family discord was repeated when Robert named his own two sons as co-CEOs of the Mondavi Corporation in 1990. From the start, the brothers fought constantly over the company's direction. Finally, in 1994 they asked their father to name one of them company leader. They promised that whichever one he chose, the other would go along with the decision. Robert Mondavi chose his oldest son, Michael. This ended the fighting and the company went on to years of tremendous growth. Michael manages the company with a team that includes his brother and seven other major executives. Their plans are subject to the approval of an outside board of directors. Under Michael's leadership, the company has become a global force in the wine industry.[3]

Robert Mondavi was lucky that his sons realized that they needed one leader and were willing to abide by their father's decision. But it was not all luck. Clearly, Mondavi senior had imbued his sons with a strong commitment to preserving the business—so strong that they drew back when they realized that their wrangling, if unchecked, could destroy everything their father had built. He also must have taught them that problems do have solutions, that compromise can be tolerated, and that we don't always get everything we want. In other words, he had created a family business culture that could survive conflict. As I have already argued, conflict can be good, and all family businesses must endure conflict at some time or another.

Mondavi had laid the building blocks for succession, not by deciding in a high-handed way who should succeed him, but by teaching his sons to value the business and to remember that conflict need not destroy it. Dr. Harry Levinson, professor emeritus at Harvard Business School and one of the first to bring the study of psychology to the world of family businesses, feels that one of the fundamental issues in succession is the reluctance of many CEOs to let go. Lacking respect for their children's abilities or unable to imagine retiring, they do not plan for succession and don't prepare their children for it. This can be disastrous, Levinson believes, because the issue of succession is so volatile, and caution and time are required to achieve a long-lasting solution. If you want one of your children to succeed you and you don't want to trust chance to make that happen, you must start thinking about succession early in the history of your business.[4]

Most professionals agree that by the time the next generation is ready to come into the business, a formal structure should already be in place. I have already discussed many of the features of this structure. It should include criteria for family members to join the business, a strict system of accountability and rewards for family members in the business, a compensation plan based on job responsibility and performance, and a business model in which decision making is driven by strategic planning and timely goals. A clear distinction should always be made between employment and ownership so that two siblings may own equal amounts of common stock but earn unequal salaries because their responsibilities differ. This structure must also include formal problem-solving mechanisms such as referring to a board of advisers, deadlock trustee, or outside counselor if disputes reach an impasse. Lastly, CEOs must build into their family cultures the belief that protecting the family investment is dependent on the most qualified people rising to top management positions—and it is the responsibility of the family ownership to make this happen. This principle combined with tying salaries to job responsibility will give the ambitious among your offspring a strong incentive to excel in order to reach the top.

Lastly, a CEO must devise a fair method for choosing his or her successor and give his or her heirs sufficient warning about the process elected. Since in my experience it is not realistic for us to think that we can act both as responsible CEOs and as great parents when it comes to naming one of our own children to lead our companies, I strongly recommend putting the decision in their hands. But first you must raise them in a way that makes it possible for them to reach a decision. If they are not ready to make that decision by the time you are ready to retire, it is not unreasonable to name an interim, professional, nonfamily CEO to guide the company until your children are ready to take charge.

In the last analysis, even though you may cede the choice to your children, preparing for a successor in a family business is not unlike preparing for a successor in a public company. It takes time and great care and a lot of forethought, and it is ultimately the responsibility of top management. You must make it happen. The difference is, you must make it happen in a way that benefits both your business and your family.

Stepping Out of the Way

Five years before I planned to retire, I began to think about who should be ScrubaDub's next CEO. Around the same time, I became friendly with a few of the other business owners active in the Northeastern University Center for Family Business who were at the same point in their own business cycles. During one intense discussion about business succession, three people felt that it was their job and their responsibility, no matter how difficult, to name a replacement. I was one of them. Who else but me could know who was most capable? Another very prominent business leader believed he could not pick one of his two sons without alienating the other. My wife was sure I would start a major confrontation in our family if I picked one son over the other and vehemently opposed my making the choice.

At about this time, one of the other business leaders who was active at the center named the next CEO of his company in a fit of anger. His action caused a major family crisis and caused me to rethink my position. I agonized for months over how to determine who the next leader would be. I consulted our board of advisers, but they felt that after meeting quarterly for just a few years they were not equipped or qualified to make that decision. Both my sons felt that they were equally capable and would settle for a co-CEO position. But I feared that this was not a workable arrangement—I was convinced that someone should have the last word. Having witnessed the disaster caused in one family when the father made this choice, and feeling pressure from my wife not to decide, I gave my sons a one-year period to establish for themselves who would hold the position of CEO. Some of my friends at the center felt that I had taken the easy way out and had shirked off my responsibility of making the selection. But I had concluded that my decision would be worthless if Bob and Dan did not both agree with it. Since they would have to live with the choice, why not give them the responsibility to make it? In addition to giving them a year to make the decision, I gave them a budget to hire an outside consultant or psychologist if they needed to. It took them almost the full year to come up with an answer. They never used any consultants and agreed upon a shared vision for the company. Bob became CEO and his brother Dan became president. Together, they rewrote their job descriptions, clearly detailing each other's responsibilities. They agreed that if the president did not like a decision made by the CEO, he had the right to appeal to the deadlock trustee to arbitrate the disagreement. In the several years that Bob and Dan have worked under this arrangement, they have found a way to agree upon all their actions.

After the Choice Has Been Made

Unique challenges face the CEO of a family business when the time comes to choose a successor, but the challenges don't end there. Once the choice has been made, the retiring leader still has some extremely important tasks to complete. First of all, the successor must be made aware of the wide range of responsibilities that confront a new CEO. He or she will certainly have a sense of the scope of the job from watching you do it, but undoubtedly much has remained concealed. It can't hurt for the retiring CEO to run through his or her ideas about what the job requires, emphasizing in the process that it is the successor's right to do things differently. One way to make this important point is to encourage the new CEO to develop a fresh vision for the company and update the firm's mission statement and strategic plan to reflect that vision. This done, successors should be urged to turn their attention to setting long- and short-term goals, projecting capital needs, and directing the development of operating budgets and human resources to meet those goals. They should make sure that they're comfortable with the existing systems for monitoring the company's progress in marketing, operations, fulfillment, and customer service. They should be encouraged to assess the quality of their staff and surround themselves with enlightened, energetic, and creative people who will take an innovative approach to implementing their vision.

Once the successor has completed this basic overhaul of the CEO's role, he or she can turn to the task of developing the qualities that will make him or her an effective leader. I've already discussed many of these qualities elsewhere in the book, such as the ability to inspire others, good interpersonal skills, readiness with praise and encouragement, and adroit facilitation methods for guiding the consensus-management process. Other important habits of effective CEOs include driving decision making downward, reserving their own energies to focus on their companies' broad plans, and being mindful of the many pitfalls hiding in the shadows: lack of management commitment, poor follow-through on implementing strategy, inadequate linkage between departments, weak communication between field and office, faulty systems that do not support employees' efforts (communications, compensation, etc.), and lack of accurate market information. Technicians win battles, but strategists win wars. Let your successor know that they need the confidence to change direction when required and accelerate growth when possible and appropriate. Remind your successor that a good CEO also knows what *not* to do, like staying out of operations, refraining from micromanaging, and not second-guessing decisions before they have been properly tested and the results analyzed.

The most important thing is to view your role as that of a teacher and helper. None of us is born with all the skills the job demands, and any new leader can benefit from your experience and knowledge—as long as you offer your help rather than impose it, and refrain from condescending.

In a family business, a retiring first-generation CEO may need to impart a few other ideas to their successor as well. By the second generation, successful family businesses typically enter a period of strong growth. If they follow the usual pattern, second-generation children who enter the business with new ideas and plenty of energy fuel growth at a rapid pace. At this juncture, a less experienced CEO will confront the temptation to accelerate growth on several fronts. At every level of management, the possibility of speedy growth will be an exciting prospect because it promises to open the doors to new opportunities for every employee. Nonfamily managers will see growth as a way to increase their compensation. Family managers will see it as a logical next step and a wonderful way to enhance the legacy they have received. The retiring generation will regard growth as a source of additional cash to fund their retirement. And growth will look like a simple matter: a working formula and key personnel are already in place, making it easy to duplicate the business's successful format. Limited capital and the reluctance of banks to loan to growing family businesses may have controlled growth during the first generation, but these restrictions may no longer exist. If the company has built a reputation for its service or product, has a history of producing sufficient profits, and maintains large bank deposits, lenders may line up to finance added growth. This is even more likely if the second generation takes over at a time (like the present) when financial institutions must aggressively compete with other lending sources for business. This happens in a cyclical pattern and occurs when the economy is itself growing at a rapid rate, as it did between 1985 and 1987 and is currently doing. On March 16, 1998, *Fortune* magazine published an article about this phenomenon, titled "Would You Please Take My Money."[5] In addition to venture capital, a whole slew of lenders—from angels (private investors) to state and local organizations—stand ready to fund growth when the market is growing. Foreign money, pension funds, and insurance companies all can be reachable through money brokers.

With pressure to grow coming from all sides and financing easily available, who wouldn't be tempted to expand rapidly? The problem is, very few young people have ever managed a business through a recession. The situation today provides a good example of how confusing market conditions can be. *Fortune's* business confidence index peaked in November of 1997 with an unprecedented rating of 195, dropped over twenty points to 172 in December 1997, and remained confident but cautious for 1998. By 1998 the U.S. economy had enjoyed seven unbroken years of growth. Unemployment had fallen lower than it had been in a generation, and easy money was pushing expansion and competition to dizzying new heights. Still, scholars and financial pundits warned that all these factors made it a particularly risky time for small businesses. Dwight Gertz, coauthor of the book *Grow to Be Great,* says: "Managers who are convinced of the value of growth should be aware that they are pursuing a state of affairs that is not only rare, but becoming even rarer." The rush for growth is going to create more losers than it does winners. Real growth is rare.[6]

For all these reasons, your proper role, as adviser and teacher to your successor, must include pointing out how many family firms, saddled with too much debt, lost their businesses in the 1988–1989 period when federal regulators forced banks to recall many small business loans. Urge your successor to proceed cautiously, reminding him or her of the advantages of managed, slow growth, and pointing out that a thriving small business is far better than a bankruptcy or no business at all.

Discuss different approaches to growth with the new CEO. One common way to achieve growth is to buy market share with promotions and coupons that discount products and services. Although this method can produce exciting short-term returns, it can easily lead to losses if competitors meet your challenge and lower prices even further to protect their position. Fred Reichheld, in his book *The Loyalty Effect,* believes that this approach is "a sure route to the poorhouse. This is the absolute best way to acquire the worst customers, the ones who are fickle and disloyal to begin with."[7] Making acquisitions is another common way to grow, but this tactic also fails more often than it works. In the rush to buy up competitors, too many businesses overpay, creating more debt than they can manage if sales flounder. Even large companies frequently make this mistake: Quaker Oats overpaid to acquire Snapple, the beverage maker, and has since seen earnings drained away to service its debt. In a *Fortune* article discussing ways to grow your company, the author Ronald Henkoff reported that just 23 percent of acquisitions earn their cost of capital. Those companies that successfully use this method tend to look for companies with products or services that bring them added value. They choose carefully, and refuse to overpay. Another preferred method of growth, according to Henkoff, is finding new channels for your product. He points out how industry giants like Kraft, Procter and Gamble, and Nestle stood by and watched Starbucks poach customers directly from their market share by developing new channels for selling brand-name coffee (such as on all United Airlines flights and at Barnes and Noble bookstores).[8]

Traditionally, innovation and anticipating the changing needs of customers have been the safest and most effective methods of growth for family firms. When you pull ahead and stay ahead of your competition by developing a marketing advantage, growth almost always follows. Similarly, if you understand your customers' expectations better than your competition does, and you fulfill and even exceed those expectations, growth will follow.

In addition to offering general advice, you can help your successor manage growth by making prudent financial policies a major fixture of your family business culture. In our early years, ScrubaDub's growth was held back because our bank required personal guarantees from both Elaine and myself and covenants on the business's required cash flow in our annual profit-and-loss statement. In later years, we established a debt-to-asset ratio that limits expansion. In the event the economy collapsed at any time, this ratio ensured that we would be able to meet our debt obligations. My sons, now that they have taken over the business, have adopted this debt-to-asset ratio as one of the guiding principles of their tenure as family leaders of the business. This frees me from worry, although I still do what I can to prepare them to cope with hard times. The U.S. economy may be in better shape than it has been in four decades, but I know from my long years in business that this situation won't last forever. I want my sons and my business to be ready when the hard times come.

I leave you with this final thought about succession. If you have built a strong family business culture and made the transfer of power, become chairman of the board and leave the running of the business to the new leaders. Leaving is not easy, but your job now is to make it possible for the new leaders to run the business without you. Staying on can only make that more difficult. Believe it or not, there are still plenty of challenges awaiting you. I recommend that you move on.

There will be times when selling the family business is a reasonable consideration. Our next two chapters will develop the theories on when, why, and, if necessary, how to sell the business.

Key Messages from This Chapter

❖ Ensure a smooth succession.

It may seem on the surface easy for a CEO to choose their successor. As I have pointed out, a CEO's decision is not always accepted by all

parties and can end in disaster. If there is any question about
next CEO should be, let the candidates for successor settle th
among themselves. This is not the time to create a family problem.

❖ **Encourage a new vision.**

When a new leader takes over, it is important that their ideas be implemented. Encourage a new vision and a strategic plan to promote it.
Urge that the mission statement be revised to reflect the new leadership. It is important that new leaders establish their position with excitement for the company's future.

❖ **Train the new CEO.**

In public companies, by the time someone becomes CEO they have
been fully indoctrinated into the company culture. This may not be so
in the family business. Issues of growth, financial conservatism, reinvestment, and judgment have to be reinforced. Once these are discussed, however, leave the new CEO to run the company without
second-guessing his or her decisions.

❖ **Establish a debt-to-asset ratio or set financial limits.**

It is very easy for overexpansion to take place in the second generation.
The business is established, and the new leadership is ambitious. Unless financial controls are put in place, things can get out of hand.
Every industry has some units that can be measured, and prudent limits should be agreed upon.

8

When Selling
Makes Sense

My wife and I recently dined with four other couples at a restaurant
located in a beautiful Cape Cod hotel. One of the couples owned
the restaurant and the hotel and they gave us a tour before dinner. The
immaculately maintained hotel had over 120 rooms, an active lounge,
and, as we soon discovered, a fine restaurant. The employees were dressed
in attractive uniforms and they were extremely friendly. The immaculate,
modern, and artfully decorated rooms all included large hot tubs. Although it was October and most of the tourists had left the Cape, the
hotel was filled to capacity and the dining room and lounge were hum-
ming with activity. Our host explained that he had developed his own
niche market by creating a hotel that catered to consumers who wanted a
romantic getaway. He did very little advertising and did not belong to a
national reservation service or national hotel affiliation, but while most
other Cape hotels were forced to cut back or close down for the winter,
this establishment kept breaking volume records. Most of his visitors had
heard about the hotel from other customers.

It was clear that this entrepreneur had done everything right. He had
trained his employees well, reinvested every year to keep his hotel in top
shape, served the highest-quality food, and demonstrated that he cared
about his customers in everything he did. The rewards of his success were
plentiful. While his son and a capable general manager ran the hotel, he
spent the winter in Florida, where he had a beautiful home in an exclusive golf community. He also belonged to one of the finest country clubs

on the Cape, so he was able to play golf year round. His Massachusetts home stood in a wonderful location overlooking Cape Cod Bay. He had been living this way for over ten years when Elaine and I had dinner with him. Nonetheless, during the evening we learned that despite his more than comfortable life, the steady growth of the hotel, and its effective operation by his manager and son, our host was selling his business. I asked him why he didn't just retire and sell the hotel to his son and manager. He said that they could not afford to buy the property and he questioned whether their passion for the business matched his own. "I've promised to set them up in another business when the hotel is sold, though," he said. Everyone else at this dinner party—all of whom had sold their businesses outside their families to retire—agreed with him. The general feeling was that as he approached the end of his life, his obligation was to ensure the security of his family. By selling the hotel, he accomplished this while escaping from the daily headaches of running a business. Also important was that his son would have a new start. None of the other couples saw any loss in selling the business outside the family rather than passing it on.

I subsequently heard a different perspective from a friend of the family, however. It turned out that the entrepreneur allowed the manager and his son little authority to make decisions. From wherever he was living, the founder continued to exert almost total control over even day-to-day decisions. He spoke to them daily, often from the golf course. If given the chance, I'm sure the manager and the founder's son would have loved to buy the business, but the founder was adamant that selling was the best course. From the outside looking in, it seemed that this niche business could continue for some time. With a little training and some experience handling the responsibility, the current management should have been able to run the business successfully. Contrary to popular belief, statistics show that more often than not the second generation in a family business builds a sound business to greater heights. Unfortunately, however, too many entrepreneurs, like the hotel owner, don't think that the next generation is capable of running their business. They assume that everything that can be achieved with the business has been achieved; they can't imagine anyone else moving the business beyond their accomplishments. Sometimes, as in this case, the temperament of the entrepreneur makes selling out the only way for him to get peace of mind. Many of these entrepreneurs feel that the only way to protect their families' futures is by converting the business into more secure assets.

Why Family Businesses Get Sold

During the years in which Elaine and I were preparing our sons to take over our business, we asked many of our contemporaries who had sold their businesses to explain why they decided to sell. Many said they were just plain tired of fighting the battle. Others hadn't planned well and could not afford to let their children take over the business, because they needed the sale money to support their retirement. Others said that they had no qualified successor to run the business—their children had chosen other careers and their grandchildren were too young. (If I probed a little further, I often discovered that these entrepreneurs had encouraged their children to pursue other careers rather than join the family business.)

Investment bankers told me that when family businesses are passed to the third or fourth generations, many are sold out of sheer greed. For example, one entrepreneur I knew passed his business on to two or more children. The business grew and through the natural pruning process one family eventually owned all the stock. That family successfully passed the company to their children, and shortly thereafter the children sold. In another case, one brother in a third-generation business bought out the other, who had no children interested in the business. The brother who took over the business paid his brother around $10 million for his half-share and a few years later sold the company for $30 million. Not surprisingly, these two families no longer speak to each other. In a similar situation, two sons of a third-generation business bought out their uncle and father. A few years later they sold the company for three times what they had recently paid their families for it. In both these cases, a "clawback" provision in the original purchase and sale agreement would have been helpful. Clawback provisions require the seller to share any excess revenues from another sale of the business during a specific period of time after the buyout.

I have named many other reasons for selling out elsewhere in this book, and I haven't concealed my strong belief that most of the reasons people give for selling are based on inadequate information, poor planning, or what I consider to be an insufficient appreciation for the benefits of keeping a family business in the family. But, as I have also said, there can be sound financial and strategic reasons for selling.

When to Sell and When Not to Sell

While I was doing research for this book, professional advisers to family businesses constantly reminded me that there are many sound reasons for selling out. They would repeat the common rationalizations we have all heard, but rarely did I hear the one reason I could readily agree with: "New technology will affect our long-term viability as a successful company." This to me is the only logical reason to sell a successful business. If my grandfather had owned a business that sold ice at the time when refrigerators were being invented, I certainly wouldn't fault him for selling out if he received a good offer. Similarly, if I had owned a movie theater that specialized in showing old movies at the time when VCRs were making revival houses obsolete, I would have sold in a second if I could have found a buyer. Sometimes new technology threatens the long-term viability of a family business because management gets tired and cannot keep up with the industry. This often takes place when it becomes clear that staying competitive requires a major investment. First-generation owners at a late point in their careers typically want to protect their net worth and are reluctant to take any sizable risks. The important question for a business owner in this situation should not be "How big an offer can I get?" but "Will investment keep the company competitive over the long term?" If the answer to this question is yes, then I think that before selling out, an owner needs to ask one more question: "How much do I need to retire without worrying about the future?" Once this question has been answered, he or she may discover that it's possible to refinance the company to fund that retirement and reinvest enough to make the company viable for the future. Why is this a better solution than selling out? I have already discussed the negative aspects of leaving wealth rather than opportunity to your heirs. If no family member has joined the company or currently possesses the capabilities to run it, you can make it possible for the company to continue growing and preserve the asset for future family members by replacing the family leadership with professional management.

Many family businesses have done this with remarkable success. One example is William H. Kaufman, of Kitchener, Ontario. This company, started in 1907 by William Kaufman, manufactures a line of industrial footwear. Three generations later, no Kaufman was ready to run the company when the existing leadership wanted to retire. The next two presidents, both nonfamily members, continued expanding the business.

During this period, I'm sure that the Kaufmans were strongly tempted to sell the company. When each of the last three generations had begun preparing to retire, they faced tax problems and other barriers to financing their retirement. When a business makes it through three generations, however, a culture develops that helps keep it going. And in 1996, a fourth-generation family member—the current president, Tom Kaufman—was ready to take the helm. Tom Kaufman intends to continue growing the company by expanding into designer footwear. In addition to Tom Kaufman, three other children not in the business share the rewards of the company's success. Looking upon their role as that of professional caretakers rather than entrepreneurs, all four members of the fourth generation attend succession-planning courses in order to learn how to manage their relationship. If the business is successful enough, they know that future generations will continue to benefit from the family business. If not, a pruning of ownership will take place and one family will buy out the others.[1]

Another persuasive argument frequently offered to justify selling involves the so-called category killer companies. Home Depot and chains like it have put thousands of small lumber and hardware stores out of business. Other "superstores" have forced the closing or sale of many family businesses. Can you survive when one of these giant merchandisers comes to your town? Maybe. Here is a story of how one family business not only survived but continued to grow. Harvey's hardware store opened in 1953 in the small suburban town of Needham, Massachusetts, twenty miles west of Boston. An opportunity to take over a failed paint and wallpaper store originally brought Harvey Katz to Needham. Harvey quickly realized that the training he had received from his father and grandfather in how to run a hardware business was worth more than simply selling paint and wallpaper. As time passed, even though seven other stores carried hardware in this small town, Harvey built his business by expanding inventory to include almost any item his customers could want. Eventually, his inventory grew so vast that he was forced to make a strategic decision: Should he enlarge the store or hire more employees to help customers find what they want? Figuring that the cost of more help would be less than the cost of additional rent, Harvey decided to hire more employees. The results were astonishing. Although the average annual sales per employee in American hardware stores today is $102,000, at Harvey's the sales per employee averages $228,000, or more than double. The store's inventory per square foot is over three times the national average for hardware stores, and Harvey's total annual sales average $503 per square foot compared with the national average of only $129 per square foot. Harvey achieved this remarkable result by carefully training each employee in the principles of customer service. Although Harvey's does not resemble a Home Depot with wide aisles and endless product displays, it carries many products Home Depot does not carry. Many customers discover Harvey's because a salesperson at one of the huge chains advises them to try Harvey's for an item the chain does not carry. At Harvey's, these customers are welcomed by a clerk as soon as they enter and taken directly to the item they need. If a customer wants additional help, these clerks will explain what else he or she needs to complete their project. Because of this astonishing level of service, hardware stores have come and gone in Needham but Harvey's continues to thrive. In 1997 *Inc.* magazine featured Harvey's Hardware in an article titled "Best Hometown Businesses in America." Harvey has now retired (although he's still frequently at the store), and the business is run by his two sons. Harvey gifted the stock to them over several years and they flipped a coin to see who would become the president after their father stepped down. Equal stockholders, they run the business as a partnership. Harvey's retirement is funded by a pension fund he set up at least ten years before he retired and by the rent on the property.[2]

Here's another example of a company that competed successfully with Home Depot. In 1995 Lucas Lumber Company in Oceanside, Long Island, New York, owned by the Lucas brothers, found itself in deep trouble. Lucas Lumber was a supplier of wood and raw materials used to build and remodel homes. Home Depot had moved into its market and just about killed its consumer business. The company had no new trade business and regular customers were defecting. Sales had slipped from $6 million to $2.85 million in less then three years, and ten major trade accounts made up 50 percent of the company's business. The retail showroom had become shabby, and several employees were performing poorly. At this moment of crisis, the Lucas brothers called in a business consultant.

The consultant conducted a target-market analysis and discovered that trade customers made up 90 percent of Lucas Lumber's existing business and consumers accounted for only 10 percent. The consultant recommended that the company change its focus to serve trade accounts exclusively and close its doors to the public. Following his advice, the Lucas brothers renamed the company Contractor Express and set out to add ten new trade accounts of $100,000 each. To do this, they remodeled their showroom and held seminars to help current trade customers grow their contracting businesses. They produced a new brochure and developed an aggressive marketing program to show contractors that the firm understood and was dedicated to their needs. They commissioned a new logo, purchased new trucks for delivering materials to contractors' building sites, constructed offices on their premises for contractors to use, and promoted the theme "Building Materials—Fast." The Lucas brothers also retrained their staff, emphasizing customer service and empowering them to cater to their customers' emergency needs. By 1997 Contractor Express posted sales of $6 million and was heading for $10 million in 1998.[3] You can find stories like this all over America, in every category invaded by the killer chains. What each story has in common is a dedicated family determined to keep the business going and keep it in the family. With few exceptions, these families have also made a big commitment to customer service and employee excellence.

This is not to say that there is never a time when selling all or a piece of a family business shouldn't be seriously considered. One good reason to analyze this option arises when the business has grown to the point where too much of a family's wealth is involved and some diversification is warranted. (In examining a lot of family-controlled companies that have reached this point, I've concluded that it is almost always preferable to stay private and grow through debt, however.) If the company foresees a time in the future when it can no longer compete effectively in its industry, then selling out is a responsible decision. In these cases, I favor fighting any impulse to hoard the wealth the sale brings. Sharing the proceeds with members of previous or concurrent generations who have sold their stock to consolidate ownership in the hands of those running the business will not only save your family from what may be a terrible rupture, it will set a standard of caretaking and generosity that will be felt in your family for years to come. Unfortunately, instead of regarding the business, if sold, as belonging to the whole family, too often the generation that decides to sell keeps all the rewards, causing hurt feelings, anger, lawsuits, and family feuds.

Is Going Public the Best Exit Strategy?

Rather than selling a business in its entirety, many family business owners who need cash—to fund the retirement of an older generation or to invest in new technology—follow the suggestion of professional advisers who recommend selling some stock on the open market. An initial public offering (IPO) can convert some of the owners' paper stock into cash, allowing them to diversify their investments and increase their discretionary income. It can put additional capital into the business to finance growth and the stock can be used to make acquisitions. There is also prestige attached to being a public company, and an IPO creates a ready market for stock owned by family members should they need money.

When all is said and done, going public can have many disadvantages as well. The biggest one is the need to explain every decision from then on. In a family business built on providing top-notch service to customers, most of management's energy goes into understanding customer needs and finding ways to meet their demands. The management of a publicly traded entity must shift its attention to different issues. The prime job of the company's leadership becomes serving the needs of shareholders rather than those of customers. And with shareholders come analysts, underwriters, lawyers, and a whole new list of time-sensitive reporting responsibilities. Financial information about the company, as well as other data that you had been able to keep confidential, must now be disclosed to the Securities and Exchange Commission. And now that your profitability is a matter of public knowledge, new competition may be attracted to your industry.

The problems begin during the pre-IPO process, when the multiple demands of preparing for the offering take away from the normal running of the business. New personnel must be hired. You must pick an underwriter, then oversee the preparation of a prospectus. Then you must help the investment community understand the company and create interest in the operation. Once the offering is successful, you must devote time and energy to a whole new group of people who are only interested in how the company is doing each quarter.

Management often becomes absorbed in the ebb and flow of the market. Gone is the spirit and excitement of long-term planning to outwit the competition. Instead, everyone becomes preoccupied with the daily price of the stock and what can be done to enhance its value. The CEO must be prepared to increase his or her workload and time commitments in order to meet the demands of shareholders. At the same time, his or her salary and those of other owners and key employees are subjected to the constant scrutiny of outsiders. The board of directors takes on a more formalized role requiring fiduciary responsibility, and as a result typically becomes more conservative. Friends who served as professional advisers may have to be replaced by larger, costlier firms. If you are unlucky, you may even face legal suits by shareholders who believe that they have identified a weakness in the company's operations or a promise that was not kept. Eager not to lose money for the many friends, family members, and community folks who invested in the company, the CEO struggles under a lot of new stress. The typically conscientious nature of a family business leader may cause him or her to feel more concerned about results than an outside CEO might. Balancing the market's short-term expectations with the long-term needs of the business creates added stress. Worse, it may actually threaten the future viability of the business—and with it the careers of family members still working for the company. The very things that made the business successful in the first place may no longer be possible when obligations to shareholders become a prime concern. Innovation, long-range planning, and going to extreme lengths to exceed customer expectations may be sacrificed in favor of short-term goals such as dramatically increasing sales and rapidly boosting the business's market value. Very often this leads to a takeover bid on the company stock that eliminates family control.

With all this added work and anxiety, cashing out to diversify your retirement portfolio or meet estate taxes does not seem to provide sufficient justification for taking a successful family firm public. The use of public money as an exit strategy is at best risky and at worst a disaster. Of course, it is not unheard of for a family business to become a public company with family owners still maintaining control. However, if you choose this route and hit a string of bad years or make one poor management decision, the roof can fall in. You then become a target for investment bankers looking for opportunities in depressed-valued stocks.

A little bad luck can even cause the family owners of a well-run public family business to lose the company. This is what happened to Stop & Shop, a leader in both the supermarket and discount department store industries and a public company that was third-generation-family managed. The company first went public in 1925. Over the intervening years, additional stock was issued for both succession and expansion purposes. Although the family did not maintain total control, Stop & Shop was run by a combination of family leaders and professional managers, and together they produced above-average returns for stockholders. Unfortunately, the chain fell victim to the takeover frenzy of the 1980s, which focused particularly on retail companies. During the 1987–1988 recession, a corporate greenmailer (an anti-takeover maneuver in which a company purchases another company's stock at a price above that available to other stockholders), helping to protect the management in place, took advantage of Stop & Shop's depressed stock value and launched a hostile attack. The company was "put in play" and, after a forced auction, a well-known leveraged buyout (LBO) firm bought and took over Stop & Shop. The family had not intended to sell their interest but circumstances beyond their control forced the end of the family connection in the third generation.[4] If the culture of this family business had made a priority of keeping the business family-controlled—as it has for the Grahams, who own the *Washington Post*—maybe the board of directors would have acted more prudently before issuing new stock that ultimately gave the family little recourse as the business was wrenched from them.

Of course, there are ways of going public and retaining control of a family company. The history of the Robert Mondavi Winery provides a good example of a family business that was fortunate enough to have a board of directors with the know-how and the commitment to keep the family in control and still go public. The winery went public in 1993 for two reasons: the Mondavis needed to replant their vineyards after a devastating plague, and they wanted to shelter the family from inheritance taxes when Robert Mondavi dies. Since the IPO, about eight thousand shareholders hold 47 percent of the business, but the Mondavi family retains 92 percent of the voting power.[5] The way the IPO was structured, the family's equity share would have to drop to 12 percent before they would lose control of the board of directors. Given the limits the IPO placed on shareholder control, selling shares was no easy matter. The offering opened at $13.50 and quickly tumbled to a low of $6.25 in August of 1994. In September of 1997 the stock had risen to $47, fueled in part by the bull market but also by aggressive action to take the company global by the second-generation CEO, Michael Mondavi. Michael's vision for the company has led to expansion throughout California and to joint ventures around the world. The winery currently has plans to spend $80 million for vineyard acquisitions over the next five years. The success of the early phases of Michael Mondavi's program enabled Mondavi to make a secondary offering of stock in 1995 and appeal to large institutional and private investors to hold their stock for the long run. In contrast to Mondavi's growth using public funds, Kendall-Jackson Winery, Mondavi's largest competitor, has chosen to stay private. Like Mondavi, Kendall-Jackson has been buying large tracts of California vineyards and has established its own wineries in Chile and Italy. Current company president Jess Jackson says: "Once you go public, you have to change your vision to the short-term. Volume goes up, prices go down and quality goes down." He vows never to go public.[6]

Both families have a passion for excellence and offer wonderful examples of family-run businesses that have chosen differing courses but so far have managed to preserve the qualities that made them successful in the first place. Mondavi's board of directors has chosen public equity financing and partnership joint ventures for their growth strategy. Kendall-Jackson's board has chosen debt financing and company-owned vineyards to support their growth. Will the demands of the market force changes on Mondavi? Can they control quality with partners operating some of their vineyards? Time will tell.

Studies show that how well a family business controls quality as it grows can be a major determinant of whether that business survives. I wouldn't claim that total family ownership is a requirement for controlling quality—it just typically makes it easier. But many family businesses have gone public and continued to grow without sacrificing quality. One of these is Coors Brewing Company. Coors now ranks as the fifth largest brewery in the United States.[7] Founded in 1873 in Golden, Colorado, Coors was run as a sole proprietorship until 1923, when the founder, Adolph Herman Joseph Coors, distributed shares to family members, but kept most for himself. He then convinced the family to put the stock he'd distributed in trust without dividends in order to reinvest the profits and grow the company. This strategy proved successful until 1978, when the company went public to pay estate taxes for the retiring generation of family leaders. The IPO was carefully constructed to keep over 50 percent of the shares under family control, however. All the company's voting stock is in trust and only family members who work in the business can be trustees. Despite this careful planning, the current generation faces some interesting problems. Four Coors brothers work in the business, and all of them are said to have difficult personalities. They are surrounded by a mix of in-laws and spouses with different backgrounds and values, as well as twenty-three grandchildren. To find ways to make this tangle of relationships work for the company rather than against it, the Coors family has commissioned a study that will set standards for family members who want to work in the company and establish guidelines for joining and rising within the family business hierarchy. It is too early to tell whether the Coors family will be able to retain control of this business in the next generation, but they are taking important steps to try to make that possible.

A large family-owned company that has stayed privately owned is the Johnson Wax Company. The fourth-generation leader of this company, Sam Johnson, in an article titled "Why We'll Never Go Public,"[8] explained how Johnson Wax has managed to stay private. Even though going public makes it easier to diversify family investments and settle estates, the Johnson family thinks the burden is too great. Concerned about responding to the diverse expectations of thousands of shareholders, the Johnsons also fear the sort of takeover that has wrested control away from many family business owners in the past decade and a half. In addition, they believe that a totally private firm has a competitive edge because it does not need to disclose information about company actions, plans, and performance. At the same time, the private company can closely monitor its public competitors and act accordingly.

Sam Johnson also points out that to keep shareholders content, public companies must focus most of their energies on enhancing short-term earnings. Since a family-controlled company can measure its success in decades rather than in quarters or years, it can choose to accept lower earnings. Under these circumstances, certain tax write-offs can be viewed as long-range opportunities rather than drawbacks. Johnson also points out that the CEO of a public company is beholden to thousands of individuals and interests and must spend his time responding to all of them instead of using his time to run his business. Countless hours can be consumed by government agencies and stockholders complaining about a company's earnings. The actual monetary costs of going public can also be substantial. Public companies must spend hundreds of thousands of dollars a year on legal fees, registration fees, filing requirements, and publishing costs for their quarterly and annual reports.

Johnson mentions, as well, the problems created by stock-market ups and downs that, through no fault of management, can disrupt an entire management group. Constantly working under the threat of a hostile raider, when a takeover usually means the speedy purging of top management personnel, these executives must function at a distinct disadvantage compared with private-company executives, who can focus more energy on their jobs because they typically feel more secure. This means that they can use their talents to the fullest and the company can benefit accordingly.

Sam Johnson makes a number of other interesting points. He observes that family-controlled firms can make quick decisions and move more quickly to implement them, as Johnson Wax did in 1975 when it was the first in its industry to remove fluorocarbons from its products. Sam Johnson also commented on the restrictions public ownership can place on philanthropic activity. A public firm's shareholders may not believe in giving profits away. This means that the family firm enjoys more freedom to contribute to its community without needing to answer to anyone other than family members. In addition to the many gratifications philanthropy provides, we all know that it can also be good for business. Sam Johnson concludes by reemphasizing his belief that Johnson Wax continues to be a market leader because remaining private has given his family the freedom to focus on long-term planning.

Recent data support Sam Johnson's belief in the benefits of remaining private. Except for approximately three thousand companies earning over $500 million annually, privately held companies outnumber publicly held companies in all other ranges of gross revenues. The family business universe approaches and possibly exceeds the entire publicly owned universe in size and scope of economic activity.[9]

But remaining private in and of itself does not guarantee success. Sam Johnson makes a strong case for outside board members as a way to keep each generation on the ball. And ultimately, it will be your board of directors who should help you decide whether to go public or stay private. If you do decide to go public, the quality of your board and the preparations they help you make for your public offering can make all the difference in keeping the family business intact. To a board of directors made up of just family members, the idea of going public can be a tempting idea. This is not to say that nonfamily board members would not agree, but they do bring wider experience to analyzing the decision. If you are just considering going public, the first thing you should do is make sure you have well-qualified nonfamily members on your board to advise you.

Making the Decision to Sell

I have gone to great lengths to demonstrate the value of passing a family business on to another generation. But what if you have received an offer that you genuinely believe is too good to refuse? How can you test that belief? Are there ways to find out whether it is the best offer you can get for your business? Let's assume that for several reasons you think the time has come for you to sell your business. Before making a final decision and announcing your intentions publicly, I strongly urge you to discuss alternative approaches with your professional advisers. In Chapter 9, I discuss the many advantages of conferring with experienced investment bankers before you make up your mind to sell, and hiring them to manage and orchestrate the sale should you decide that that's what you want to do. Questions an investment banker can help with include: Should you sell the corporation or just the assets? Can you (and should you) sell the business and retain the real estate? What will be your tax liability under different terms of sale? What kinds of buyer can you hope to find? These are issues you should explore while making your decision. At the same time, there are a number of steps you can take to make your business a better prospect for a sale should you decide that selling is your best course.

Considering alternative ways to sell

If you have a choice, you should try to sell the corporation rather than simply the business assets. In that way, you will be taxed only on the gain in your stock value under the new, lower capital gains tax rate. Any savvy buyer will prefer to buy just the assets, however, and avoid taking on legal responsibility for your liabilities and any hidden problems that may exist in your corporation. But if you allow your buyer to take only the assets, you will be forced to pay taxes twice—once on your profits from the sale of the assets at the corporate level and again at the individual level when you liquidate the corporation to get your money out if no selection is in place. In order to avoid an assets-only sale, you may have to indemnify the buyer on those liabilities that concern him or her. This could include product liabilities, contract problems with suppliers or distributors, and potential lawsuits from employees regarding their pension funds. Another option is to put a portion of the sale proceeds into an escrow account for a limited period of time. Although escrow and indemnification agreements may help you avoid an asset sale, they can create a long-term liability on your estate unless they are drafted by a lawyer who specializes in this type of agreement. So be careful while negotiating with a potential buyer not to agree to anything without consulting your attorney first. On the other side of the coin, some contracts you hold—such as favorable leases or raw-material purchase contracts—might be beneficial to a new buyer and could be used to persuade him or her to buy the corporation instead of just the assets, especially since most third-party contracts are difficult to renegotiate at their old favorable terms.

Alternatively, you may qualify for a tax-free reorganization. Under this arrangement, you accept the other company's stock in exchange for your stock. This can work to your advantage if you are selling to a public company where there is potential for appreciation in the buyer's stock value. But you must have faith in the abilities of your buyer and the new management because you will be required to hold the stock for a minimum period before you can sell it on the open market.

Pricing the business

If you cannot convince a buyer to purchase the stock of your company, it will be necessary to allocate the total purchase price among the assets being sold. The IRS requires that the seller and buyer agree on this allocation, which can affect the ultimate tax liability of the seller. Generally, a sophisticated buyer is interested in valuing your company on a multiple of earnings before interest and taxes (EBIT). Some buyers will just recast your statements, taking out your salary and other perks you have allowed yourself. Be sure to include an experienced business-tax specialist in your team of advisers for the sale.

Researching your potential tax liabilities and your state's tax policies

By now it should be clear that understanding your tax liability under different scenarios may play a significant part in determining the terms of a sale you are willing to accept. Since a stock sale could leave more money on the table but keep your taxes lower, you might consider encouraging a stock sale by lowering your selling price. One way to avoid the issue of a stock sale versus asset sale would be to elect S-corporation status at least ten years prior to a sale. Electing S-corporation status allows a sale on stock or assets passed directly to stockholders. This can avoid appreciation of assets and the double taxation you would face if you remained a C corporation. The election of S-corporation status must have been made ten years prior to the sale. The benefits of converting from C-corporation to S-corporation status only becomes fully effective at the end of the ten-year period.

These are some of the federal tax issues to consider, but don't forget that you will also be subject to your state's tax policy. Some states apply a sales tax to asset sales, others tax real estate separately, and still others levy a tax on stock transfers. In addition, most states have bulk-sales laws that require you to notify your creditors of a pending sale. This gives creditors the opportunity to repossess their goods or obtain payment prior to your leaving town. Once again, be sure to have a qualified professional and attorney go over the details of any sale to establish these liabilities before you enter into an agreement to sell.

Increasing your bottom line

By preparing your business for sale you can do a lot to increase its value, and the best way to prepare the business is to make meaningful changes that will have a positive impact on your cash flow. Increase sales by extending hours, advertising more, or adding more salespeople. Control expenses by cutting down on perks to family members, and get tough on expense controls that you have been ignoring. Also, clean up any dirt you may have in your business "closet" (every business has some). Capitalize a few of those assets that you would have expensed. Get rid of old inventory that might make a potential buyer nervous about your business. Sell off assets that are nonproductive. Buy back from the corporation at book value any personal-use assets like your car. Have your accountant check your depreciation schedules to be sure they are in proper order.

Try to settle any pending legal claims such as employee lawsuits, product liability claims, or IRS audits. If you haven't already done so, this is a good time to separate your business real estate from the corporation so that you may be able to retain it and lease it back to your buyers as an added source of revenue. You may have to pay some taxes when the real estate is purchased at market value, but the stepped-up basis will provide you with an added tax shelter.

If the real estate must go with the sale, be sure to check on the environmental issues. Any buyers will want to know that you have no asbestos or lead-paint problems. Confirm, as well, that there is no land contamination from prior use or a leaking underground oil tank. Most buyers today will require a Phase 1 environmental audit conducted by an environmental consulting company. It's best to know whether you have any problems before you run into an urgent need to sell, because it can often take a few years to clean up a problem and the wait can kill a good deal.

Getting your business appraised

Prior to putting your business up for sale, you should hire an appraiser to study your industry and give you an approximate value using two or three accepted valuation methods. You may be able to get free appraisals in the proposals of potential investment bankers.

Once you have decided how you want to sell the business, you must prepare the company to be sure you get the best possible deal. Then you will need to position the company for the sale, possibly help create a market for it, and find a buyer. Lastly, you will need to negotiate the form or forms of payment you will accept, and close the transaction.[10]

Preparing and Positioning the Company

Essentially, there are two ways for owners to prepare their companies so that shareholder value is maximized upon sale of the company: create intrinsic value and eliminate issues that buyers may use against the seller during negotiations. The means by which management can create intrinsic value are beyond the scope of this book, but many other books address this subject in detail. As for eliminating certain issues: All companies have strengths and weaknesses. No amount of expert representation in the mergers and acquisitions (M and A) marketplace can overcome deficiencies in the competitive capabilities of a company being sold. To the extent that you can address and effectively deal with your company's weaknesses in advance of a sale, your company's value in the M and A marketplace will be enhanced. Some of the common weaknesses of middle-market companies that can have significant impact on the ultimate price obtained from a buyer include:

- inconsistent revenue growth;
- lack of management depth;
- overdependence on key customers;
- deficient managerial accounting, information, and control systems;
- failure to achieve the company's targeted market niche or erection of barriers to entry;
- neglect of environmental issues.

If any of these problems characterize your firm, you should begin addressing them in preparation for a sale long before you make the final decision to go forward.

In addition to creating intrinsic value, management teams can head off issues that often arise in the M and A process and might reduce the ultimate purchase price. For example, during final negotiations with a buyer, sellers of middle-market companies often find themselves confronted with accounting-oriented and other due-diligence issues that could have been avoided; at this late stage in the process, they can cost a seller dearly. This is because, if the sale is properly managed, a selling company will have a number of companies interested in acquiring it. During this phase of the search, the seller's negotiating leverage is at its zenith. Once the winning bidder is selected, however, the buyer holds most of the negotiating leverage. This occurs because the company being sold is effectively taken off the market and the winning bidder is given exclusive rights to perform due diligence as part of negotiating a purchase agreement. Problems that emerge at this point in the process can be difficult and costly for a seller to overcome. For this reason, every owner should remedy problem areas well before the negotiating leverage shifts to the buyer.

Key Messages from This Chapter

❖ Consider nonfamily management.

If you have an exciting company, are a leader in your industry, and have no family member to succeed you, consider interim professional management. You can use all the techniques discussed to pass your business on to your heirs and save the estate tax bill. The company can support your lifestyle and you can still leave a legacy of opportunity for another generation.

❖ Decide if an IPO is for you.

I have demonstrated conditions when an IPO makes sense, but the reality is that few companies can successfully do it and still maintain control. For the majority of successful family businesses, slow growth with a long-range vision is a more secure path. Many companies that have gone public did so in order to retire a senior generation. With proper planning this is not necessary.

❖ Use the "clawback" provision.

If you are selling your stock to another generation or to another family member, this idea can protect you for at least five years. The provision states that if the company should get sold at a substantially higher market value then what you received for your stock, you are entitled to some of the proceeds. Having this provision in your purchase-and-sales agreement can prevent a major family confrontation.

❖ Consider S-corporation status.

There are many advantages of S-corporation status over conventional C-corporation status. The major one is to avoid double taxes (once on the profits and again when you take it out of the corporation). If you think that selling your company down the road is a possibility, this is another reason to choose S-corporation status. To take full advantage of it you must be an S corporation for ten years.

9

Navigating a
Successful Sale

In order to get more information on how family business owners can successfully navigate the sale of their businesses, I interviewed William Jarrett Jr., managing director of Goldsmith, Agio, Helms and Company, a well-known national investment banking firm based in Minneapolis, Minnesota, that focuses on selling middle-market companies. Although Jarrett made many of the same points that I have already made, I think it is worth discussing his ideas in detail because of his breadth of experience and the special perspective he brings as an investment banker. Jarrett told me that the process of selling a privately owned company typically takes six to nine months if professionally managed by an experienced investment banker. He also said that this complex process often requires the assistance of a whole team of experienced professionals—not only investment bankers, but lawyers, accountants, and sometimes actuaries, environmental engineers, and other specialists. Jarrett also pointed out that this process is typically very emotional, dealing as it does with the sale of something into which a family has poured years of hard work and high hopes. As a result, it invariably creates tension, anxiety, and anticipation among family business owners. When it works well, he said, it also holds the potential for great rewards and fulfillment.

To make this demanding and difficult process go as smoothly as possible, Jarrett suggests the following preparations:

- find the right investment banker to orchestrate the sale process, augment your management resources, and protect your interests;

- prepare conservative financial statements that disclose all material events and facts; make proper adjustments for nonbusiness and nonreoccurring expenses;
- determine the right amount of disclosure for potential buyers during the competitive bid stage of the sale process;
- devote sufficient resources to writing a highly credible, informative, and compelling "confidential memorandum" describing your company;
- preserve a certain favorable M and A accounting opportunity to allow for pooling of interests;
- implement employment agreements with management;
- create an expansive list of potential domestic and foreign buyers.

I discuss each of these steps in detail below.

Finding the Right Investment Banker

To sell a middle-market company, a family business owner must enter the growing, complex, dynamic, and crowded mergers and acquisitions (M and A) marketplace. This marketplace is no place for amateurs. The M and A market has changed substantially since the beginning of the current bull stock market fifteen years ago. It will certainly continue to evolve. The good news for family business owners is that the economy and the financial markets, including the stock and debt/lending markets, have grown steadily stronger and more robust since the early 1980s. In this environment, the M and A market has flourished, achieving record transaction activity, dollar volume, and pricing levels. Today, the buyers of middle-market companies can be divided into two broad categories: strategic buyers, including large, and usually publicly traded, domestic and foreign corporations; and financial buyers, primarily buyout and venture capital groups (often referred to as private equity groups).

The unprecedented resources and huge acquisition appetites of both these groups continue to drive today's record-setting M and A market. Strategic buyers—the large corporations—can utilize their enormous borrowing capacity and, sometimes, their high-priced common stock to pay for acquisitions. The smaller financial buyers—primarily buyout and venture capital groups—have successfully raised hundreds of billions of dollars in equity capital over the past five years, primarily from institutional investors, to finance acquisitions and investments. In the past decade, over a thousand private equity groups have accumulated thousands of "portfolio" companies. Almost always, these financial buyers will acquire companies on a leveraged basis, bringing in the companies' management teams as equity investors in the portfolio companies they manage. This ensures that owners and managers feel a shared incentive to maximize shareholder value.

If you care about the long-range future of your firm, keep in mind that the larger strategic buyers usually acquire companies with the intention of keeping them forever, while many financial buyers purchase intending to liquidate their investments within three to seven years. In fact, most financial buyers are under contractual obligation to do so. For the most part, these buyout and venture capital groups raise millions of dollars in equity from investors—pension funds, insurance companies, banks, and other financial institutions as well as wealthy individuals—that require the private equity groups to build a portfolio of investments and invest their capital according to certain established investment parameters (e.g., company size, industry, location, etc.). Since these portfolios must be accumulated and liquidated within a ten to twelve-year time frame, these financial buyers are forced to sell their portfolio companies or, much less often, common stock in these companies via initial public offerings (IPOs). These forced sales combined with the relentless, aggressive buying activities of both strategic and financial buyers have been responsible for dismantling thousands of well-known and highly regarded businesses, and they are changing the face of many American industries.

Making the process of choosing the right buyer even more complicated, middle-market companies are now being subjected to increased competition from both sides of the market: from smaller, more nimble companies establishing new niches, often based on new business models or technologies, and from larger companies that are focusing their energies and resources on one or a few select, core markets and competing directly with middle-market companies in those targeted markets.

Owners who go it alone, without the guidance of experienced M and A professionals, face a variety of risks: leaving millions of dollars on the table, being left at the altar, tainting the company's reputation in the industry, giving vital confidential information to competitors, or losing key employees and customers. Simply screening prospects to eliminate buyers who are just looking but cannot afford your price and those who just want information can be time-consuming and tricky. In addition, you could end up with a huge tax liability—or none at all—depending on how the deal is structured.

With all the potential pitfalls, I can't overemphasize the importance of finding the right investment banking firm to represent you early in the process, perhaps even before you have made a final decision to sell. It should be a reputable firm with an excellent reputation in the M and A market, extensive experience with mergers and acquisitions of firms your size, and good references from past clients. The firm should also make a commitment to provide sufficient people and resources to the project throughout the life of the project. Most of all, you should feel comfortable with the lead banker and the members of the investment banking team working on the project, since you will be working closely with them for an extended period of time. You should trust and respect them and feel that they trust and respect you. To reassure you that the interests of the investment bankers you choose stay aligned with your interests, the bulk of your investment bankers' fee should be contingent on the successful sale of your company.

Steve Goldsmith, founder and head of Goldsmith, Agio, Helms, suggests the following list of what a good investment banker does while selling a company:

- increases the number of potential acquirers, both domestically and internationally, in the competitive sale process;
- organizes the competitive sale process to meet the seller's needs and then pushes it through all three phases of the sale process: (i) preparation, (ii) market-making and negotiations, and (iii) due diligence, documentation, and closing;
- allows the client's managers to focus on their expertise—managing the business—not the resource-draining company sale process;
- determines key issues and properly positions the company before the client goes to the M and A marketplace;
- imparts credibility to the sale process and avoids any perception that the transaction is a hard sell;
- is proactive in providing strategic and tactical advice throughout the process;
- acts as a buffer between the seller and buyer on difficult issues;
- is a sounding board on a myriad of business and, particularly for individual owners of companies being sold, personal issues;

- creates a sense of urgency;
- garners the top value for the client, thereby paying for the investment banker's contingent fee, probably many times over.

Taking the time to interview several firms and choose carefully can make an enormous difference in the final price you receive for your business. Once selected, your investment banking firm's initial responsibilities should focus on producing a confidential memorandum that describes your business for interested parties and assembling a list of potential buyers.

Preparing Conservative Financial Statements

In the negotiation of a purchase agreement, contention tends to center on two issues:

- the accuracy and thoroughness of the seller's representations and warranties regarding product liability, collectability of receivables, salability of inventory, and the extent to which the seller will take responsibility for problems he or she doesn't know about;
- the limitations to the buyer's remedies for such liabilities, which are typically designated in terms of minimum amounts ("baskets") for which the seller will take responsibility, maximum amounts ("caps") the seller will pay, and a limitation period ("survival" or "sunset" period), after which the seller's responsibility ends.

To head off a lot of wrangling about these issues, you should seek to minimize potential due-diligence issues before embarking on a sale. Buyers who stumble onto unpleasant surprises during the due-diligence process are more likely to negotiate for more favorable terms with respect to representations and remedies.

In addition to clearing up lingering legal problems and outstanding liability issues, you should prepare your financial statements with great care. To make the sale process go more smoothly, consider:

- upgrading the quality of your company's financial statements either by expanding the scope of your accounting firm's review or audit or by changing to a more prestigious accounting firm;

- reporting financials in the same manner and using the same accounting principles as do the leaders in your industry;
- utilizing segment reporting to accentuate otherwise hidden, but
  valuable, sources of revenue;
- aggressively taking reserves for possible write-offs of receivables;
- aggressively writing off inventories;
- creating adequate reserves for returns, product warranties, vacation pay, severance/retirement benefits, and so on.

Pay particular attention to opportunities to create reserves in advance
of the sale. Certain buyers may look for inadequate reserves and then demand a reduction of the purchase price to compensate for the adjustment.
These reductions may not in fact be related to any fundamental inaccu-
racy they've discovered in your company's cash flows or in its intrinsic
value; they are based purely on accounting adjustments to the balance
sheet. So creating sufficient reserves or making reserve adjustments up
front and disclosing them to potential buyers early in the process can prevent subsequent contentious and painful downward adjustments in the
purchase price later in the process.

Determining the Right Amount of Disclosure

Working with your investment banker, carefully consider the amount of
disclosure you want to present to qualified and interested potential buyers. Sellers are prone to disclose an insufficient amount of information;
some do so hoping to conceal hidden company weaknesses; others don't
enlist the type of professional aid they need to do the job right. Many of
them pay for this lapse down the road, because bids made on the basis of
incomplete information are almost always revised downward during final
negotiations with the winning bidder. Even worse, incomplete disclosure
can lead to a loss of the seller's credibility, resulting, at best, in a slower,
more difficult due-diligence and negotiation process, at worst, in a failed
deal and a tainted reputation for the seller.

Sometimes, however, a seller goes too far in disclosing information, allowing potential buyers to gain access to important information prema-
turely. In highly competitive and rapidly changing industries, such as the
information technology industries, this can have a devastating impact on
the seller's competitive strategy and future marketability. If you do feel a

need to protect trade secrets in the early stages of the sale process, be sure to hire a reputable and experienced investment banker who will vouch for the viability or efficacy of your protected business process. Eventually, however, you will probably need to reveal a lot of sensitive information before any buyer will commit to a deal. When to disclose sensitive information is a crucial decision in the process of selling a company, and should be carefully made with your closest advisers. Of course, certain buyers, once they get information such as your customer lists, technological data, and business plans, may decide it would be cheaper to build their own business rather than buy yours. For this reason—and here again your investment banker will play a big role—it is essential to know as much as you can about your potential buyers when you start narrowing the field. Your banker should also insist on obtaining ironclad confidentiality agreements from every serious buyer before disclosing the identity of your company.

Writing a Compelling Confidential Memorandum

Once you have decided to sell your company and hired a good investment banker, your next task is to create an informative and compelling confidential memorandum that describes your business for potential buyers. This should be a selling piece that will interest potential buyers in looking more deeply at your company. It should contain an overview of your industry, an accurate assessment of your market position, descriptions of your key products and customers, and a business plan for the future. All financial information should be accurate and straightforward, and all projections should be reasonable. Admit any problems and explain both their source and your plans for solving them. If you leave anything out or exaggerate, you risk killing the deal further down the line; you might even find yourself sued for fraud.

Note that private companies' financial statements often include expenses that are nonbusiness in origin or expenses that will no longer be incurred by the company under new ownership. In preparing financial statements, most private companies are less concerned about reported earnings than the typical public company, but more concerned about minimizing taxes. At the time of a sale, however, it is important to show buyers an accurate income statement, both past and future, that has been adjusted for such expenses.

Also, onetime, nonrecurring expenses can often be adjustments. As long as all of these adjustments are both reasonable and supportable, buyers will base their valuations on these adjusted earnings. Almost certainly, this will result in higher valuations and a higher ultimate selling price for the seller.

Over the past two decades, as M and A activity has accelerated, the increasing demand of buyers for sufficient disclosure has produced a dramatic increase in the quality of these confidential memorandums. You should therefore not stint on the resources you devote to creating this memorandum—the competition is fierce and a poor-quality memorandum will hamper you throughout the attempted sale process. The confidential memorandum fulfills several functions. If done well, it should enable an interested buyer to accurately estimate the appropriate price range to discuss with the seller. Buyers of every type have finite resources to spend on acquisitions and many acquisition opportunities to examine. Therefore, they want to avoid a protracted education process about your business. By including historical financial statements, market and industry research, management biographies, and detailed projections, you can help buyers determine fairly quickly whether they want to investigate purchasing your company.

You, the seller, have other goals—primary among them the need to differentiate your company in a very crowded market. Providing interested buyers with a comprehensive and thorough confidential memorandum will in itself help distinguish your company from many, if not most, of the other middle-market companies being sold. Your memorandum's substance and scope and the quality of its organization and writing style will reflect on the capability and professionalism of your company's management. Many sellers focus exclusively on history, facts, and numbers, however. Although all of these are extremely important, if your memorandum can project a compelling image as well, you will be starting ahead of the pack. Keep in mind that, in addition to being a disclosure document, the confidential memorandum should be a marketing document—selling what is often referred to as your company's "sizzle." Describe the current and potential competitive strengths of your company, explain why your company is poised to move ahead of its rivals, or—without giving away too many company secrets—showcase a few of your novel approaches or original ideas. If you have assembled a particularly dynamic young management team or earned an unusually high degree of brand loyalty from customers, highlight these facts. Later in the process, you should be prepared to sell your company's sizzle effectively. This means analyzing potential buyers to determine which of your company's strengths, prospects, and potential synergies will have the most appeal. Selling the sizzle, including those intangibles that may excite certain key buyers, becomes increasingly important as negotiations go on and you learn more about each potential buyer's desires and needs.

The confidential memorandum should also convey your company's potential in the absence of certain current constraints. For middle-market companies, these constraints can include insufficient capital for expansion or modernization, undeveloped distribution channels, inadequate marketing capabilities, out-of-date technology, and management limitations.

As previously discussed, the confidential memorandum must also contain the right amount of disclosure—not too little and not too much. Its accuracy and level of detail should minimize opportunities for buyers to claim adjustments to the purchase price later. Although later in the process you will allow selected buyers to visit the company and interview your management team, the confidential memorandum is the most important disclosure vehicle for conveying information to the marketplace at large. Like a prospectus for a public offering of common stock, your confidential memorandum should describe in detail the history of your company and its current business, management, and financial results. It should also analyze the condition and prospects of your company's competition and the industry as a whole. Finally, the confidential memorandum should state your preferred transaction structure for the sale, if you have one, and give potential bidders the requisite sale-process information.

Using Pooling-of-Interests Accounting

Pooling accounting, which can be used in mergers involving stock-for-stock transactions, allows a buyer to make an acquisition without reporting the cost of goodwill. From the buyer's position, goodwill represents the difference between the market value of assets versus the purchase price. From the seller's position, goodwill is the value of its brand in the marketplace. Since the stock market evaluates companies largely upon reported earnings per share, public companies, or private companies that may someday want to go public, do not like impairing their financial statements and reported earnings by recording their goodwill costs.

To make your company attractive to as many potential buyers as possible, you should therefore take steps to preserve your ability to enter into a pooling-of-interests transaction. Since the Securities and Exchange Commission (SEC) and the accounting profession have many complex—and changing—rules for determining if a transaction qualifies for pooling-of-interests accounting, you should talk to your accountants about these rules. In particular, inform yourself of the rules pertaining to transactions that produce material changes in the ownership of your company, such as instituting stock option plans, repurchasing shares, or recapitalizing the company. Such changes could preclude your company from entering into a pooling-of-interests transaction for an extended period, which could last several years. This is particularly important if you are hoping to sell a technology company, since pooling-of-interests transactions are particularly prevalent in the booming technology sector, which is also one of the most active sectors for M and A transactions.

Implementing Employment Agreements with Management

The talents of your senior management team can have a significant impact on your company's sale price since acquisition targets that offer buyers the prospect of adding effective management talent to their organizations are more highly valued in the M and A marketplace. Therefore, it is important to make sure that key management stays in place during the sale process and for at least a limited time after the transaction is concluded. Senior managers will probably need to be involved in the sale process in any case. To avoid having one or more of them leave and to provide the necessary assurances to future owners, preparation for a sale should include signing employment agreements with key management at your company. Typically, sellers entering into the sale process like to get three pledges from management: (1) to participate in the sale process with loyalty and enthusiasm; (2) to agree to remain with the company for the new owners; and (3) to agree not to leave and compete against the company. For example, each key manager could pledge in a written agreement to:

- participate in the process and stay through closing;
- work for the buyer for one to three years at the same or stipulated compensation;
- abide by a reasonable noncompete (no solicit, no raid, etc.) restriction if he or she leaves.

In return for these pledges (and, often, to show appreciation for years of loyal and quality service), a seller frequently needs to offer some form of compensation to key managers. One common form of compensation is a "closing bonus." The selling owner creates a bonus pool from which management can be compensated (on a percentage or flat basis) from the proceeds of the sale upon closing. Obviously, this compensation is the liability of the seller, not the buyer. An alternative form of compensation is a severance agreement. If structured correctly, this form of compensation can become the liability of the buyer. Under such an agreement, the owner of a company being sold promises key managers severance of, say, two to three times their annual compensation if they should be fired within a specified period of time. This agreement can be designed to survive a change in ownership for a period of, say, two years. If the buyer terminates a manager without cause, the buyer will then be obligated to pay that manager two or three times the remaining compensation owed him or her between the time of termination and the end of the second year. Some companies devise agreements with management that contain a mixture of the two compensation alternatives, and variations on these themes are certainly possible.

Regardless of the structure of the agreement, you should try to execute some form of agreement before beginning the sale process—and better yet before you have even made your final decision to sell. Should you begin the sale process without these agreements in place, you may lose key managers or key managers may refuse to cooperate, hampering your efforts to sell. If you attempt to obtain these agreements after the sale process is under way, your buyers may be reluctant to incur the expense of these contracts, particularly if they were not disclosed in the information upon which buyers based their initial bids.

Finally, given that few buyers will be prepared to install a whole new management team immediately after they acquire your company, having these management agreements in place prior to the sale process can enhance the company's attractiveness—and value—in the eyes of most buyers.

Creating a List of Potential Buyers

The final task in preparing to enter the M and A market is to create a list of potential buyers for your company. This list is just a working document and should be lengthy, including national and international firms and a wide variety of choices. Let's look at the types of buyers that may be attracted to your business in order of greatest return. If you are a company with a hot product and some market recognition, you may be able to sell your company to the public. This would be done through an initial public offering (IPO). Plenty of investment bankers scouting the marketplace in search of potential public offerings will be eager to advise you on your potential success. If you meet the criteria for an IPO, you will immediately need to involve your banker, accountant, and attorney in the process. I have already discussed the steps and the work necessary to go public above. It is a time-consuming, demanding exercise but well worth the effort if your company is large enough and has charisma.

The next best group of potential buyers will be companies that want your business because it fits into their long-range plans. These companies will include your direct competitors as well as similar companies that want to expand into your market. Other types of companies may want your business or your product line because it will add a new distribution channel to their products. Perhaps one of your suppliers wants to branch out into a different segment of the marketplace. Buyers in this group can be very attractive because they may be willing to pay more than a buyer just looking for a return on an investment. If you can demonstrate a strategic fit between your company and another segment or subsegment of the market, you may be able to attract more then one interested company. This creates the potential for a bidding war between competitors who want to prevent your company from falling into the hands of one of their rivals, and this can drive your price up. But this sort of thing doesn't happen by chance—a lot of planning and preparation is required to create excitement and a sense of urgency in the right boardrooms.

As I have already discussed, private equity groups represent a large, well-capitalized, aggressive, and growing group of buyers of middle-market companies. Many of them are trying to build companies through acquisitions, internal growth, and synergy. They seek to build market share in consolidating industries. In this way, they resemble strategic buyers, with whom they often compete in making acquisitions. In structuring their deals, private equity groups generally require the management of the company to be investors and continue to manage the company. Buyout groups usually encumber the acquired companies with significant amounts of debt and the liquidating event for management may not occur for five or more years.

The next group of potential buyers includes both individuals and holding companies interested in a financial opportunity. Individuals in this category tend to be former executives of large companies looking for a company to own and run themselves. Holding companies are looking for well-run businesses that they can oversee. In both cases, these buyers will scrutinize your financial statements to be sure that they can get a reasonable return on their investment; they will also take a close look at your management team, which they will need to help run the company.

Your own employees make up another potential buying group. They can be attractive buyers both because they understand the risks and returns involved and because they may have some sentimental attachment to the company; these two factors may convince them to pay a higher price than outsiders. This group may be least able to finance the purchase, however, and you may have to take back some paper, such as a mortgage or other form of loan. But if you have confidence in the management your employees will install, this may give you a good opportunity for long-range income. Employees with a vested interest in the company cannot help being committed to its success, and more often than not they will increase productivity. In addition, this group typically prefers to separate the real estate (which is in your best interest) in order to reduce the size of the transaction. You could even help them raise the purchase money through your own bank, which may not want to lose your account. Of course, along with the opportunity for greater return comes the greatest risk of failure. If you decide to consider your employees as potential buyers, you can also sell the company to them through an ESOP (employee stock ownership plan). This is a qualified retirement benefit plan in which the retirement plan purchases the company stock. This type of transaction offers tax advantages to both the seller and the ESOP, but be forewarned that implementing an ESOP is time-consuming and can be expensive. Expert advice is needed to explore this alternative.

Now that you know something about the types of buyers out there, how do you find the right one? To start with, you must proceed with great care. You want to avoid an uncontrolled spread of rumors linking the sale to financial problems. This may prompt suppliers to look for new customers or customers to look for new sources. With this in mind, finding buyers by advertising in the *Wall Street Journal* is not the recommended route. But what if you know someone or some firm that has expressed interest in your company? You think this party possesses the right set of skills to manage your business successfully; you are persuaded that this buyer has the resources to meet your price; and the idea of avoiding all the headaches of a full-blown search for buyers appeals to you. You just want to sell the company and get out. William Jarrett Jr. says that this is almost always a terrible mistake, and selling a company via unilateral negotiations should be avoided at all costs. Jarrett's firm studied thirty recent M and A transactions in which it acted as financial adviser to the seller. At the start of each engagement, each client predicted the most likely buyer. These predictions were almost all wrong. After the successful completion of a competitive-bid sale process, the predicted buyers prevailed in only four (13 percent) of these thirty transactions. Of these same thirty clients, eight had become clients only after they had received a unilateral acquisition offer. Instead of entering into unilateral negotiations, the recipients of these offers retained Goldsmith, Agio, Helms. Subsequently, the competitive-bid sale process resulted in purchase prices for these eight companies ranging from 20 to 43 percent higher than the initial, unilateral offer prices. The results of this study support Jarrett's observations of the M and A market over many years. To avoid "leaving millions of dollars on the table," he says, a business owner should always create a market for the company via a competitive-bid process. After you have prepared and positioned your company for the sale, the competitive-bid process involves three essential stages:

- creating a market for the company;
- selecting the buyer;
- closing the transaction.

Each of these stages is discussed below.

Creating a Market

The private M and A market does not always serve the best interests of family business owners. This can be demonstrated by the high internal rates of return (IRRs) achieved by financial buyers over recent years, primarily from buying middle-market companies. In most cases, it is hard to argue that the sellers of those companies failed to make the best deals they could. Because financial buyers have consistently produced such great results in this market, with IRRs often in excess of 30, 40, and even 50 percent, they are now raising record amounts of new capital. The inefficiency of the M and A market for private middle-market companies can be attributed in part to the inherent negotiating weaknesses that sellers of middle-market companies too often grapple with or fail to anticipate. On the buyer's side of the negotiating table, the inexperienced family business owner often confronts an army of experienced and well-supported M and A professionals. Most owners of middle-market companies possess little experience with the complexities and nuances of selling a company. If they also fail to retain qualified investment banking advisers, they are almost guaranteed to leave a lot of their company's value on the table.

As noted above, preconceived notions on the part of a seller about the best and most likely buyer tend to be wrong. Too often, the most obvious buyer perceives the seller's company as merely a market-share fold-in acquisition. Looking at the acquisition as a "build or buy" decision, this type of buyer is frequently unwilling to pay a premium price. A superior bet can be buyers who compete in "adjacent" markets and want to expand the scope of their business. Although the seller may be unfamiliar with these buyers, they may be more willing to pay a premium price because building is not an option for them. Figure 9.1 demonstrates how the purpose of the acquisition can affect the value of the acquisition.

As this example indicates, expanding the scope of your search for potential buyers requires creativity, strategic thinking, and knowledge—based on both experience and thorough research—of the market and individual buyers. Your aim should be to identify buyers who can see a significant value-added purpose in acquiring your company and will therefore be willing to pay higher valuation multiples. In order to maximize shareholder value and adjust for the imperfections of the M and A market, you should also try to create the broadest possible market and identify buyers of different types and different ambitions. Finally, in completing your list of potential buyers, be sure that your bankers screen all prospects thoroughly. They should look at their transaction track records, funding and financing capabilities, ability and commitment to move quickly, and operating philosophy. Goldsmith, Agio, Helms reports that about 15 percent of qualified buyers will be willing to sign a confidentiality agreement. Of those, 10 percent will submit bids attractive enough to warrant visits with company management.

At this stage, it is vitally important to avoid disclosing any information that might help the buyer identify the company for sale. Even before sending a prospective buyer your confidential memorandum, you should obtain a confidentiality agreement. Thereafter, confidentiality must be

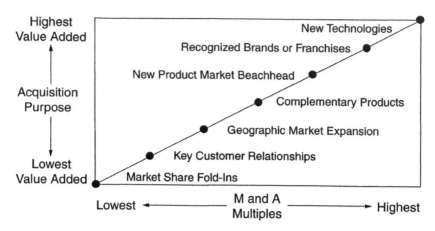

FIGURE 9.1   Creating a Market

stressed at each stage to all participants in the process. Once again, your investment bankers can perform a valuable service by concealing your name and your company's name in their initial approach to potential buyers. As potential buyers study your confidential memorandum, they may consult with your investment bankers to get their questions answered and figure out whether your firm will be a good "fit" for them. This process can vary significantly by buyer. During this process, you need to know that your bankers have the experience to release sensitive information only when it is appropriate to do so. Confidentiality is important at your end too. During the sale process, it is essential that your business be run as usual. Leaks and rumors about the sale of the company can disrupt business operations by influencing the behavior of managers, employees, customers, suppliers, competitors, and executive recruiters looking to lure away suddenly insecure managers. Foreign buyers typically take the longest time to arrive at a valuation conclusion, while domestic strategic buyers already familiar with the industry and market of a selling company generally arrive at a valuation conclusion quite quickly. For this reason, your bankers may suggest a staged process for sending out confidential memorandums so that foreign buyers receive copies first, domestic buyers, second, and strategic buyers, third. This way, all of the potential buyers will be ready to proceed with their initial bids at about the same time.

Typically, responses to the high-quality confidential memorandum of a private, middle-market company for sale will vary widely. Usually the highest preliminary bids will be about twice the lowest bid, with most bids clustered toward the middle of the range (resembling a bell-shaped curve).

In the Goldsmith, Agio, Helms study of thirty M and A transactions, buyers' preliminary bids ranged, on average, from 56 to 95 percent of the ultimate purchase price. Once you have received preliminary bids, your next objective is to cultivate the outliers at the high end of the bell-shaped curve. Ideally, by creating competitive tension among these final bidders, you should be able to extract the best possible terms and conditions.

Selecting the Buyer

Your next step will be to invite a handful of the leading potential buyers to visit your company and meet with management. The number of finalists can range from four to six at the low end to a dozen or more at the high end. In addition to their initial price bid (which is usually stated as a range), you should select these finalists based on their:

- degree of demonstrated interest in your company;
- rationale and basis for interest, including an overview of their plan for assimilating and growing your company;
- responsiveness throughout the early stages of the process and development of relationships with your management;
- proposed terms, structure, and timing;
- financing resources and contingencies;
- track record in completing transactions in a timely and cooperative manner.

You should arrange site visits for each buyer at a separate time, without identifying competing buyers. These visits should include a professional, well-orchestrated management presentation, tours, and extensive Q and A sessions; visits can last from several hours to an entire day. Once again, an experienced investment banker can help you prepare for and conduct these presentations.

After the site visits, your bankers will orchestrate one or more additional rounds of bidding depending on buyer responses. If these competitive rounds of bidding are well managed, this is when your shareholder value will be maximized. The sale process should be highly customized at this point, with each buyer receiving specially targeted information supporting the argument that that buyer will uniquely benefit from acquiring your company.

At this point in the process, you must also evaluate the various structural and payment alternatives offered by the potential buyers. Is the buyer proposing to purchase stock or assets? If it's a stock purchase, will there be a 338 (h) (10) election? The answers will have a big impact on your tax liabilities and therefore on the net value you ultimately receive from the sale. These tax issues will depend in part on how you have legally structured your business—as a C corporation, S corporation, limited-liability company, partnership, or something else. Each bid will also have to be evaluated in terms of the form of payment proposed. Is the buyer offering cash, stock, notes, or a combination? Will the buyer require a noncompete agreement or an earn-out provision? The answers to all of these questions will have a big impact on the present value of the offers you receive.

You should carefully evaluate each bid with the assistance of your investment banker (and possibly your lawyer and accountant, too). This evaluation should be based on the buyer's track record for completing similar transactions, the strategic fit of the two organizations, and any financing or other contingencies that are part of the offer. After you select and notify the winning candidate, the usual next step is to negotiate a letter of intent. Sometimes, however, a buyer and seller will proceed directly to negotiation of the purchase agreement. Doing so is to your advantage because it speeds up the due-diligence and documentation process and thereby minimizes the amount of time the company is off the market. If for some reason the deal falls through, the seller can restart negotiations with one of the other final bidders—perhaps without the new buyer even knowing that discussions with another buyer have fallen through. Thus, by skipping the letter of intent, the process retains greater competitive tension and, consequently, you, the seller, retain more negotiating leverage.

Closing the Transaction

Once you and your buyer agree to terms and your lawyers have drafted the letter of intent (or a less definitive alternative, called a term sheet), it is time for you to draw up a purchase agreement and for the buyer and its financiers to complete their due diligence. At this point in the process, all of your preparation (or lack of preparation) will bear fruit. If you have properly prepared for the sale, your company continues to operate as planned, and if your legal counsel is experienced and skillful, then this final stage of the transaction should create few surprises or problems for either the seller or the buyer.

Make sure that your investment banker stays involved and actively manages this important phase of the transaction. Important business issues underlie most document negotiations and it is your investment banker's responsibility to bring out these issues and expeditiously resolve them. For example, an experienced M and A investment banker will be familiar with the common environmental, accounting, legal, and regulatory issues that may arise and will be able to resolve them without damaging your interests or delaying the schedule for closing. Your investment banker can also assist in preparing the schedules and exhibits required by the lawyers in drafting a purchase agreement.

The time required to complete the sale will vary depending on a number of factors. These include:

- needs of the seller;
- strength of the M and A and financing markets;
- number of qualified buyers who showed strong interest in the company;
- financing contingencies of the selected buyer;
- experience and speed of the selected buyer and its lawyer and other professional advisers;
- experience and speed of the seller's professional advisers, particularly its investment bankers, who must effectively orchestrate and drive the sale process.

At the very least, once the sale process has been initiated, it generally takes at least six months to consummate the transaction: two months to prepare the company for sale, two months to obtain final bids and select the winner, and two months to document and close the transaction.

Story of a Successful Sale

In the summer of 1997, Jay Everett, the owner of Midwood, a national consumer and marketing services firm based in the Midwest, visited the offices of an investment banking firm.[1] Everett told the investment banking firm that he was interested in selling his business. Over the previous few years, various companies had inquired about Everett's interest in selling Midwood and he had been approached again just prior to his visit to the investment bank. In response to one of these inquiries, Everett had entered into discussions that resulted in a preliminary bid of about $50 million for the company. Believing this to be a reasonable offer, Everett conferred with his lawyer. The lawyer suggested that he get the perspective of an experienced M and A advisory firm. The Minneapolis investment banking office Everett approached examined Midwood's financial results, its prospects, and its industry. It also analyzed the public equity market valuations of public companies similar to Midwood that had shares of common stock actively traded on one of the major exchanges. The investment banking firm also studied the valuations of M and A transactions involving target companies similar to Midwood.

Based on this research and the firm's own considerable experience in representing middle-market companies, the investment bankers concluded that Everett had chosen the optimum time to sell Midwood and that he could get far more for it than $50 million. The timing was right for a variety of reasons. First, the M and A market was robust. After hitting a cyclical low in the early 1990s, the M and A market had climbed quickly and steadily to record levels of both transaction activity and dollar volume by the mid-1990s. Moreover, the M and A market for companies providing consumer marketing services—Midwood's industry—was strong. Several organizations, including both strategic corporate and financial buyers, were looking to acquire companies in this industry. Their aim was to achieve economies of scale, offer a bigger bundle of services to corporate customers, and consolidate the market. Finally, Midwood was a growing, profitable marketing services company that had carved out an attractive niche in coupon fulfillment. To make matters even better, during the sale process Midwood's growth and profitability exceeded its plans. Not only did this increase the company's base earnings and growth rates—key determinants in valuing any company—it added to buyers' perception of the capability and credibility of Midwood's management team, another key determinant in valuing a company.

Although the timing appeared to be right for Jay Everett to sell Midwood, he hesitated. Like many owners of middle-market companies, this decision was not an easy one. Since M and A valuations are based largely on the most recent corporate earnings and cash flow, many sellers, even owners of highly profitable companies, want to defer taking action until after achieving expected higher levels of earnings. By waiting, however, sellers run a variety of risks. While they wait, M and A market-valuation multiples may decline, their companies may fail to reach anticipated levels of earnings, earnings could plateau and therefore be assigned a lower valuation multiple by potential buyers, or key potential buyers may satiate their acquisition appetites purchasing other companies. In addition, sellers who decide to wait often don't discount the values they hope to receive in the future to account for the time value of money as well as the inherent business risks.

Let's suppose, for example, that a company has just recorded earnings before interest and taxes (EBIT) of $20 million and expects to record EBIT for the next year of $25 million (a 25 percent increase). This company receives an offer of $160 million (or eight times EBIT for the most recent year) but elects to wait until next year, when it will have a higher base of historical earnings. After waiting a year and achieving its expected earnings, the company unexpectedly finds itself with much weaker growth prospects. Now, buyers are willing to pay only six times EBIT for the slower-growing company. Applying a multiple of six to the higher $25 million EBIT produces a valuation of only $150 million, $10 million less than the $160 million offered the previous year. And this is before the company has taken into account the time value of the money.

In Midwood's case, after considering the strength of the M and A market, the company's growth record and position in a consolidating industry, as well as its bright prospects, Jay Everett decided that the time was right to sell. The sale process, managed by the investment bankers he'd hired, produced a dozen bids, each of which were well in excess of $100 million—far above the "reasonable" bid of $50 million he'd obtained in a unilateral negotiation.

In November 1997, six months after deciding to sell his company, Everett announced that he had sold Midwood Corporation to a group that included Midwood's management team (except for the selling owner) and was led by a large private equity group based in New York City. This buyout group had previously acquired dozens of companies, some in businesses closely related to Midwood's. The group acquired Midwood intending to combine the company with its other consumer-marketing services companies. After creating operating synergies among these combined holdings, the buyer planned to take public the larger, integrated company with an initial public offering of common stock. While the vast majority of owners of middle-market companies cannot hope to achieve results comparable to those achieved by Jay Everett, achieving surprisingly good results in the M and A marketplace is not that unusual if both the timing and execution of the transaction are right.

It must be clear, however, that the process of selling a middle-market, privately owned business places enormous demands upon the seller. Perhaps the two most important factors that will help you achieve success are correctly timing the sale and employing a competitive-bid process to find the right buyer. But if you decide to sell, you can do a great deal to ensure a successful transaction by being prepared, committing the considerable requisite resources, hiring experienced advisers, and—last but not least—persisting.

Key Messages from This Chapter

❖ Navigate a successful sale.

If selling makes sense, this chapter can pay you big dividends. The chances are that there are many more buyers than you may be aware of. Finding them through the services of a reputable investment banker is time well spent. This allows you to focus on the business, not on the resource drain that a company sale can produce. Use the guide in this chapter to help you find the right investment banker for your company.

❖ Avoid unilateral offers.

Consolidators enter an industry with a preset EBIT formula. Although this offer may seem high when first made, there are other potential buyers who may pay more. Local competitors are one example. While strategic buyers (those in your industry) seem logical, the opportunity to involve financial buyers in today's world are just as likely. The big message here is to get many buyers interested in bidding for your company.

❖ Be mindful of document preparation.

The greatest anxiety in the sale of a company can come after an offer has been made and accepted and the buyer is doing due diligence. If the documents presented contain inaccurate or exaggerated facts, the buyer will take advantage and renegotiate for more favorable terms. Follow the recommendations given in this chapter to prepare your documents and avoid this unnecessary step.

❖ Negotiate a management-employment agreement.

To achieve the highest value for your company, you must keep key management in place. Prior to putting the company on the market, negotiate with existing management a noncompete agreement. This may require a bonus provision if the company is sold.

10

A Legacy
of Opportunity

To summarize the thoughts in this book, let's look at a hypothetical case of how the owners of a family business with a healthy, well-developed family business culture might respond when they receive a dazzling offer to sell their business. Two cousins, Connor and Jason, succeeded their parents as co-CEOs of a small quality printing business in South Carolina. In their family succession plan, they received some of the business's stock from their fathers as gifts and purchased the remainder over a ten-year period to fund their parents' retirement. Connor and Jason continued to grow the company, increasing sales and market share. Three years into their purchase, a public company wishing to enter their market made a generous offer for the company. The offer equaled twice the market value of the company and three times the book value. Both their accountant and their attorney agreed that this offer deserved serious consideration.

The cousins called a family council meeting to discuss the offer. Although they had the legal right to make the decision, some other relatives received rent from the business property. At the family meeting, their aunt Terri reminded the cousins that the family was committed to passing the business on from one generation to the next. She pointed out that Connor and Jason had purchased the company at a reduced value with the obligation of protecting it during their tenure for the benefit of the family. After the meeting, Connor voted against the sale on the grounds that the company was healthy and growing with no serious threat to its market position. Jason voted to sell because of the large amount of money at stake and the advice of their accountant and lawyer.

Under the terms of the corporate bylaws, the deadlock trustee was asked to break the tie. Before voting, the deadlock trustee called a board of advisers meeting and listened to the opinions of the outside board members. They felt that, with so much money at stake, they could not make a recommendation. The deadlock trustee then studied the company's strategic plan and the written family plan. He found clear direction in the documents that encouraged continuation of the business as long as it was viable and competitive. He voted with Connor not to sell the business. The documents clearly stated the family's values and intentions. The purpose of the family business was not for whoever owned it at any given time to get as rich as the business made possible. Ownership was just a right passed on by inheritance to use both for one's own benefit and for the benefit of the family as a whole. It was not the right of any one generation to capitalize on the efforts of previous generations, who themselves had already given up collecting the market value of the business in order to pass it on.

Let's look at another example. In this case, two brothers, Alex and Ian, jointly ran a linen supply business that provided linens to most of the hospitals in a large Midwestern metropolitan area. Alex and Ian's great-grandfather had started the business a hundred years earlier and it had been passed down for three generations. By the time the brothers took over, the family had in place a family plan, a stock redemption agreement, an outside board of directors, column voting, and a deadlock trustee. Alex had no children interested in the business and at age sixty-three decided to retire. The corporation paid Alex for his stock at book value over five years as required in the redemption agreement. The book value of the business at the time Alex retired was $8 million. Ian, who had a college-age son who eventually hoped to join the business, voted Alex's trust until the total purchase price was paid out and the trust was dissolved.

Under Ian's leadership, the company continued to grow in sales and market share. Three years after Alex received the last payment for his stock, a company with new laundering technology threatened the future of the business. This company offered to buy the company from Ian for $30 million, which by then was three times the company's book value. Recognizing the serious competitive threat, the board, including its outside members, agreed to the sale. But because of the family culture, the board and Ian also agreed to revalue the sale to Alex under a formula that would give him a portion of the proceeds as if the sale had taken place at the time of his retirement. In addition, they made a special distribution of 10 percent of the proceeds ($3 million) to family members who had no ownership in the business. They did this by issuing warrants or stock options to family members before they started to negotiate the sale. This distribution included the family of an aunt—Ian and Alex's father's sister—who had never worked in the business but had always been included in family council meetings during her lifetime.

Although there was no requirement to do this, Ian knew that his good fortune was partly due to the efforts of the previous three generations who had passed on the company—discounting the stock—for far less than it would have been worth if they had sold it. Having enjoyed the opportunity that his forebears' generosity made possible, he felt an obligation to share part of the proceeds with the rest of the family when he sold the business, even though it cost him additional taxes. He reasoned that if the opposite had happened and the business had failed before the five-year payoff was complete, his brother would have been forced to share in the loss—why shouldn't he share in the good fortune, too?

You might feel that it was unnecessary for Ian to pass on any of the sale proceeds to family members who had already sold their shares, arguing that they accepted a price for their stock and have no legal rights to further compensation. Although this is true—they had no legal rights—I believe they had a moral right to some of the proceeds. After all, they could have sold their shares for full market value too. But they had made a commitment to the family and had put the good of the family ahead of their own enrichment. Having accepted the moral obligation to do this as part of their family heritage, they'd acted accordingly. When Ian decided it was time for the business to be sold, he didn't also decide that his family's tradition of sharing the benefits of the business automatically came to an end.

Unfortunately, Ian's actions were unusual. Nowadays, very few people feel any such obligation to their families. They contend that once family members have sold their stock, their rights come to an end. But they fail to take into account what might have happened if the heirs who finally sold the business had originally been forced to buy their shares on the open market. Faced with competitive bidding, they would probably have been forced to incur substantial debt. This debt might have prevented them from being successful. Only because they received much of the stock and value as part of an inheritance plan—paying only a fraction of the business's actual value—were they able to increase the value of the business in the first place. It is my contention that this enormous advantage brings with it additional obligations. When a family business gets passed from one generation to another, the transaction cannot be compared to the buying of a business on the open market.

I believe that in a responsible and caring family culture—the direct opposite of our competitive business culture—those inheriting a business accept it as a loan to grow and nurture and then loan to the next generation. They don't regard themselves as sole owners of the company. Therefore, if during their guardianship the business can no longer continue and the asset must be converted to cash, they don't believe that the proceeds belong only to them. They feel instead that those proceeds should be shared by all living members of the family that participated in the business's growth. After all, the efforts of each previous generation contributed to the business's value when it was sold; the selling owner didn't create that value out of whole cloth. For these reasons, if the families that own family businesses are to thrive—a separate issue from whether their businesses survive—those families must develop a culture that overcomes the general business value concept. This reasoning is based on the belief that if someone purchases a family business at a reduced value only because he or she is related to the current owner, that new owner inherits some responsibilities that differ from the responsibilities of the general business community.

I believe this idea of inherited legal rights is part of the American value system that has gone astray. A family business is too important an asset to just give away. If you are the original owner, then without question you have the right to sell rather than pass the benefits of the business on to your heirs. But once a family tradition of passing on a business has been started, why should a few members of a future generation garner the benefits of three or four generations of hard work? Each generation passes the business to the next at some sacrifice.

We can see in both these cases that a strong family culture, supported by sound written systems, can lead family business owners to truly make the most of an offer that is too good to refuse, whether by selling out and generously distributing the profits or by refusing to sell and recommitting themselves to carry on their proud family tradition of stewardship and mutual obligation. I believe that this kind of strong family culture creates a family bond that most families wish for and few achieve. Add a tradition of family philanthropy and you have a wonderful recipe for family unity and pride. Family pride in a business can be seen by all children, and helps instill a sense of responsibility as well as gratitude for their good fortune. It's a completely wrongheaded notion that a family business's only value is its market value. Family businesses possess far more value—to the families that own them, to the communities in which they function, and to American society as a whole—than can be calculated in mere dollars and cents. I also believe that this idealistic view of succession is practical, rewarding, and worth working toward.

I am not suggesting that any rights be taken away from succeeding generations; sound reasons for selling a business frequently arise. But a moral culture must be in place that puts a heavy burden on each generation running the business to keep it in the family. This should be articulated in writing and every board member should be aware of the family policy. Under these circumstances, when a tempting offer comes along, nonfamily board members have some history on which to base their decision.

I also think that the kind of moral culture I am proposing extends to issues beyond the sale of a family business. This kind of moral culture should inform everything a family does while it owns the business as well as when it sells out. Let me give you an example. In a third-generation family-owned mechanical engineering firm in Rhode Island, a job as head of the human resources department opened up. The CEO's daughter, who had graduated from college a few years earlier and was working for an insurance agency, applied for the position. Although she had no training or experience in the field, she argued that she didn't need an advanced degree to be a good judge of people and to read a résumé. She was an extremely personable young woman, thoughtful and responsible, and her father, the CEO, was inclined to agree that she could do the job and do it well. But he decided that, as a responsible executive, he should at least send his daughter out into the work world to gain some training and experience before giving her the job. He discovered that a large architectural firm for which his company frequently worked had an opening in its human resources department, and his daughter applied for the job and was hired. Does this mean that he felt his CEO's hat was more important than his parental hat? That his business meant more to him than his daughter? I don't think so. First of all, I would argue that decisions made in the best interest of the business are in the best interest of the family in the long run, for the business helps keep the family together. Second, I'm convinced that setting and observing firm rules for entry into the business is actually better for your children in the long run. It teaches them that life will not always be easy, shows them the benefits of setting goals for themselves and working to achieve them, and earns them the respect of their colleagues in your business when they finally join it.

But what if a decision were less clear-cut—if the CEO were forced to choose between the best interests of his family and the best interests of the business? In this same Rhode Island engineering firm, the CEO's oldest son eventually became vice president. When this son was thirty-eight, his wife and the mother of his three children was diagnosed with a rare form of cancer. During the months when she was undergoing treatment, the son's attention was clearly distracted from the needs of the business. The firm was busy at the time, with several demanding projects under way and aggressive deadlines to be met. In the corporate world, balancing the needs of the business with the needs of his family might have caused the young vice president enormous stress. But in this family firm, in which two cousins, his brother, his sister, his father, and his uncle all worked, no one expected him to perform his job as usual. His father, the CEO, divvied up some of his responsibilities among the rest of the family and made it clear that he shouldn't worry about the business until his wife was out of the woods. Fortunately, his wife recovered, and a year later he was back at work and going strong.

This is the way I think it should be. What's the point of having a family business if we can't take care of our loved ones when they're in trouble? In a family business, in times of personal crisis, I think the needs of the family should always come first. I also think that there are times when the parental role must take precedence over the business role. Sometimes the need is small, and only a soft word of concern is necessary; sometimes the need is financial and the business can make a personal loan to a family member.

In a strong family culture, one person's misfortune does not impel others to ask for equal treatment. None of the young vice president's family members who worked in the business asked permission to spend a year doing light duty on their jobs because he had been allowed to do so. No one thought that his taking time off was unfair, and no one complained. Without a strong family culture built on love and respect, however, this type of situation has the potential to develop into a serious family conflict.

The ability to help a family member in need is part of what makes family business culture unique, special, and worth preserving. It also distinguishes family business culture from general business culture, because it makes clear that the business exists, essentially, for extrabusiness reasons. It doesn't exist solely to make money and to be successful, like most businesses; it exists to take care of a family.

We have now come full circle. If you have a successful family business, nurture and cherish it, because it is sure to become more valuable in future generations. If you consider selling it, look carefully at the after-tax results and compare the earnings potential with that of the going business. If you must sell, be generous with the proceeds, and consider converting your proceeds into another business. This can keep your family working together, and prevent a lot of the problems caused by inherited wealth. Just including family members in the process of investing the proceeds can comprise another family business. The Pitcairn family, which sold its interest in Pittsburgh Plate Glass in 1923, invested the proceeds of the sale into the Pitcairn Trust Company. Today, over one hundred family members hold a beneficial interest in the trust, which boasts assets of over $1 billion. An elected board manages the company according to the directives of a written mission statement, the Pitcairns hold annual family meetings, communicate with one another constantly, and have all signed a stock redemption plan for any family member who wishes to end his or her participation to cash out.[1] Although the trust has enormous holdings today, it began modestly in 1923. Growth came from using estate-planning tools such as discounted values to pass the beneficial interest from one generation to the next. So if you must sell, consider starting a new family business in order to carry on your proud family tradition of leaving the next generation a legacy of opportunity and mutual responsibility.

Once my sons joined ScrubaDub, I enjoyed working with them every day to build our family business. I looked forward to going to the office each morning, and now that I have retired I relish the years that we worked together. My office is still waiting for me when I come to Boston, and I spend about one week in four there. A few weeks ago when I was in the city, I shared an experience that seemed to encapsulate all that a family business can give to a family. The school year had ended and my twelve-year-old grandson had a few days off during the week before leaving for summer camp. Because of his heavy weekend sports obligations while school was in session, we had missed an annual spring sailing trip that I know he loves. That Monday morning, I was at ScrubaDub for a meeting when it occurred to me that his father and I could adjust our Wednesday schedules and take Mat and a few of his friends sailing to Martha's Vineyard. I suggested this to Dan, we both changed our Wednesday appointments, and early that morning took four twelve-year-olds to Cape Cod. In the afternoon, while we were playing tag football on the beach, my son looked at me and said, "Where else but in a family business could this day have happened?" Having my son recognize what the business meant for our family—no amount of money could give me more satisfaction.

In the hundreds of interviews I conducted to write this book, I met dozens of people whose circumstances fully warranted their selling of a family business. Feeling as though they had no choice, these people would say to me, "I know I shouldn't feel so bad about letting go of the business. My children will still receive the benefits." But they never seemed convinced by their own words. As I hope I have demonstrated in this book, I'm convinced that most of them did have a choice. With adequate planning, enough information, and a different way of thinking about the decision, I believe that they might have responded very differently, leaving a legacy of opportunity instead of accepting the offer that seemed too good to refuse.

Appendix: The Family Business Universe

There are many definitions of a "family business." Such entities can range from very small enterprises run out of the family home to large public companies. The evidence is, however, that most family businesses are a part of the fast-growing middle-market segment of the economy. The issues and problems are essentially the same in every country of the world. Family businesses have been defined as businesses that are owned and managed by one or more family members.[1] Researchers have estimated that 90 percent of businesses in the United States are family owned and control somewhere between 30 and 60 percent of the nation's gross domestic product and approximately half of the total wages paid.[2] This could fall somewhere between $2 and $3 trillion in annual production of goods and services.

Family Business Surveys—Highlights

The University of Connecticut, MassMutual 1996: 1,002 respondents.

- 57 percent intend to pass on their ownership to a close relative.
- Source of conflict: management role, 25 percent; money, 24 percent; company vision, 24 percent.
- 53 percent have a written estate plan.
- 57 percent have no written plan for passing control to the next generation.

American Family Business Survey MassMutual, Kennesaw State University, Loyola University, 1997: 3,000 respondents.

- 53 percent expect the CEO to retire in the next ten years.
- 32.6 percent of CEOs over the age of sixty-one have not selected a successor.
- 23.1 percent have not completed estate planning.
- 56.6 percent routinely take advantage of the annual $10,000 gift exclusion.
- 36 percent have formal stock redemption plans.
- 69.7 percent do not have a written strategic plan.

Inc. *magazine, "Estate Planning When I'm Gone" (January 1990). Source: "Pulse of the Middle Market 1989," BDO Seidman, New York City: 1,873 respondents.*

- 42 percent are using lifetime gifting of business shares.
- 25 percent are using joint asset purchase.
- 20 percent have used employee stock ownership plans.
- 10 percent have a grantor-retained income trust.
- 3 percent have gone public.

Northeastern University Center for Family Business, "Little Known Facts About Family Businesses," Family Business Quarterly (1998).

- 80–90 percent of all businesses are family businesses.
- One-third of the Fortune 500 companies are family businesses.
- Fewer than one-third of family business survive to a second generation.
- Less than 10 percent make it to the third generation.
- Average life of a family business is twenty-four years.
- Major cause for lack of survival is "lack of planning."

Notes

Introduction

1. "Little Known Facts About Family Business," Paul Karofsky, *Northeastern University Center for Family Business Newsletter* (1996).

2. "Time to Go," Steven Lipin and Gabriella Stern, *Wall Street Journal* (February 28, 1997).

3. "Second Generation Entrepreneurs in Family Business Face New Challenges," Marcy Syms, *Family Ink,* a Newsletter of the George Rothman Institute at Fairleigh Dickinson University (summer 1996).

4. "Taking Stock of Family Owned Firms," Sharon Nelton, *Nation's Business* (October 1996).

5. "Family Firm and Community Culture," J. H. Astrachan, *Family Business Sourcebook,* vol. 1, no. 3 (Marietta, GA: Business Owners' Resources, 1988), pp. 165–189.

6. "The Succession Conspiracy," Ivan Lansberg, in *Family Business Sourcebook,* 2d ed., edited by Craig E. Aronoff, John L. Ward, and Joseph H. Astrachan (Marietta, GA: Business Owners' Resources, 1996).

7. Confirming this assumption, the November 7, 1997, issue of the *Kiplinger Washington Letter* reported that corporate consolidation was taking a toll on civic leadership, especially where big out-of-town companies buy locally-owned businesses. The publication went on to say that new owners usually have less interest in heading up local charity drives and raising money for hospitals, museums, symphony orchestras, theaters, school bands, and so on. Some of these large companies even tell their managers not to get involved in the community, Kiplinger discovered. As Kiplinger concluded, this means that fewer people must bear more of the civic load in many places around the country.

8. *Secrets of a Strong Family,* Nick Stinnett and John DeFrain (Boston: Little, Brown, 1986).

9. Arthur Andersen/MassMutual 1997 American Family Business Survey.

Chapter One

1. "Die Broke," Stephen M. Pollan and Mark Levine, *Worth* (July/August 1995).

2. *Family Business, Risky Business: How to Make It Work*, David Bork (New York: American Management Association, 1986), p. 116.

3. *Keeping the Family Business Healthy: How to Plan for Continuing Growth, Profitability, and Family Leadership*, John L. Ward (San Francisco: Jossey-Bass, 1987), p. 57.

4. *Your Family Business: A Success Guide for Growth and Survival*, Benjamin Benson (Homewood, IL: Dow Jones-Irwin, 1990).

5. *Grow to Be Great: Beating the Downsizing Cycle*, Dwight L. Gertz and Joao Baptista (New York: Free Press, 1995); *Customer Connections: New Strategies for Growth*, Robert E. Wayland and Paul M. Cole (Boston: Harvard Business School Press, 1997).

Chapter Two

1. *Keeping the Family Business Healthy: How to Plan for Continuing Growth, Profitability, and Family Leadership*, John L. Ward (San Francisco: Jossey-Bass, 1987), p. 211.

2. "Living Lessons," Knight Kiplinger, *Family Business Advisor*, Kiplinger Washington Editors (spring 1997).

3. "Managing Your Career," Hal Lancaster, *Wall Street Journal* (October 15, 1996).

4. "Culture and Continuity in Family Firms," W. Gibb Dyer Jr., *Family Business Review*, vol. I, no. 1 (spring 1988).

5. "Thriving on Health Food," S. C. Gwynne, *Time* (February 23, 1998), p. 53.

6. *The Leadership Challenge: How to Get Extraordinary Things Done in Organizations*, James M. Kouzes and Barry Z. Posner (San Francisco: Jossey-Bass, 1987).

7. "Living Lessons," Kiplinger.

8. Austin Kiplinger, *Kiplinger Washington Letter* (October 4, 1996).

9. *Keeping the Family Business Healthy*, Ward, p. 159.

10. "The Succession Conspiracy," Ivan Lansberg, *Family Business Review* (summer 1988); *Organizational Dynamics*, Manfred F. R. Kets De Vries (New York: American Management Association, 1993); *Your Family Business: A Success Guide for Growth and Survival*, Benjamin Benson (Homewood, IL: Dow Jones-Irwin, 1990), p. 49.

11. *Keeping the Family Business Healthy*, Ward, pp. 159, 199.

Chapter Three

1. "Family Firm and Community Culture," J. H. Astrachan, *Family Business Sourcebook*, vol. 1, no. 3 (Marietta, GA: Business Owners' Resources, 1988), pp. 165–189.

2. Quoted in *Managing with a Conscience: How to Improve Performance Through Integrity, Trust, and Commitment*, Frank K. Sonnenberg (New York: McGraw-Hill, 1994), p. 124.

3. Quotes from Winston S. Churchill, 1874–1965, WSC Quote Page, http://muse2.msfc.nasa.gov/churchill/wsc1.html.

4. *The Leadership Challenge: How to Get Extraordinary Things Done in Organizations,* James M. Kouzes and Barry Z. Posner (San Francisco: Jossey-Bass, 1987), p. 93.

5. "Labor Letter," no author credited, *Wall Street Journal* (February 18, 1987), p. A1.

6. *Managing with a Conscience,* Sonnenberg, p. 178.

7. "Worker Satisfaction Found to Be Higher at Small Companies," Jeffrey Tannenbaum, *Wall Street Journal* (May 5, 1997).

8. *Cultural Change in Family Firms: Anticipating and Managing Business and Family Transitions,* W. Gibb Dyer Jr. (San Francisco: Jossey-Bass, 1986).

9. "Rugg Lumber—Stewardship of a 5 Generation Family Business," *UMass Family Business Center Newsletter,* Fall 1995, Shel Horowitz.

10. *The Leadership Challenge,* Kouzes and Posner, p. 13.

11. See *The Customer Comes Second,* Hal F. Rosenbluth and Diane McFerrin Peters (New York: William Morrow, 1992).

12. Rosenbluth International, Corporate Internet PR, December 1994.

13. "Many Happy Returns," Case and Conlin, *Inc.* (October 1990), p. 31.

14. *The 100 Best Companies to Work for in America,* Robert Levering and Milton Moskowitz (New York: Doubleday, 1993).

Chapter Four

1. "Conflicts That Plague Family Businesses," Harry Levinson, *Harvard Business Review* (April 1971).

2. "Preparing the New CEO; Managing the Father-Daughter Succession Process in Family Businesses," Collette Dumas, *Family Business Review* (summer 1990).

3. "Conflict Resolution," meeting address by Bobby Gordon, Northeastern University Center for Family Business, 1996.

4. *The Family in Business,* Paul C. Rosenblatt et al. (San Francisco: Jossey-Bass, 1985).

5. "Managing Your Career," Hal Lancaster, *Wall Street Journal* (October 15, 1996).

6. *Keeping the Family Business Healthy: How to Plan for Continuing Growth, Profitability, and Family Leadership,* John L. Ward (San Francisco: Jossey-Bass, 1987).

7. *Family Business, Risky Business: How to Make It Work,* David Bork (New York: American Management Association, 1986).

8. *Family Business Compensation,* John Ward and Craig Aronoff, Family Business Leadership Series, vol. 5 (Marietta, GA: Business Owners' Resources, 1993).

9. "Can't Agree on the Company's Future Strategy," Dal Dearmin and Marc Scullin, *Northeastern University Family Business Quarterly* (fall 1997).

10. "10 Myths About Outside Boards," John Ward and Craig Aronoff, *Nation's Business* (April 1993); *Passing the Torch: Succession, Retirement, and Estate Planning in Family-Owned Businesses,* Mike Cohn (New York: McGraw-Hill, 1992); "The Importance of Outsiders in Small Firm Strategic Planning," Richard Robinson Jr., *Academy of Management Journal* (March 1982).

11. *Your Family Business: A Success Guide for Growth and Survival,* Benjamin Benson (Homewood, IL: Dow Jones-Irwin, 1990), p. 150.

12. "Outside Boards and Family Businesses: Another Look," Marc A. Schwartz and Louis B. Barnes, *Family Business Review* (fall 1993).

13. *Keeping the Family Business Healthy,* Ward, p. 44.

14. "10 Myths About Outside Boards," Ward and Aronoff.

15. Our board meetings are scheduled quarterly and run from 4:00 P.M. to 10:00 P.M. We work through dinner and distribute detailed written minutes within a month after each meeting.

16. *Keeping the Family Business Healthy,* Ward, p. 11.

17. "Outside Boards and Family Businesses: Another Look," Marc A. Schwartz and Louis B. Barnes, *Family Business Review* (fall 1991).

18. *Personal History,* Katharine Graham (New York: Knopf, 1997), p. 619. The rest of her quote offers a wonderful paean to the special qualities of family businesses: "I think that family-owned companies bring special qualities to the table and that family members can bring singular attributes to a business enterprise. Possibly, quality may be nourished most easily by a family whose perspective extends beyond the immediate horizon. There are exceptions, to be sure, but family members can provide stability and continuity, and family ownership can prevent takeovers, which is important to smooth operations in the period of disruptive and often ill-considered mergers and acquisitions. We never took success for granted."

19. "Heartbreak Hotel," no author credited, *Boston* (June 1996), p. 64.

Chapter Five

1. "The '97 Tax Plan—What It Means To You," Lynn Asinof, *Wall Street Journal* (July 30, 1997), p. C24; "Estate-Tax Cut On Small Business May Not Aid Many," Michael Selz, *Wall Street Journal* (July 30, 1997), p. 10.

2. *Passing the Torch: Succession, Retirement, and Estate Planning in Family-Owned Businesses,* Mike Cohn (New York: McGraw-Hill, 1992), p. 10; *Keeping the Family Business Healthy: How to Plan for Continuing Growth, Profitability, and Family Leadership,* John L. Ward (San Francisco: Jossey-Bass, 1987), p. xv.

3. "Funeral Parlors Become Big Business," Robert Tomsho, *Wall Street Journal* (September 18, 1996).

4. "Industry Focus," Robert Tomsho, *Wall Street Journal* (September 18, 1996).

5. "Have a Nice Death," Peter Goodwin and Sara Baseley, *The Guardian* (February 27, 1996).

6. http://www.Loewngroup.com/home.nsf/public/highlights.

7. "Loewen Group Plans $80 Million Charge," Tamsin Carlisle, *Wall Street Journal* (September 15, 1997), p. 10a.

8. Loewen Group press release (May 14, 1996).

9. "Roll-up Trends: Main Street Meets Wall Street," no author credited, *Houston Business Journal* (January 12, 1998).

10. "Funeral Home Chain Exploits Demise of Tradition," Marc Ballon, *Inc.* (April 1998).

11. "Is Big Back or Is Small Still Beautiful?" David Friedman, *Inc.* (April 1998).

12. "Special Report—Rushing Away from Taxes," Christopher Drew and David Cay Johnston, *New York Times* (December 22, 1996).

13. "Buy-Sell Agreements After Chapter 14," Roy M. Adams, David A. Herpe, James R. Carey, *Trusts and Estates*, vol. 32, no. 5 (Argus, 1993).

14. *Passing the Torch*, Cohn, p. 110; "Special Report—Rushing Away from Taxes," Drew and Johnston.

15. "Tax Report: A Special Summary and Forecast of Federal and State Tax Developments," *Wall Street Journal* (April 8, 1998), p. 1.

16. "Should You Leave It to the Children," Richard I. Kirkland, *Fortune* (September 19, 1986).

17. Ibid.

18. "The Dynasty Trust: Protective Armor for Generations to Come," Pierce H. McDowell III, *Trusts and Estates*, vol. 32, no. 10 (Argus, 1993). A detailed description of effective estate planning methods and wealth-transfer techniques can be found in *Passing the Torch*, Cohn. Dy. T.

Chapter Six

1. "Sam Steinberg's Non-Lasting Legacy," Shell Horowitz, University of Massachusetts Family Business Center newsletter (winter 1996).

2. "Elegant Estate Planning," Susan E. Kuhn, University of Massachusetts *Related Business* newsletter (spring 1995).

Chapter Seven

1. "A Loser's Revenge," Steven Berglas, *Inc.* (July 1997).

2. George Berkowitz related his story at a meeting of the Northeastern University Center for Family Business and again in October 1995 at a family business owners' conference at the University of Massachusetts. The Berkowitz family story was reported in detail in "Family Schism: The Legal Sea Foods Saga," no author credited, UMass Family Business Center newsletter (spring 1995).

3. "The Rising Sun," Kim Marcus, *Wine Spectator* (October 31, 1997), p. 80.

4. "Conflicts That Plague Family Businesses," Harry Levinson, *Harvard Business Review* (March–April 1971).

5. "Would You Please Take My Money," Eileen P. Gunn, *Fortune* (March 16, 1998).

6. *Grow to Be Great,* Dwight L. Gertz (Joao, PA: Baptista Free Press, 1995), p.23.

7. "The Loyalty Effect," Fred Reschheld, Thomas Teal, Harvard Business School Pub. (March, 1996).

8. "Growing Your Company: Five Ways to Do It Right," Ronald Henkoff, *Fortune* (November 25, 1996).

Chapter Eight

1. "Kaufmans Keep It in the Family," Gayle MacDonald, *Globe and Mail* [Kitchener, Ont.] (February 10, 1997).

2. Interview with Harvey Katz, October 1997.

3. Case study supplied by Jim Iseman, Business Growth Marketing Inc., 301 Madison Avenue, New York, N.Y.

4. Interview with Carol Goldberg, June 1996.

5. "The Rising Sun," Kim Marcus, *Wine Spectator* (October 31, 1997).

6. Kim Marcus, in the *Wine Spectator* article cited above, compared the growth strategies of Mondavi and Jackson and reported that Jackson was unfazed by Mondavi's growth. "If they're copying us, it's a compliment to our vision," Jackson said. He then went on to make his statement about never going public.

7. "Family Brew at Coors," Jim Klaes, *Family Business Forum News,* University of Texas at El Paso College of Business Administation (July 1996).

8. "Why We'll Never Go Public," Samuel C. Johnson, *Family Business* (May 1990).

9. "Financing Family Business: Alternatives to Selling Out or Going Public," D. R. Dreux, *Family Business Review* (1990), pp. 225–243.

10. I am indebted to William Jarrett Jr., of Goldsmith, Agio, Helms and Company, for much of the material in this section.

Chapter Nine

1. The specific facts pertaining to this transaction, the name of the company, and the name of its owner have been changed.

Chapter Ten

1. "How to Invest in Family Businesses," Louis Moscetello, *Family Business* (February 1990).

Appendix

1. "Methodological Issues and Consideration in Studying Family Businesses," W. C. Handler, *Family Business Review* (1989), pp. 257–276.

2. *Family Business Management: Concepts and Practice,* A. B. Ibrahim and W. H. Ellis (Dubuque, IA: Kendall/Hunt, 1994).

Index

Printed in the United States
53011LVS00004B/229-231

9 780738 203201